Crafting Nonfiction

Lessons on Writing Process, Traits, and Craft

Linda Hoyt

PRIMARY

*first*hand

HEINEMANN

DEDICATED TO TEACHERS

DEDICATED TO TEACHERS

*first*hand
An imprint of Heinemann
361 Hanover Street
Portsmouth, NH 03801
www.heinemann.com

Offices and agents throughout the world

"Dedicated to Teachers" is a trademark of Greenwood Publishing Group, Inc.

© 2011 by Linda Hoyt

Interior design: Karen Billip and David Stirling
Cover design: Lisa Fowler and Jenny Jensen Greenleaf
Composition: Eclipse Publishing Services
Cover photos: Bill Miller
Text illustration: K–2 students of Mrs. Hoyt and colleagues

Library of Congress Cataloging-in-Publication Data

Hoyt, Linda.
  Crafting nonfiction, lessons on writing process, traits, and craft / Linda Hoyt.
    p. cm.
  Includes bibliographical references and index.
  ISBN 0-325-03147-9
  1. Authorship. 2. Authorship--Vocational guidance. I. Title.
  PN145.H69 2011
  808'.02—dc22
                                    2010046029

ISBN 10: 0-325-03147-9
ISBN 13: 978-0-325-03147-7

Printed in the United States of America on acid-free paper
15 14 13 12 11 ML 1 2 3 4 5

ACKNOWLEDGMENTS

Every time I write a page of acknowledgments, I worry that I might omit someone who has helped me shape my thinking, shared an anecdoctal moment from their classroom, or passed along a sample of amazing student writing. The list I share below is a group of people who have contributed to my work, my own professonal growth, and offered questions that stimulate my ongoing effort to better understand how to serve children. They are among the many to whom I owe a debt of gratitude.

Maura Sullivan, Tina Miller, Debra Doorack, Charles McQuillan, David Stirling, Stephanie Levy, and Smokey Daniels, Heinemann *first* hand. You are a WOW in every way.

Tony Stead, fellow nonfiction devotee. Working together has been a grand adventure. Thanks so much.

Kelly Boswell, writing partner, friend, esteemed colleague.

Teresa Therriault, co-author of *Mastering the Mechanics*, best buddy, literacy counselor, and fellow traveler.

Marie Govro and Leah Starkovich, trusted reviewers and amazing educators from Gilbert Park Elementary. Thanks for the feedback and the fabulous cookies!

Barbara Petruccio, Doreen Osmun, Sandi Gordon, and fellow educators from Hudson, Ohio. Oh, my! Working with you and sharing your celebrations of learning have been a joy. Thank you for all of the wonderful writing samples and amazing moments with students.

Kathy Porterfield, Linda Sproul, Jennifer Patterson, Michael Shay, and teachers at Wilsonville Primary School. You offered counsel and professional thoughtfulness at a time when this project was but a dream. Thank you for your encouragement and generous sharing of student work.

Barbara Coleman, Kristy Thomas, and teachers at Wingate Elementary. Thank you for testing lessons, reflecting on possibilities, and helping me find a path that took these lessons to a higher level.

Jan McCall, Anne Pergiel, and Marie Davis, Kinnaman Elementary School. You joined the call when we had little more than wet clay. Thank you for your faithful testing of lessons and feedback. You are the best!

Jodi Wilson, Angela Duff, and Eba Farzana, Holmes Elementary. You believe in possibility, and it shows in the work of your writers. You raise the bar, open the door, and set high standards. The result is amazing.

Ann Stewart, sharp-minded, kind-hearted, and always focused on kids.

CONTENTS

Just as a florist takes pride in creating the right balance between structural elements, color, and form in a display of flowers, young writers find satisfaction in knowing how to add the artistic touches that craft elements, literary devices, and process bring to nonfiction writing.

— *Linda Hoyt*

TEACHING NONFICTION WRITING

Years ago, nonfiction resources were mostly black and white. Occasionally, there was a three-color line drawing or a grainy black and white photo. The text was written in tight, constrained sentences, and there was no sense of audience or sentence fluency. With these materials in hand, teachers often struggled to entice children into the world of nonfiction writing. Writers who absolutely vibrated with descriptive language and enthusiasm as they watched a butterfly chrysalis slowly release its treasured contents wrote pieces like "Butterflies have wings. Butterflies are pretty." There was a picture at the top of the paper, and the writing appeared in the bottom half. This flat, lifeless writing did not result from a lack of interest or a lack of descriptive vocabulary in their oral language bank. These nonfiction writers were modeling their writing after the only model they had—the nonfiction books in their hands.

Evolving Perspectives

Thankfully, today's nonfiction texts are loaded with gorgeous photographs, visually enticing page layouts, well-placed text features, and enticing language. If we were to apply the rubrics we utilize in scoring student writing to the nonfiction writing of superstars like Seymour Simon, Nicola Davies, Gail Gibbons, Walter Wick, Steve Jenkins, and Karen Wallace, their writing would score over the top on all traits.

Just as nonfiction resources have changed, beliefs about the role of nonfiction writing have changed as well. Nonfiction writing used to be saved for the intermediate grades, for a time when writers went from "learning to write" to "writing to learn." Thankfully, we now know that writers get better at writing *by writing* and that if we want writers to be proficient and strategic, they need to have extensive nonfiction writing experiences from the beginning.

Today's nonfiction brings excitement to both educators and children, fostering a fertile setting in which developing nonfiction writers can read, think, and write as they explore their innate interest in the world around them.

Nonfiction Writing Is Natural

Young children want to know about and understand the world around them. So writing about the world they know and understand is absolutely natural. They may begin by profiling in pictures and writing the slow progress of a caterpillar across their hand or the way the sun catches the wings of a butterfly as it lands on a flower. What is important is that innate curiosity and writing come together as powerful partners in inquiry and that we show young children how to create writing that is worthy of their lively imaginations and growing expertise with language.

Raise Expectations: Believe They Can

Writers in kindergarten and first and second grade become excited when they have opportunities to create interesting sentence structures, make powerful word choices, and add sensory images. They love presenting the facts they gather with voice, thoughtful organization, and nonfiction text features. Their vivid imaginations spring to life when they experience nonfiction writing that richly describes a setting, an animal, or the flare of electricity within a lightbulb, so it is important to believe in the power of these writers as they create nonfiction texts of their own. It is important to believe they can.

Children Copy What They See and Hear

It is no secret that children are experts at replicating the actions of role models in their lives. They listen to their parents talk and then use what they hear in their own oral language. They watch a teacher read aloud with expression and drama, and soon young readers are reading with expression and drama, too. It stands to reason, then, that if we model nonfiction writing that is richly constructed with varied sentence structures, powerful word choices, and fascinating punctuation—if we demonstrate Modeled Writing in which we take our best shot at writing like Seymour Simon, Steve Jenkins, or Nicola Davies—young children will consciously work at enriching their own nonfiction writing.

Build on your students' natural curiosity to generate the energy they need to read and write about their world.

We must demonstrate to our students that we are writers, too. It is only through the act of writing that we can show students that we value writing and its role in our learning lives.

—Lynne Dorfman and Rose Cappelli, *Nonfiction Mentor Texts*

Dynamic Demonstrations: Show Them How

Modeling is one of the most effective of all teaching strategies (Pearson and Fielding, 1991). When students see and hear an expert writer in action, they can imagine what is possible in their own writing. This means that, with the exception of writing models created to demonstrate drafting and spelling, modeled writing should look like it was written by an adult—not a child. During read-alouds, we read as an adult, delivering the reading selection with fluency, expression, and dramatic interpretation. We don't read aloud like a young child, so the same high standard for performance and delivery should be evident when we write in front of children.

Modeled writing is a time to pull out all the stops and generate nonfiction text that elevates expectations and paves the way for excellence. This is a time to let writers observe the creation of intriguing nonfiction writing that has fascinating facts plus inviting sentence formations, sizzling interjections, and mood-altering phrasing. This is a time to create a model that writers can aspire to emulate. By raising the standard for your modeled writing, you will lift your writers as well.

> The frog is hungry after his long sleep, but he waits patiently. Suddenly, his bulging eyes fixate on a dozing fly. His long, sticky tongue darts out and . . . Snap! The unsuspecting insect pops into a greedy mouth. Yum.

Sample Modeled Writing

The Power of Close Observation: Tuning In Kids as Observers

As nonfiction writing is modeled, children need to be reminded to tune in and look closely. Young writers need to understand that they will be expected to utilize the writing techniques and craft elements that you are modeling. Target their attention by thinking out loud as you write, using phrases such as "Watch how I . . .," "Notice the way I . . .," or "Tune in, writers, I am about to show you. . . ." This kind of close observation, guided and targeted by

When students see and hear an expert writer in action, they can imagine what is possible in their own writing.

your think-aloud language, will help writers understand that they are not gathered around the chart to be entertained. They are there to learn *how* to engage in a particular writing behavior.

Through close observation, writers are more likely to notice the techniques that empower nonfiction writing, tune in closely during a think-aloud, and hold their breath in awe as they watch how onomatopoeia and creative punctuation bring voice and life to a piece of writing.

As close observers unencumbered by paper and pen, young writers are free to notice details and see the natural path a nonfiction writer takes as she flows from thinking to writing and back to thinking. Through careful observation of their teacher as a writer, young learners gain critical understandings that empower them when they pick up their pencils to craft nonfiction texts of their own. And who could be better at offering those opportunities for close observation than the teacher they know and trust—the teacher who can take their hands and show them how to bring life into nonfiction writing?

Through careful observation of their teacher as a writer, young learners gain critical understandings that empower them when they pick up their pencils to craft nonfiction texts of their own.

> Did you know that sharks are sharp-toothed, meat-eating, fast-swimming predators? With twenty rows of razor-sharp teeth, they can bite 300 times harder than a human!

> Small as a pinecone and bald as a newborn mouse, baby Panda nestles into his mother's fur. Peep!

Sample Modeled Writing

In a setting where explicit modeling and think-alouds are offered every day so writers can see what they need to do and listen to a proficient writer think out loud, writing blossoms into a state of richness that could never be achieved through assignments alone. When we have higher expectations of ourselves as writing educators and of our students as developing writers, amazing things are possible. The important point is that your writers need to watch you engage in modeled writing every day. Empowered by the rich vocabulary and interesting language structures from your modeled writing, oral language will grow hand in hand with proficiency in nonfiction writing.

Crafting the Text: Be Conscious and Deliberate

When you generate nonfiction writing in front of students, you have an opportunity to explain that the words don't just roll off your pen like magic. Let your young writers know that even adults have to think about facts and then decide how to share them with a reader so the facts are exciting to read. Even adults take conscious time to think of interesting ways to open sentences, insert text features, and consider word choice. These conscious and deliberate choices that all writers need to make are the difference between flat, monotonous nonfiction writing and nonfiction writing that sparkles.

The *New York Times* proclaimed Seymour Simon, author of more than 250 nonfiction books for young readers, the dean of the children's science book field. *Kirkus Reviews* declared, "Simon may have done more than any other living author to help us understand and appreciate the beauty of our planet and the universe."

As literacy educators, we have much to learn from Seymour Simon. Even with his vast experience as a nonfiction researcher and writer, Seymour Simon utilizes a "list of craft elements" that he keeps by his side when he is writing (Simon, 2010). He knows that his job is to create a book loaded with facts on a particular topic, but he is steadfast in also infusing craft elements that will make the content more interesting and accessible. When I asked if he would share a few thoughts for inclusion in this book, he wrote the following.

CRAFTING MY BOOKS

When I write my books

about space or animals or weather, I'm always aware of my readers and how my writing must explain and clarify yet still be exciting and interesting. I'm explaining difficult concepts in many of my books so I try to make connections to a young reader's world and understanding. One of the ways I do this is to make comparisons such as this one from my book *Stars:* "With powerful telescopes, we can see that the stars are as many as the grains of sand on an ocean beach." I also try to use strong verbs to dramatize the text. In my book *Icebergs and Glaciers*, I wrote, "When glaciers move, they grind and crush everything in their path."

I try to write effective leads in all kinds of ways, such as getting the reader to participate by doing something physical, writing exciting visualization, drama and suspense, comparisons and analogies. In my book *The Heart*, the first pages open with "Make a fist. This is about the size of your heart . . . . It weighs only about ten ounces, about as much as one of your sneakers." I also like to ask questions of my readers. I use descriptive detail as a story line in many of my texts. In my view, writing exciting nonfiction is not that different from writing exciting fiction.

—Seymour Simon

Seymour Simon's conscious and deliberate infusion of craft elements and literary devices propels fact-laden nonfiction content into writing that is highly engaging for readers—rich in detail and sensory connections. Following the lead of Seymour Simon, we too can be conscious and deliberate in creating nonfiction that is both factual and exciting.

ABOUT *CRAFTING NONFICTION*

Crafting Nonfiction is designed to provide an array of simple, ready-to-use minilessons that can be slipped into writers workshop or into the nonfiction writing you provide in science, social studies, health, and mathematics. The goal of these lessons is to support you in providing top-quality nonfiction writing instruction that is embedded with craft and graced by process—with a minimum of preparation time.

As you dip into the lessons, you will find that there is a strong emphasis on cracking open the thinking that goes on inside the head of a writer as text is created. Samples of teacher language provide think-alouds that invite your writers inside the writing process and expose the joy of crafting text that is both factual and artfully written. You'll also find lessons that provide strong support for trait-based instruction, offering writers tips on word choice, sentence fluency, research and ideas, voice, conventions, and presentation.

There are no worries about taking the time to create fascinating passages for modeled writing. Samples for modeled writing are right here in these pages to springboard your thinking. You can use them as they are written or use them as a seed from which your own ideas can grow.

These lessons are, by design, short and focused. Each lesson can and should be completed in 15 minutes or less so that writers have time to do what they most need to do—write!

A Few Tips for Using This Resource

This resource is organized into two major sections: Process and Traits and Craft. Within each major section, you'll find subsections that are designed to make lessons organized and easy to find.

Process lessons are grouped according to the stages of the writing process. In Planning and Research, you will find a wealth of resources that range from modeling how to identify facts in a photograph to how to add factual detail to an illustration to how to use the key word strategy. In the Drafting section, lessons focus on helping writers get their thinking onto the page using picture alphabet cards, stretching words to say them slowly, or writing about a picture. Revising is the section where you will find helpful modeled writing lessons on how to add details, how to combine sentences, how to add ideas by cutting and pasting, and how to tune up sensory images. In the sections Editing and Presenting, the lessons turn toward audience and focus on spacing, spelling, and publishing.

The section Traits and Craft contains rich lessons that focus on the artistic side of writing. In this section, lessons are organized around traits of quality nonfiction writing, with craft elements woven into each section. The traits are as follows:

- Ideas
- Organization and text features
- Word choice and sentence fluency
- Voice and audience
- Conventions (punctuation, grammar, sentence structure, capitalization, spelling consciousness)

Features of a Lesson

Each lesson is focused on a narrow topic—a behavior that writers can absorb and attempt to apply immediately in nonfiction writing. The structure of the lesson is repeated throughout this resource, providing a familiar, predictable routine for both you and your students.

As you view the page, be sure to notice the When to Use It feature. This is designed to assist you in lesson selection.

Another feature you will want to notice is Turn and Talk. It is important to anticipate that there will be times for students to turn and talk woven right into the fabric of the lesson. This is essential processing time when discourse is distributed so all writers are talking, thinking, and reflecting on the learning that you are modeling. It is often helpful to have writers come to your meeting area with a "thinking partner" and for the thinking partners to sit together on the carpet. Since thinking partner matchups are already in place, you won't need to waste valuable lesson time while students try to find someone with whom to discuss the learning.

Most importantly, be sure to notice the sample modeled writing. This sample can be copied as is and save you the time of getting creative. Or you can use the modeled writing as a starter for your own thinking and shift the content toward a subject that is current within your classroom.

Steps of a Lesson

- *Focus the Learning* is a brief explanation of why this lesson is helpful to primary-age writers and often provides tips for ensuring success with the target learning.

- *Model* is the heart of the lesson. In this step, you will find think-aloud language that you may want to consider as you demonstrate and consciously show your writers how to infuse the target learning in a piece of nonfiction. The Model portion of the lesson is divided into two steps to provide a pause for turn and talks.

  This portion of the lesson is essential and worthy of a bit of advance thought. This is your vitally important opportunity to make your thinking transparent and show your students how proficient nonfiction writers construct a message, take notes, play with different sentence openers—and lift their nonfiction writing so it is not boring! So it is a good idea to read the sample text and think-aloud in advance and decide if you are going to use it as is or modify it to make it your own.

- *Analyze* is a time to reread the modeled writing and reflect. Because rereading is one of the most important process tools we can teach writers, you want to make it clear that writers *always* reread and reflect on what they have created. Let your writers watch you start at the beginning and read aloud, touching each word as you go. Let

them hear you noticing places in your work where you applied the target learning or places where you are thinking you might revise to make a sentence more exciting or descriptive. Analyze includes a final turn and talk, plus a sum-up for the lesson that should refocus your writers on the target learning and prepare them to pick up their pencils.

- *Variations* Differentiation is an essential key to lifting nonfiction writers toward the highest possible levels of success. You will notice that this section has suggestions for Less Experienced Writers and More Experienced Writers. These tips can be used to modify the overall lesson, support additional lessons if they should be appropriate, or guide your thinking as you plan for guided writing groups and confer with individuals.

- *Links to CD-ROM* Note cross-references that will give you tips on additional lessons that can be linked to this lesson to provide additional support or offer an opportunity to stretch and extend the learning.

Tools to Have on Hand

Most lessons call for you to model a piece of writing, thinking aloud as you construct the text. Therefore, you will need a good supply of chart paper and markers. Once models are created, you and your students will want to return to them for reference and ongoing support. You'll need a strategy for saving your modeled writing. Some teachers find it helpful to place modeled writing on hangers and simply hang them from a clothes rack. Others use a spiral tablet of charts and flip back and forth as needed.

Selecting Lessons

Selecting a lesson from this resource is like going to a restaurant and preparing to order. As you view the menu, you have the joyful challenge of selecting meal items that best match your personal needs and interests. I encourage you to treat this resource like a menu of possibility. As you view the menu options, pick and choose from lessons that support observable needs in your learners or guide your planning for guided writing and conferring.

Target Specific Needs

Formative assessments, your observations of writers during one-on-one conferences, and your analyses of student writing samples can and should guide your thinking and lesson selection. This resource is an opportunity to do what teachers do best—match instruction to learner need.

Examples of how to analyze a writing sample and then select specific lessons from this resource begin on page 18 of this resource.

Target a Particular Trait

Your students may benefit from lessons that focus on a particular trait, such as word choice or organization. Knowing that we need to help writers develop across the full spectrum of traits, you may want to work through these sections in order. Or you may see a need in your students, such as creating a clear beginning, middle, and end, that would lead you to a particular trait, such as organization.

Most of all, ensure that your writers experience modeled writing and support with an array of lessons representing each trait so their nonfiction writing development is structurally and artistically sound. When students have repeated exposure to quality models that demonstrate how to include a particular trait and when they have the opportunity to integrate that trait into their writing, achievement soars!

Organize by Time of Year

Early in the year, when you are establishing routines and understandings for writers workshop, you might focus on the lessons for process—especially planning, drafting, and revising. As the school year progresses and writers develop fluency and begin to consider publication, you might add lessons on editing and presenting.

If you are engaging writers in a unit of study on persuasion, report writing, procedural text, or written response, you might select lessons that best support the features of the unit. For example, when students are writing reports, you could select focus lessons that pertain to research or to specific text features such as bold words or a table of contents.

Weave Lessons Throughout the Day

Nonfiction writing can take its place at any time of the day— almost in any place in the school.

Across the Curriculum

With so much content crowding our instructional day, we need to integrate content across the curriculum. These lessons can be used to teach writing in connection with science, social studies, health, or mathematics. For example, if students are learning about frogs in science, you might consider choosing lessons that teach students how to research, take notes, and create a labeled drawing. Likewise, if you are engaging in a mathematics unit on graphing, you might choose the lessons that teach how to locate and use facts from a visual or how to create a chart or table.

In Writers Workshop

Writers workshop is grounded by an opening minilesson. The lessons and modeled writing presented in this resource will slip naturally right into your workshop routines, saving you time and elevating the nonfiction writing of your students.

Be Flexible!

However you choose to utilize the lessons in this book, realize that all of them can be used for whole-class minilessons, for small-group supports, or as vehicles to lift one-on-one conferences.

ONGOING, FORMATIVE ASSESSMENT: INFORMANT TO INSTRUCTION

Ongoing, authentic assessment is the heart of teaching. However, assessment is only useful when it is used to guide our instructional decisions. As teachers, it's imperative that we become careful observers, collecting writing samples to analyze, listening in on partner conversations between writers, conferring with individuals, and using expert kid-watching skills during guided writing sessions.

When we observe writers, analyzing writing samples and behaviors closely, we can determine which students are integrating the writing technique from modeled writing into their work. Close observation will make it clear which students might benefit from additional support in a small-group writing lesson or a one-on-one conference in which the skill, process, or craft element is modeled again. These careful observations will also guide you to know if the entire class may benefit from another modeled writing focused on the same writing technique.

Each piece of writing that you examine will broaden your base of understanding for your writers and improve the scaffolds you offer in conferences, in guided writing sessions, and in modeled writing demonstrations.

Analyzing Nonfiction Writing Samples: Observe, Reflect, Plan

The following nonfiction writing samples, reflective of those you might see in a primary classroom, offer invaluable insights into the development of each writer. As you analyze a writing sample, it is important to first identify the strengths of the writer and then to consider teaching moves and specific craft lessons that will best lift the development of this nonfiction writer.

As with all formative observations, it is important to note that while every writing sample provides valuable information, it takes a review of many samples over time to fully understand the strengths and areas of need for a learner. This is especially true with nonfiction writing, as each text type includes different text structures, features, and conventions.

MoM
plese
seind
me
pensils *Some*
Love
Maggie

Maggie's Note to Mom

Maggie's Note to Mom

Strengths of this writer:

This note is an authentic, functional nonfiction text type. Maggie has a greeting, a complete message, and a closing. She has used enough sounds that all words are decipherable, and her handwriting is neatly done.

Observations and possible teaching moves:

It would be great to confer with Maggie to celebrate this writing with her, pointing out the many strengths of what she has done. She is writing in a column down the center of the page rather than using the width of the available paper. It would also be helpful to guide Maggie in comparing the use of space to other writing she has done. If other writing samples suggest that she needs assistance with space management, a modeled writing in a small-group setting to work on spacing would help focus her on its importance.

Suggested lessons from this resource:

- Planning, Lesson 5, Planning Page Layout and Paper Selection
- Drafting, Lesson 5, Use Mostly Lowercase Letters
- Presenting, Lesson 3, Page Layout Includes Effective Use of Margins
- Capitalization, Lesson 2, Proper Nouns: Names and Places

Amazing Sunrise

Strengths of this writer:

Sydney has a piece that is organized by time and is easy to follow. She's provided enough letters and sounds so that the piece can be read easily.

Observations and possible teaching moves:

This writer has a lot to say, but she needs to narrow the topic and develop just one little nugget of her day. A reader would love to hear rich details about a particular sunrise and what made it so amazing, but instead Sydney has written a "dawn to dusk" narrative. She may need a nudge toward finding that golden moment in her day and developing that into a more focused piece of writing.

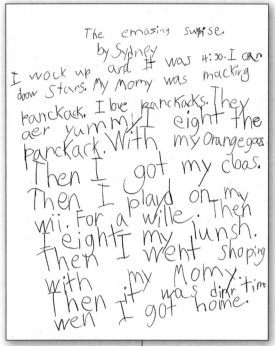

Amazing Sunrise

Suggested lessons from this resource:

- Revising, Lesson 1, Revising to Add Details
- Revising, Lesson 10, Tuning Up Sensory Images
- Ideas, Lesson 3, Narrow the Topic
- Organization, Lesson 1, Main Idea Maintained Throughout
- Spelling Consciousness, Lesson 3. Strategic Spellers Pay Attention to Syllables

Recycling Poster

Recycling Poster

Strengths of this writer:

This writer has made a clear and concise poster. It's easy to read and gets right to the point!

Observations and possible teaching moves:

This writer might be ready to learn how authors use bold words to add emphasis to posters and to differentiate between upper- and lowercase letters. This writer may also benefit from a short guided lesson on how pictures and words can go together. The writer has written about recycling bins but has drawn a picture of a trash can.

Suggested lessons from this resource:

- Organization, Lesson 2, Pictures and Words Work Together
- Text Features, Lesson 6, Bold Words
- Voice and Audience, Lesson 8, Show Excitement in Writing (Exclamation Point)
- Voice and Audience, Lesson 9, Include Humor or Surprise

Delaney's Persuasive Letter

Strengths of this writer:

What a delightful piece of writing! Delaney has crafted a convincing text that would make any teacher consider a classroom pet. She's combined sentences to make a piece that is pleasant to read and flows nicely.

> Dear Mrs. Flagel,
> Please get a classroom pet. We will take care of it! You won't have to worry one bit. We will feed it, get it a cage, and when it's older (like a dog) We will take it for walks! We will also give it baths.
>   With hope,
>   Delaney

Delaney's Persuasive Letter

Observations and possible teaching moves:

The writing is clear and organized, but it needs a little pizzazz! I might consider teaching Delaney how to insert those extra details that could make the piece even more effective. She might also benefit from analyzing how each sentence begins and revising the beginning words to add variety.

Suggested lessons from this resource:

• Organization, Lesson 5, Details Support Main Idea
• Organization, Lesson 7, Craft a Satisfying Ending
• Word Choice, Lesson 1, Use Descriptive Words and Phrases
• Sentence Fluency, Lesson 3, Varied Sentence Beginnings

To-Do List

To-Do List

Strengths of this writer:

This (busy!) writer has beautifully organized this to-do list by time of day. He's done a nice job underlining the different times of day and has spaced his bullets down the left-hand side of the page, just as he should. The addition of the frowny face at the end of the piece adds some voice.

Observations and possible teaching moves:

This writer has done a great job of stretching words to include many of the sounds, but he could benefit from some additional support with spelling. In a conference with this writer, it would be good to ask him if there are any words that *he* thinks need to be "fixed up." You could then show him how writers use resources around the room to help them as they spell familiar words.

Suggested lessons from this resource:

- Spelling Consciousness, Lesson 3, Strategic Spellers Pay Attention to Syllables
- Spelling Consciousness, Lesson 4, Strategic Spellers Use a Variety of Resources

Labeled Bear Diagram

Strengths of this writer:

This writer has done an effective job of creating a visual with factual information. She has utilized a title (BEAR) and has included and labeled all of the important parts of the bear and his surroundings (sun and cloud).

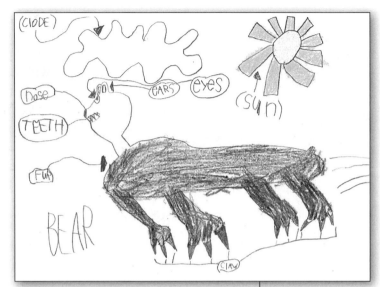

Labeled Bear Diagram

Observations and possible teaching moves:

This writer might be ready to learn how writers can use a visual like this to develop a piece of writing. As you confer with this student, you might show her how writers can take one label in a drawing and write a little bit about it. For example, she might write a page about the bear's claws. This might lead her to conduct further research and would stretch her as a writer.

Suggested lessons from this resource:

- Drafting, Lesson 1, Write About Your Pictures
- Ideas, Lesson 4, Infuse Interesting Details
- Text Features, Lesson 2, Headings Help Your Reader

Frog Sentence

Frog Sentence

Strengths of this writer:

The writer of this piece has used some great action to engage the reader. She's also incorporated powerful verbs and onomatopoeia, which enhance the writing. The illustration and the speech bubbles add a whimsical touch.

Observations and possible teaching moves:

Other than some quick teaching on how to capitalize the beginning of each sentence, it would be good to challenge this writer to rewrite this sentence from a different point of view, perhaps shifting to first person. It would be informative to chat with this writer to see if she could continue the piece to elaborate on *what* the frog catches and what the frog does once the food is caught. It appears that this writer has more information that could be shared on this topic!

Suggested lessons from this resource:

• Organization, Lesson 5, Details Support Main Idea
• Craft, Lesson 3, Shifting Point of View
• Capitalization, Lesson 1, Capitalize Beginning of Sentences

Key Word Sentence

Strengths of this writer:

This child has gathered information using the key word strategy and then has used those words to develop a sentence. He's even added a little detail by telling the reader *where* the puppies run.

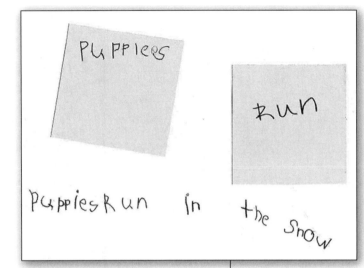

Key Word Sentence

Observations and possible teaching moves:

This writer may benefit from a small-group lesson on how to identify additional facts by looking at a visual. The writer can then add more detail (key words, text, or illustration) to enrich the piece.

Suggested lessons from this resource:

- Research, Lesson 1, Identify Facts in a Visual
- Research, Lesson 4, Create a Visual that Contains Facts
- Ideas, Lesson 2, Write About Pictures
- Organization, Lesson 5, Details Support Main Idea

As bravley as a lion

The crayfish move to get it food

The Brave Crayfish

The Brave Crayfish

Strengths of this writer:

This writer has used action to engage the reader and paint a picture of this crayfish. I'm dying to know more!

Observations and possible teaching moves:

This writer may be ready to add interest with compound descriptors. You could challenge her to describe the crayfish and then add more details to help teach a reader something new about how the crayfish goes about catching its prey.

Suggested lessons from this resource:

- Ideas, Lesson 7, Teach Your Reader Something New
- Word Choice, Lesson 2, Target Powerful Action Verbs
- Word Choice, Lesson 8, Compound Descriptors and Hyphens
- Voice and Audience, Lesson 11, Draw Your Reader into the Setting

RECORD KEEPING FORMS

Keep Track of Writers' Growth: Class Record-Keeping Grid

A class record-keeping grid is a helpful tool for recording and keeping track of your modeled writing as well as your students' attempts to employ process, trait, or craft elements from your demonstrations. All you need to do is list your modeled writing lesson topics across the top of the grid and then note when you observe the target in an example of student writing. You will quickly be able to differentiate instruction, providing extra assistance for those who need it.

Class Record-Keeping Grid

Writers	Draw pictures before you write	Add labels to drawings	Count the words in a message	Revise to add details	Add words with a caret	Combine sentences (and, so, but, or)	Make the setting stand out	Beginning, middle, end
Ji	9/8	9/16	10/14					
Alina	9/8	9/8	9/16	9/21	9/21	10/1	10/15	
Margetta	10/1	10/4	10/7					
Yolisa	9/8	9/22		10/15	10/1			
Angie	9/7	9/7	9/22	9/22	9/22			10/7
Harvey	10/1	10/4	10/15					
Ryanne	9/21	9/21			10/14			
Dominic	9/15	9/22	10/1		10/1			
Taylor	9/9	9/9	9/9	9/16	9/16	9/21	10/1	10/15
Marcos	9/22	10/7	10/1	10/7				
Brady	9/8	9/22	10/14					
Carson	9/7	9/21	10/4	10/4	10/4			
Angelina	10/4	10/4	10/7					

LINKS TO CD-ROM:

Keep Track of Your Lessons: Demonstration Lesson Tracker

A lesson tracker can help you plan instruction and keep an eye on the topics you are teaching. This broad look will help you evaluate the balance of your instruction both across the writing process and within your grouping structures. The Demonstration Lesson Tracker pictured here is one of 17—one for each section in this book—on the accompanying CD-ROM.

Demonstration Lesson Tracker: Planning

Planning		Date Modeled		Date Modeled		Date Modeled	
		Whole Class	Small Group	Whole Class	Small Group	Whole Class	Small Group
1	Draw Pictures Before You Write						
2	Talk Before You Write						
3	Create a Labeled Diagram						
4	Map Out Your Writing with Informational Pictures						
5	Planning Page Layout and Paper Selection						
6	Gather Information with the Key Word Strategy						
Other							

LINKS TO CD-ROM:

Monitor Progress: Trait Scoring Guide

The scoring guide that follows is designed to support your ongoing assessment of trait development in the writers in your classroom. You can use the guide "as is" or use it as a springboard to create your own scoring guide.

Trait Scoring Guide

	Just Beginning (1) _____	Developing (2) _____	Getting Stronger (3) _____	Wow! (4) _____
Content and Ideas (the meaning and core communication of the piece)	The writer has difficulty selecting a topic and offers few details.	The main idea is present, but there are few details and specifics.	Details are present and related to the broad topic. The writing is focused enough and rich enough in details to satisfy a reader's curiosity.	The topic is narrow and very well developed. Substantial details are provided in a manner that interests the reader.
Organization and Text Features (the internal structure of the piece, and the text and graphic features that support the piece)	The writing lacks a beginning or ending, and the writing lacks organization. No text features are included in the writing.	A beginning and ending are present but not well developed. The order and structure are not clear. A few text features, such as title and labels, are used.	The beginning and ending are more clear, and the order and structure are logical. Additional text features are included (labels, title, boldface words, and captions).	The beginning and ending are well crafted. There is a clear order and structure. Numerous text features are included in the illustration and text (labels, title, boldface words, captions, cutaways, diagrams).
Style (rich vocabulary and the way words flow from sentence to sentence)	Vocabulary is basic. Sentences are simple and do not flow together. The writing is choppy or incomplete.	The writing includes functional words but seldom selects words that are interesting. Sentences are of similar length, and many start the same way.	Verbs are becoming active and nouns more precise. Sentences have variety in length and beginnings. The piece can be read aloud with ease.	Action verbs and precise nouns are used in a way that adds interest to the piece. Adjectives create clear sensory images for the reader. There is a smooth flow to the writing. The piece invited expressive oral reading.
Conventions (punctuation, grammar, sentence structure, capitalization, spelling consciousness)	Lack of conventional spelling affects readability. Other conventions are not present.	Spelling is close to conventional and can be read. End punctuation and capitalization are used.	Spelling is strong. Grammar, punctuation, and sentence structure are close to conventional.	Spelling of even more difficult words tends to be correct. A variety of punctuation marks are used.

REFERENCES

Anderson, J. 2005. *Mechanically Inclined: Building Grammar, Usage, and Style into Writers Workshop.* Portland, ME: Stenhouse.

Angelillo, J. 2002. *A Fresh Approach to Teaching Punctuation: Helping Young Writers Use Conventions With Precision and Purpose.* New York: Scholastic.

Barone, D., and L. M. Morrow, eds., *Literacy and Young Children: Research-Based Practices,* 226–242. New York: Guilford Press.

Bridges, L. 1997. *Writing as a Way of Knowing.* York, ME: Stenhouse.

Britton, J., T. Burgess, N. Martin, A. Mcleod, and H. Rosen. 1975. *The Development of Writing Abilities.* London: Macmillian.

Boushey, G., and J. Moser. 2009. *The CAFÉ Book: Engaging All Students in Daily Literacy Assessment and Instruction.* Portland, ME: Stenhouse.

Calkins, L. et al. 2003. *Units of Study for Primary Writing.* Portsmouth, NH: Heinemann.

Common Core State Standards. 2010. Washington, DC: Council of Chief State School Officers and the National Governor's Association.

Culham, R. 2004. *Using Picture Books to Teach Writing With the Traits.* New York: Scholastic.

Dorfman, L., and R. Cappelli. 2009. *Nonfiction Mentor Texts.* Portland, ME: Stenhouse.

Duke, N. 2004. "The Case for Informational Text." *Educational Leadership* 61 (6): 40–44.

Duke, N., and S. Bennett-Armistead. 2003. *Reading & Writing Informational Text in the Primary Grades: Research-Based Practices.* New York: Scholastic.

Glover, M. 2009. *Engaging Young Writers Preschool-Grade 1.* Portsmouth, NH: Heinemann.

Greiner, A. 2007. "Eleven Research-Based Tips for Improving Writing Instruction." *Center for Performance Assessment*

Newsletter, May 1, 2007. Denver, CO: Center for Performance Assessment.

Hoyt, L. 1999/2009. *Revisit, Reflect, Retell.* Portsmouth, NH: Heinemann.

———. 2000. *Snapshots: Literacy Minilessons Up Close.* Portsmouth, NH: Heinemann.

———. 2003. *Make It Real.* Portsmouth, NH: Heinemann.

———. 2004. *Navigating Informational Text.* Portsmouth, NH: Heinemann.

———. 2005. *Spotlight on Comprehension.* Portsmouth, NH: Heinemann.

———. 2007. *Interactive Read Alouds, K–1.* Portsmouth, NH: Heinemann.

———. 2007. *Interactive Read Alouds, 2–3.* Portsmouth, NH: Heinemann.

Hoyt, L., M. Mooney, and B. Parkes. 2003. *Exploring Informational Texts: From Theory to Practice.* Portsmouth, NH: Heinemann.

Hoyt, L., and T. Therriault. 2008. *Mastering the Mechanics K–1.* New York: Scholastic.

Hoyt, L., and T. Therriault. 2008. *Mastering the Mechanics 2–3.* New York: Scholastic.

Moline, S. 1995. *I See What You Mean: Children at Work with Visual Information.* Melbourne, Australia: Longman.

Mooney, M. 2001. *Text Forms and Features: A Resource for Intentional Teaching.* Katonah, NY: Richard C. Owen.

Murray, D. M. 1984. *Write to Learn.* New York: Holt, Rinehart.

Newkirk, T. 1989. *More Than Stories: The Range of Children's Writing.* Portsmouth, NH: Heinemann.

Pearson, P. D., and L. Fielding. 1991. "Comprehension Instruction." In *Handbook of Reading Research*, Vol. 2, edited by R. Barr, M. Kamil, P. Mosenthan, and P. D. Pearson, 815–860. New York: Longman.

Portalupi, J., and R. Fletcher. 2001. *Nonfiction Craft Lessons.* Portland, ME: Stenhouse.

Purcell-Gates, V., N. K. Duke, and J. A. Martineau. 2007. "Learning to read and write genre-specific text: roles of authentic experience and explicit teaching." *Reading Research Quarterly* 42: 8–45.

Ray, K. 1999. *Wondrous Words.* Portsmouth, NH: Heinemann.

Ray, K., and L. Cleaveland. 2004. *About the Authors: Writing Workshop with Our Youngest Writers.* Portsmouth, NH: Heinemann.

Ray, K., and M. Glover. *Already Ready: Nurturing Writers in Preschool and Kindergarten.* Portsmouth, NH: Heinemann.

Routman, R. 2004. *Writing Essentials: Raising Expectations and Results While Simplifying Teaching.* Portsmouth, NH: Heinemann.

Saunders-Smith, G. 2009. *Nonfiction Text Structures for Better Comprehension and Response.* Gainesville, FL: Maupin House.

Simon, S. 2010. Presentation at the International Reading Association Conference, Chicago, IL.

Stead, T. 2001. *Is That a Fact? Teaching Nonfiction Writing K–3.* York, ME: Stenhouse.

———. 2003. "The Art of Persuasion." *Teaching Pre K–8,* November/December.

Stead, T., and L. Hoyt. 2011. *Explorations in Nonfiction Writing: Kindergarten.* Portsmouth, NH: Heinemann.

———. 2011. *Explorations in Nonfiction Writing: Grade 1.* Portsmouth, NH: Heinemann.

———. 2011. *Explorations in Nonfiction Writing: Grade 2.* Portsmouth, NH: Heinemann.

MASTER LESSON CHART

🔍 Research

	K	1	2
1 Identify Facts in a Visual	●	●	

RELATED LESSONS: *Organization:* Lesson 2, Pictures and Words Work Together

	K	1	2
2 Locate and Use Important Words and Phrases: Alphabox	●	●	●

RELATED LESSONS: *Planning:* Lesson 6, Gather Information with the Key Word Strategy
Word Choice: Lesson 1, Use Descriptive Words and Phrases
Word Choice: Lesson 2, Target Powerful Action Verbs

	K	1	2
3 Locate and Use Facts from Multiple Sources		●	●

RELATED LESSONS: *Planning:* Lesson 6, Gather Information with the Key Word Strategy
Research: Lesson 2, Locate and Use Important Words and Phrases: Alphabox

	K	1	2
4 Create a Visual with Factual Attributes	●	●	●

RELATED LESSONS: *Planning:* Lesson 3, Create a Labeled Diagram
Ideas: Lesson 7, Teach Your Reader Something New
Ideas: Lesson 4, Infuse Interesting Details

	K	1	2
5 Place Labels on Illustrations	●	●	

RELATED LESSONS: *Planning:* Lesson 3, Create a Labeled Diagram
Text Features: Lesson 3, Questions Make Great Headings

	K	1	2
6 Use *I Remember!* to Summarize Information	●	●	●

RELATED LESSONS: *Research:* Lesson 8, Use the Very Important Points (VIP) Strategy
for Key Information

	K	1	2
7 Sketch to Stretch: Visual Summary	●	●	●

RELATED LESSONS: *Planning:* Lesson 1, Draw Pictures Before You Write
Research: Lesson 4, Create a Visual that Contains Facts

	K	1	2
8 Use the Very Important Points (VIP) Strategy for Key Information	●	●	●

RELATED LESSONS: *Planning:* Lesson 6, Gather Information with the Key Word Strategy

	K	1	2
9 Use a Pocket Organizer		●	●

RELATED LESSONS: *Organization:* Lesson 9, Multiple Pages Are Used:
Page Breaks Support Units of Meaning
Drafting: Lesson 7, Turning Notes into Sentences

	K	1	2
10 Using a Research Notebook	●	●	●

RELATED LESSONS: *Research:* Lesson 3, Locate and Use Facts from Multiple Sources

🔍 Planning

	K	1	2
1 Draw Pictures Before You Write	●	●	●

RELATED LESSONS: *Drafting:* Lesson 1, Write About Your Pictures
Research: Lesson 7, Sketch to Stretch: Visual Summary

MASTER LESSON CHART

Planning *(continued)*   K   1   2

2 Talk Before You Write   ● ● ●

RELATED LESSONS: *Planning:* Lessons 1, 3, 4
                     Research: Lesson 1, Identify Facts in a Visual

3 Create a Labeled Diagram   ● ● ●

RELATED LESSONS: *Research:* Lesson 5, Place Labels on Illustrations
                     Text Features: Lesson 5, Diagrams with Labels

4 Map Out Your Writing with Informational Pictures   ● ● ●

RELATED LESSONS: *Organization:* Lesson 3, Plan the Beginning and the End . . . Then the Middle
                     Organization: Lesson 9, Multiple Pages Are Used:
                     Page Breaks Support Units of Meaning

5 Planning Page Layout and Paper Selection   ● ●

RELATED LESSONS: *Text Features:* Lessons 2–10

6 Gather Information with the Key Word Strategy   ● ● ●

RELATED LESSONS: *Research:* Lessons 1, 2, 5
                     Text Features: Lesson 6, Bold Words

Drafting   K   1   2

1 Write About Your Pictures   ● ● ●

RELATED LESSONS: *Planning:* Lessons 1–4
                     Research: Lesson 7, Sketch to Stretch: Visual Summary

2 Stretching Words . . . Listening to Sounds   ● ●

RELATED LESSONS: *Spelling Consciousness:* Lesson 2, Stretching Words . . . Writing Sounds You Know

3 Using a Picture-Alphabet Card   ● ●

RELATED LESSONS: *Spelling Consciousness:* Lesson 4, Strategic Spellers Use a Variety of Resources

4 Count the Words in a Message   ● ●

RELATED LESSONS: *Revising:* Lesson 2, Adding Words with a Caret
                     Revising: Lesson 8, Deleting Extra Words

5 Use Mostly Lowercase Letters   ● ●

RELATED LESSONS: *Capitalization:* Lessons 1–4

6 Scratching Out . . . Changing Your Mind   ● ● ●

RELATED LESSONS: *Revising:* Lesson 2, Adding Words with a Caret
                     Revising: Lesson 5, Adding Ideas by Cutting and Taping

7 Turning Notes into Sentences   ● ●

RELATED LESSONS: *Research:* Lesson 6, Use *I Remember!* to Summarize Information
                     Sentence Fluency: Lesson 4, Varying Sentence Beginnings with Prepositional Phrases

MASTER LESSON CHART

Revising

	K	1	2
1 Revising to Add Details	●	●	●
RELATED LESSONS: *Ideas:* Lesson 4, Infuse Interesting Details *Word Choice:* Lesson 3, Select Words that Show Order or Sequence			
2 Adding Words with a Caret	●	●	●
RELATED LESSONS: *Word Choice:* Lesson 6, Adding Action: Group "ing" Words Together *Organization:* Lesson 5, Details Support Main Ideas			
3 Revising a Lead to Make It Stronger	●	●	●
RELATED LESSONS: *Organization:* Lesson 6, Create an Inviting Lead *Voice and Audience:* Lesson 11, Draw Your Reader into the Setting			
4 Sentence Combining		●	●
RELATED LESSONS: *Sentence Structure:* Lesson 3, Compound Sentences *Sentence Structure:* Lesson 4, Introductory Phrases or Clauses			
5 Adding Ideas by Cutting and Taping		●	●
6 Revising to Add Variety to Sentence Beginnings		●	●
RELATED LESSONS: *Revising:* Lesson 4, Sentence Combining *Sentence Fluency:* Lesson 3, Varied Sentence Beginnings			
7 Checking the Closing	●	●	●
RELATED LESSONS: *Voice and Audience:* Lesson 7, At the End, Reveal Your Thoughts, Feelings, and Opinions *Organization:* Lesson 7, Craft a Satisfying Ending			
8 Deleting Extra Words	●	●	●
9 Recasting a Single Page as a Book	●	●	●
RELATED LESSONS: *Planning:* Lesson 4, Map Out Your Writing with Informational Pictures *Organization:* Lesson 9, Multiple Pages Are Used: Page Breaks Support Units of Meaning			
10 Tuning Up Sensory Images		●	●
RELATED LESSONS: *Word Choice:* Lesson 1, Use Descriptive Words and Phrases *Word Choice:* Lesson 2, Target Powerful Action Verbs			
11 Stick to the Main Idea		●	●
RELATED LESSONS: *Organization:* Lesson 1, Main Idea Maintained Throughout *Drafting:* Lesson 1, Write About Your Pictures			
12 Using a Revision Checklist		●	●

34

MASTER LESSON CHART

Editing

	K	1	2
1 Word Boundaries: Keep Letters in a Word Close Together	●	●	
2 Reread and Touch Each Word RELATED LESSONS: *Drafting:* Lesson 4, Count the Words in a Message	●	●	
3 Focused Edits: Reread for Each Editing Point RELATED LESSONS: *Editing:* Lesson 6, Using an Editing Checklist	●	●	●
4 Reread to Add Letters to Words RELATED LESSONS: *Drafting:* Lesson 2, Stretching Words . . . Listening to Sounds *Drafting:* Lesson 3, Using a Picture-Alphabet Card	●	●	●
5 Using Spelling Consciousness While Editing	●	●	●
6 Using an Editing Checklist	●	●	●
7 How to Peer Edit	●	●	●
8 Using Familiar Resources to Help You Edit	●	●	●

Presenting

	K	1	2
1 Handwriting Is Neat and Legible RELATED LESSONS: *Drafting:* Lesson 5, Use Mostly Lowercase Letters	●	●	●
2 Illustrations Are Detailed and Add Information RELATED LESSONS: *Organization:* Lesson 2, Pictures and Words Work Together *Planning:* Lesson 3, Create a Labeled Diagram	●	●	●
3 Page Layout Includes Effective Use of Margins RELATED LESSONS: *Planning:* Lesson 5, Planning Page Layout and Paper Selection	●	●	
4 Careful Spacing Between Words Clarifies Word Boundaries RELATED LESSONS: *Editing:* Lesson 1, Word Boundaries: Keep Letters in a Word Close Together	●	●	
5 In Final Drafts Most Words Are Spelled Correctly RELATED LESSONS: *Spelling Consciousness:* Lesson 3, Strategic Spellers Pay Attention to Syllables *Spelling Consciousness:* Lesson 5, Navigating Homophones		●	●
6 About the Author	●	●	●

MASTER LESSON CHART

◯ Ideas

	K	1	2
1 Creating a Topic List	●	●	●
2 Write About Pictures	●	●	

RELATED LESSONS: *Planning:* Lessons 1–4
Research: Lesson 1, Identify Facts in a Visual

	K	1	2
3 Narrow the Topic	●	●	●

RELATED LESSONS: *Planning:* Lesson 4, Map Out Your Writing with Informational Pictures

	K	1	2
4 Infuse Interesting Details	●	●	●

RELATED LESSONS: *Organization:* Lesson 5, Details Support Main Idea
Voice and Audience: Lesson 3, Capture the Interest of Your Reader

	K	1	2
5 Add a Little Action		●	●

RELATED LESSONS: *Ideas:* Lesson 10, Using Comparisons
Word Choice: Lesson 6, Add Action: Group *-ing* Words Together

	K	1	2
6 Make the Setting Stand Out		●	●

RELATED LESSONS: *Revising:* Lesson 10, Tuning Up Sensory Images
Word Choice: Lesson 10, Transition Words to Add Information or Conclude

	K	1	2
7 Teach Your Reader Something New	●	●	●

RELATED LESSONS: *Voice and Audience:* Lesson 3, Capture the Interest of Your Reader
Research: Lesson 8, Use the Very Important Points (VIP) Strategy for Key Information

	K	1	2
8 Separating Fact and Opinion	●	●	●

RELATED LESSONS: *Research:* Lesson 1, Identify Facts in a Visual
Research: Lesson 4, Create a Visual that Contains Facts

	K	1	2
9 Details Highlight Attributes of Subject	●	●	●

RELATED LESSONS: *Revising:* Lesson 1, Revising to Add Details
Ideas: Lesson 4, Infuse Interesting Details

	K	1	2
10 Using Comparisons	●	●	●
11 Focus on "One"	●	●	●

◯ Organization

	K	1	2
1 Main Idea Maintained Throughout	●	●	●

RELATED LESSONS: *Planning:* Lesson 4, Map Out Your Writing with Informational Pictures
Revising: Lesson 11, Stick to the Main Idea

	K	1	2
2 Pictures and Words Work Together	●	●	

RELATED LESSONS: *Drafting:* Lesson 1, Write About Your Pictures
Text Features: Lesson 4, Add Captions to Illustrations

MASTER LESSON CHART

Organization (continued)

	K	1	2
3 Plan the Beginning and End . . . Then the Middle RELATED LESSONS: *Organization:* Lesson 6, Creating an Inviting Lead *Organization:* Lesson 7, Craft a Satisfying Ending	●	●	●
4 Use a Logical Sequence RELATED LESSONS: *Planning:* Lesson 4, Map Out Your Writing with Informational Pictures	●	●	●
5 Details Support Main Idea RELATED LESSONS: *Ideas:* Lesson 9, Details Highlight Attributes of Subject *Sentence Fluency:* Lesson 6, The Rule of Three	●	●	●
6 Create an Inviting Lead RELATED LESSONS: *Word Choice:* Lesson 6, Adding Interest with *-ing* Words *Voice and Audience:* Lesson 3, Capture the Interest of Your Reader		●	●
7 Craft a Satisfying Ending RELATED LESSONS: *Voice and Audience:* Lesson 7, At the End, Reveal Your Thoughts, Feelings, and Opinions		●	●
8 Organizing with a Graphic Organizer RELATED LESSONS: Storyboard Resources CD-ROM *Ideas:* Lesson 3, Narrow the Topic *Organization:* Lesson 3, Plan the Beginning and End . . . Then the Middle	●	●	●
9 Multiple Pages Are Used: Page Breaks Support Units of Meaning RELATED LESSONS: *Planning:* Lesson 4, Map Out Your Writing with Informational Pictures	●	●	●
10 Paragraphs RELATED LESSONS: *Text Features:* Lesson 2, Headings Help Your Reader *Presenting:* Lesson 3, Page Layout Includes Effective Use of Margins		●	●
11 Create a Question and Answer Book	●	●	●
12 Sharing Information as a List Poem	●	●	●

Text Features

	K	1	2
1 Choose a Title that Is Interesting RELATED LESSONS: *Voice and Audience:* Lesson 5, Pick an Enticing Title *Word Choice:* Lesson 7, Use Onomatopoeia		●	●
2 Headings Help Your Reader RELATED LESSONS: *Capitalization:* Lesson 3, Capitalize Words in a Title		●	●
3 Questions Make Great Headings RELATED LESSONS: *Research:* Lesson 9, Use a Pocket Organizer		●	●
4 Add Captions to Illustrations		●	●

MASTER LESSON CHART

Text Features *(continued)*   K   1   2

5 Diagrams with Labels   •   •   •
RELATED LESSONS: *Planning:* Lesson 3, Create a Labeled Diagram
                        Research: Lesson 5, Place Labels on Illustrations

6 Bold Words   •   •   •

7 Table of Contents   •   •

8 Insert Page Numbers   •   •   •

9 Chart/Table/Graph   •   •

10 Bullets   •   •   •

Word Choice

1 Use Descriptive Words and Phrases   •   •   •
RELATED LESSONS: *Revising:* Lesson 1, Revising to Add Details
                        Ideas: Lesson 4, Infuse Interesting Details

2 Target Powerful Action Verbs   •   •   •
RELATED LESSONS: *Ideas:* Lesson 5, Add a Little Action

3 Select Words that Show Order or Sequence   •   •   •

4 Use Words and Phrases to Focus on Location or Place   •   •   •
RELATED LESSONS: *Ideas:* Lesson 6, Make the Setting Stand Out

5 Beginning Sentences with *-ing* Words   •   •

6 Add Action: Group *-ing* Words Together   •

7 Use Onomatopoeia   •   •   •
RELATED LESSONS: *Sentence Fluency:* Lesson 2, Reading Aloud to Check Sentence Fluency

8 Compound Descriptors and Hyphens   •

9 Have Fun with Alliteration   •   •   •
RELATED LESSONS: *Text Features:* Lesson 1, Choose a Title that Is Interesting

10 Transition Words to Add Information or Conclude   •

Sentence Fluency

1 Sentences Are of Varying Lengths   •   •   •
RELATED LESSONS: *Sentence Structure:* Lesson 1, Two-Word Sentences
                        Word Choice: Lesson 5, Beginning Sentences with *-ing* Words

MASTER LESSON CHART

Sentence Fluency *(continued)*	K	1	2
2 Reading Aloud to Check Sentence Fluency	●	●	●
RELATED LESSONS: *Word Choice:* Lesson 7, Use Onomatopoeia			
3 Varied Sentence Beginnings		●	●
RELATED LESSONS: *Revising:* Lesson 6, Add Variety to Sentence Beginnings			
4 Varying Sentence Beginnings with Prepositional Phrases		●	●
RELATED LESSONS: *Word Choice:* Lesson 5, Beginning Sentences with *-ing* Words			
Revising: Lesson 6, Revising to Add Variety to Sentence Beginnings			
5 Varying Sentence Beginnings with Phrases Focused on Time		●	●
RELATED LESSONS: *Word Choice:* Lesson 4, Use Words and Phrases to Focus on Location or Place			
6 The Rule of Three		●	●
RELATED LESSONS: *Revising:* Lesson 4, Sentence Combining			
Punctuation: Lesson 4, Comma in a Series			

Voice and Audience

	K	1	2
1 Developing an Awareness of Voice	●	●	●
2 Speak Directly to Your Reader		●	●
RELATED LESSONS: *Voice and Audience:* Lesson 12, Shifting Point of View			
3 Consider: Capture the Interest of Your Reader		●	●
RELATED LESSONS: *Research:* Lesson 1, Identify Facts in a Visual			
4 Pick a Topic You Find Interesting	●	●	●
RELATED LESSONS: *Text Features:* Lesson 1, Choose a Title that Is Interesting			
5 Pick an Enticing Title	●	●	●
RELATED LESSONS: *Word Choice:* Lesson 9, Have Fun with Alliteration			
Text Features: Lesson 1, Choose a Title that Is Interesting			
6 Make Your Writing Sound Like <u>You</u>	●	●	●
RELATED LESSONS: *Planning:* Lesson 2, Talk Before You Write			
7 At the End, Reveal Your Thoughts, Feelings, and Opinions		●	●
RELATED LESSONS: *Ideas:* Lesson 8, Separating Fact and Opinion			
Organization: Lesson 7, Craft a Satisfying Ending			
8 Show Excitement in Writing		●	●
RELATED LESSONS: *Punctuation:* Lesson 5, Comma: After Introductory Element or Clause			
9 Include Humor or Surprise	●	●	●
10 Voice Shifts with Your Audience			●

	K	1	2
Voice and Audience *(continued)*			
11 Draw Your Reader into the Setting		●	●
RELATED LESSONS: *Organization:* Lesson 6, Create an Inviting Lead			
Word Choice: Lesson 4, Use Words and Phrases to Focus on Location or Place			
12 Shifting Point of View	●	●	●

Punctuation

	K	1	2
1 End Punctuation (statement)	●	●	
RELATED LESSONS: *Sentence Structure:* Lesson 1, Two-Word Sentences			
2 End Punctuation (question)	●	●	●
RELATED LESSONS: *Organization:* Lesson 11, Create a Question and Answer Book			
3 End Punctuation (exclamation point)	●	●	●
RELATED LESSONS: *Voice and Audience:* Lesson 8, Show Excitement in Writing			
4 Comma in a Series		●	●
RELATED LESSONS: *Word Choice:* Lesson 6, Add Action: Group *-ing* Words Together			
5 Comma: After Introductory Element or Clause			●
RELATED LESSONS: *Word Choice:* Lesson 4, Use Words and Phrases to Focus on Location or Place			
Word Choice: Lesson 5, Beginning Sentences with *-ing* Words			
6 Use a Variety of Punctuation Elements	●	●	●
RELATED LESSONS: *Word Choice:* Lesson 7, Use Onomatopoeia			

Grammar

	K	1	2
1 Singular and Plural Nouns	●	●	●
2 Subject and Verb Agreement		●	●
3 Verb Tense		●	●
4 Pronoun Order	●	●	●
5 Single vs Double Subject	●	●	●
6 Open with an Adverb	●	●	●
RELATED LESSONS: *Sentence Fluency:* Lesson 4, Varying Sentence Beginnings with Prepositional Phrases			
7 Use Stellar Adjectives	●	●	●
RELATED LESSONS: *Word Choice:* Lesson 1, Use Descriptive Words and Phrases			
Word Choice: Lesson 8, Compound Descriptors and Hyphens			

MASTER LESSON CHART

Sentence Structure

	K	1	2
1 Two-Word Sentences	●	●	●
2 Simple Sentences	●	●	●
3 Compound Sentences		●	●
4 Introductory Phrases or Clauses		●	●
5 Appositives: An Interrupter that Clarifies or Explains			●

1 Two-Word Sentences
RELATED LESSONS: *Sentence Fluency:* Lesson 1, Sentences Are of Varying Lengths
Word Choice: Lesson 2, Target Powerful Action Verbs

2 Simple Sentences
RELATED LESSONS: *Editing:* Lesson 5, Using Spelling Consciousness While Editing

3 Compound Sentences
RELATED LESSONS: *Revising:* Lesson 4, Sentence Combining

4 Introductory Phrases or Clauses
RELATED LESSONS: *Sentence Fluency:* Lesson 3, Varied Sentence Beginnings
Sentence Fluency: Lesson 4, Varying Sentence Beginnings with Prepositional Phrases

5 Appositives: An Interrupter that Clarifies or Explains

Capitalization

	K	1	2
1 Capitalize Beginning of Sentences	●	●	
2 Proper Nouns: Names and Places	●	●	
3 Capitalize Important Words in a Title	●	●	●
4 Capitalize for Emphasis	●	●	●

1 Capitalize Beginning of Sentences
RELATED LESSONS: *Drafting:* Lesson 5, Use Mostly Lowercase Letters

2 Proper Nouns: Names and Places

3 Capitalize Important Words in a Title
RELATED LESSONS: *Text Features:* Lesson 1, Choose a Title that Is Interesting
Text Features: Lesson 2, Headings Help Your Reader

4 Capitalize for Emphasis

Spelling Consciousness

	K	1	2
1 Spelling Consciousness: Notice When Words Are Not Spelled Correctly	●	●	●
2 Stretching Words . . . Writing Sounds You Know	●	●	
3 Strategic Spellers Pay Attention to Syllables	●	●	●
4 Strategic Spellers Use a Variety of Resources		●	●
5 Navigating Homophones			●

1 Spelling Consciousness: Notice When Words Are Not Spelled Correctly
RELATED LESSONS: *Editing:* Lesson 5, Using Spelling Consciousness While Editing

2 Stretching Words . . . Writing Sounds You Know

3 Strategic Spellers Pay Attention to Syllables

4 Strategic Spellers Use a Variety of Resources
RELATED LESSONS: *Editing:* Lesson 8, Using Familiar Resources to Help You Edit

5 Navigating Homophones

Research

The Heart of Nonfiction Writing

Research and the gathering of factual information is the heart of nonfiction writing. This is the time when writers explore the world around them, reflect on their learning, separate fact from opinion, and consider how to share their understandings with others. Research may take the form of observation, reading, real-life experience, or focused listening and reflection. In all cases, writers must learn to determine importance, synthesize their understandings, and prepare to transfer their thinking to print.

LESSON	K	1	2	RELATED LESSONS
1 Identify Facts in a Visual	●	●		*Organization:* Lesson 2, Pictures and Words Work Together
2 Locate and Use Important Words and Phrases: Alphabox	●	●	●	*Planning:* Lesson 6, Gather Information with the Key Word Strategy *Word Choice:* Lesson 1, Use Descriptive Words and Phrases *Word Choice:* Lesson 2, Target Powerful Action Verbs
3 Locate and Use Facts from Multiple Sources		●	●	*Planning:* Lesson 6, Gather Information with the Key Word Strategy *Research:* Lesson 2, Locate and Use Important Words and Phrases: Alphabox
4 Create a Visual that Contains Facts	●	●	●	*Planning:* Lesson 3, Create a Labeled Diagram *Ideas:* Lesson 7, Teach Your Reader Something New *Ideas:* Lesson 4, Infuse Interesting Details
5 Place Labels on Illustrations	●	●		*Planning:* Lesson 3, Create a Labeled Diagram *Text Features:* Lesson 4, Add Captions to Illustrations
6 Use *I Remember!* to Summarize Information	●	●	●	*Research:* Lesson 8, Use the Very Important Points (VIP) Strategy for Key Information
7 Sketch to Stretch: Visual Summary	●	●	●	*Planning:* Lesson 1, Draw Pictures Before You Write *Research:* Lesson 4, Create a Visual that Contains Facts
8 Use the Very Important Points (VIP) Strategy for Key Information	●	●	●	*Planning:* Lesson 6, Gather Information with the Key Word Strategy
9 Use a Pocket Organizer		●	●	*Organization:* Lesson 9, Multiple Pages Are Used: Page Breaks Support Units of Meaning *Drafting:* Lesson 7, Turning Notes into Sentences
10 Using a Research Notebook	●	●	●	*Research:* Lesson 3, Locate and Use Facts from Multiple Sources

Other Lessons to Create

You might also want to teach writers how to

- write down their observations of a live animal,
- make sketches and jot notes while listening to a book on tape, or
- read a bit, write a bit, and read some more.

Identify Facts in a Visual

WHEN TO USE IT: To help writers extract information from pictures and visuals

FOCUS THE LEARNING

Photographs, illustrations, and visuals such as charts and diagrams provide essential information in nonfiction sources. Writers need to attend closely to these visuals and learn that important information can be found from sources other than print.

Model

STEP 1: Look closely at a visual and describe what you see. Make it clear that you are getting information from the picture, even though there are not any words.

Possible Think-Aloud: *Pictures are really helpful when we are researching and gathering ideas for writing. As I look at this picture of a sea turtle, I notice that it has spots on its head and really large eyes. "Spots" and "eyes" are both words I will want to include in my writing. I also see that its flippers are very thick. Since one is higher than the other, I think that sea turtles must use their flippers to help them swim. I will want to be sure to use "flippers" in my writing, too. This picture helped me notice that the flippers are thick and strong, so I will want to use "strong flippers" when I write.*

TURN &TALK *Writers, look closely at the picture. What can you learn from it? Identify words you can use in your writing based on what you see in the picture.*

Sea Turtles

Sea turtles have <u>spots</u> on their heads and very large <u>eyes</u>. They also have <u>strong flippers</u> that help them move and steer through the water.

Sample Modeled Writing

STEP 2: Demonstrate how to use the information you gained from the picture in an illustration and/or in writing.

Possible Think-Aloud: *We have learned a lot from this picture. As I begin writing, it will be important to use words I identified in the picture: "spots," "eyes," and "strong flippers." The picture helped me learn about those. I will begin by writing, "Sea turtles have spots on their heads." Did you notice that I remembered to use the word "spots"? As nonfiction researchers we need to pay attention to pictures because we can learn a lot from them even before we read the words.*

TURN &TALK *Think together about something else that I could write based on what we see in the picture. Design a terrific sentence that describes what the picture shows.*

Analyze

STEP 3: Reread and reflect.

Possible Think-Aloud: *Writers, let's check the picture one more time. Is there any other important information that I should have included in my writing? Think together. What is most important in this picture, and is it in my writing? Did I include the important words that show what I learned from the picture?*

Sum It Up

When we do research, we can learn a lot from pictures and illustrations. As you gather ideas and do research for your writing, be sure to spend time looking closely at pictures. Pictures help you think about what is important and the words you will want to use in your writing. From now on, I know you will be looking closely at pictures because they will help you become a better nonfiction writer!

LINKS TO CD-ROM:
- Visual: Sea Turtle
- Visual: Science and social studies visuals

Locate and Use Important Words and Phrases: Alphabox

WHEN TO USE IT: To focus writers on collecting the content-based vocabulary they need as a foundation for nonfiction writing

FOCUS THE LEARNING

Writers are often overwhelmed by data collection as they prepare to write. When they collect important words and phrases from their reading and store them in an Alphabox, they have a rich cache of words with which they can support themselves during writing.

Model

STEP 1: Read aloud from a resource, pausing often to select words to add to the Alphabox.

Possible Think-Aloud: *As I read about how snow is formed, I am going to pause often, so we can think about the words we are hearing and decide if any of them are important words we want to add to our Alphabox.* (After reading a page or two . . .) *I am going to stop reading because I want to put some of these words into the Alphabox so I can use them later. I really liked "icy crystals." That phrase reminds me of what it feels like to have snow land on my face. It also reminds me of the shape of a snowflake. Snowflakes are little crystals. I am also going to write "close to the ground." This is important because the air close to the ground must be very cold or the snowflakes would melt before they land.*

TURN &TALK *What words do you think we could add that will help us when we write about snow?*

STEP 2: Extract words from the Alphabox, and show students how you integrate them into a piece of writing.

Possible Think-Aloud: *To begin a piece of nonfiction writing about snow, I want to set the book aside and use the words in the Alphabox to help me decide what to say. When I look at the C box in the Alphabox, I remember that air* close to the ground *must be* cold, *or the water drops will come down as rain. Watch as I use the words from the Alphabox to write, "Snow is created when water drops hit cold air close to the ground." The Alphabox really helped!*

TURN &TALK *Go back to the Alphabox and select other words that we can use in our writing. Select the most descriptive words.*

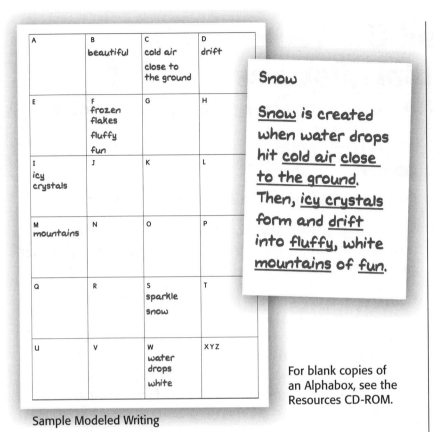

A	B beautiful	C cold air close to the ground	D drift
E	F frozen flakes fluffy fun	G	H
I icy crystals	J	K	L
M mountains	N	O	P
Q	R	S sparkle snow	T
U	V	W water drops white	XYZ

Snow

Snow is created when water drops hit cold air close to the ground. Then, icy crystals form and drift into fluffy, white mountains of fun.

Sample Modeled Writing

For blank copies of an Alphabox, see the Resources CD-ROM.

VARIATIONS

For Less Experienced Writers: Gather less experienced writers in a small group around a large Alphabox, and assist them in collecting and inserting words into the shared Alphabox.

For More Experienced Writers: Have writers use personal Alphaboxes to collect words on a topic of study and then use the words to support development of drafts. During revision, have writers double-check their Alphaboxes for words that would add important details.

Analyze

STEP 3: Reread and reflect.

Possible Think-Aloud: *Let's reread my writing and think together. Have I covered the most important ideas that we learned in the book? Are there any other words in the Alphabox that we should include in our writing about snow?*

Sum It Up

Nonfiction writers focus on important words and use them in their writing. Now that you know how to use an Alphabox, you have a great tool for collecting the important words that you want to include as labels in your drawings and in your writing, too.

LINKS TO CD-ROM:
• Teacher Tool: Alphaboxes

Locate and Use Facts from Multiple Sources

WHEN TO USE IT: To help writers assimilate information gathered from more than one resource

FOCUS THE LEARNING

All writers of nonfiction must be able to gather information from a variety of sources and organize that information into coherent pieces of writing.

Model

Post several sheets of paper in a row next to the chart of facts.

STEP 1: Display three nonfiction resources, preferably leveled selections with strong visuals. Demonstrate how to collect ideas from each of them before you begin to write.

Possible Think-Aloud: *Writers of nonfiction need to use lots of sources for their information. I have these three great books on frogs. My goal is to get information from each of them that I can use in my writing. I am going to start by thinking about frogs when they are grown up. There will probably be information about tadpoles and frog's eggs, but for now I am just going to think about grown-up frogs and collect ideas on this chart. (Open book 1 to a pre-identified point.) Here is a page about an adult frog. It says that a frog's legs are so strong it can leap up to 20 feet. I am going to save that information by combining a sketch and some words on my chart. Watch as I sketch the frog leaping, and then I write, "strong" and "20 feet." Notice that I don't try to write complete sentences. A sketch and a small number of words will help me to remember the fact.*

TURN &TALK *(Read a short passage and show the pictures from a second book with information on adult frogs.) Writers, this has some incredible information on adult frogs. If you were going to use some facts from this book, what would you want to remember? Think together about facts I should add to my chart about adult frogs. (Repeat with the third book, integrating sketches and labels with information from the previous books.)*

A frog's tongue is curled up inside its mouth until a fly goes zipping by. Then, the sticky tongue snaps out and the fly becomes the frog's dinner!

Sample Modeled Writing

STEP 2: Demonstrate how to recast an important idea from your chart into a sentence.

Possible Think-Aloud: *I am looking at the sketches and facts on my chart about adult frogs. I feel really good about my facts because I used three books. Great research begins with more than one resource. Now I am ready to turn my facts into sentences. I will use page one to tell about a frog's sticky tongue. I love visualizing how the tongue snaps out and catches flies. On my chart, I drew the tongue as curled and I wrote the word "sticky." Those are both helpful. My first sentences will say, "A frog's tongue is curled up inside its mouth until a fly goes zipping by. Then, the sticky tongue snaps out, and the fly becomes the frog's dinner!" That is a great first page. For my second page, I am going to write about the frog's bulging eyes. That fact is on my chart from my second book.*

TURN &TALK *Think together and design a great sentence about the frog's bulging eyes.*

Analyze

STEP 3: Reread and reflect.

Possible Think-Aloud: *Why is it important to find interesting facts when we write? Remember, too, to select facts with interesting and descriptive words that help your readers visualize the details.*

Sum It Up

Writers, it is helpful to use more than one resource in order to gather the very best facts for our writing. The trick is to focus on a single idea and not all of the information in each book. As I gathered my facts from the three books, did you notice that I only looked for facts about adult frogs? Next time, I could check all three books for facts about tadpoles or frog's eggs or what frogs do in the winter. Now you know how to locate and use information from more than one book. Let's start writing!

VARIATIONS

For Less Experienced Writers: In a small group, guide writers as they skim and scan the visuals to locate facts on a single focus point. Coach and assist as they take notes—sketching, labeling, and writing phrases.

For More Experienced Writers: Establish the expectation that writers use multiple sources, and have students learn to keep a list of the sources they used in each piece of writing. Have writers save their pages of notes that were gathered from multiple sources (sketches, labels, and phrases) and display them next to their finished writing.

LINKS TO CD-ROM:
- Thinking Challenge: Research with More than One Book

Create a Visual that Contains Facts

WHEN TO USE IT: To help nonfiction writers understand that nonfiction visuals contain accurate and factual information

FOCUS THE LEARNING

Writers of nonfiction need to learn that they cannot "make up" the content of visuals in nonfiction writing. It must come from a reliable source. To accomplish this, they need to read, summarize their learning, and then infuse accurate content into their visuals.

Model

You will need several apples and a knife for this lesson.

STEP 1: Display a real apple and consider its attributes, both exterior and interior.

Possible Think-Aloud: *As a nonfiction writer, I know that one of my important jobs is to create diagrams that have accurate information. I can get those facts by doing research with real things and by reading books. Today I am going to do research on an apple. I will gather all the facts I can and put those facts into a diagram. When I look at this apple, I see it is mostly red. It wouldn't be accurate to color it all red as there are little stripes of yellow along the skin. I notice the stem at the top and the way the skin of the apple slopes down to where the stem is connected. When I turn it over, I notice the place where a blossom used to be at the bottom of the apple. The skin of the apple slopes toward that area, too. I am going to try to put those facts into my diagram. Watch as I draw, and see if I am using accurate information about this apple.*

TURN &TALK *Writers, accuracy is important. Check my drawing. Does it have real facts about this apple? Is there anything else I could do to make this diagram more accurate?*

STEP 2: Cut the apple open and examine the interior. Make a second diagram showing the "facts" about the interior of the apple.

Possible Think-Aloud: *The facts in a diagram need to be as accurate as possible. As we look inside the apple, I can say that it is a fact that it has seeds. I can say it is a fact that the flesh is a creamy, white color and the skin is mostly red. My diagram needs to include those facts. This is not a time when I can use my imagination. Nonfiction writers need to get their facts straight. Watch as I put those important facts into my diagram of the interior. While I work on my diagram, please look closely at the apple slices that Andrew is passing around. See if you can think of additional facts that should be in my diagram.*

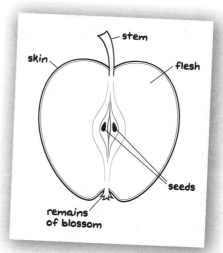

stem

skin

flesh

seeds

remains of blossom

Sample Modeled Writing

Analyze

STEP 3: Reread and reflect.

Possible Think-Aloud: *Sometimes diagrams are needed to show facts about a topic. Why is it important that the facts shown are accurate? Why would it be a bad idea to show things that might not be facts? Always remember to put only facts in your diagram.*

Sum It Up

Writers of nonfiction need to create visuals that show real facts. Sometimes we get those facts from books. Sometimes we get them from researching with real things, like our apples. The important thing is to create diagrams that show facts—not just ideas that we think might be true. Now that you know how to include facts in your nonfiction diagrams, I know I will be seeing lots of interesting information when I look at your drawings.

Place Labels on Illustrations

WHEN TO USE IT: To help writers understand that labels are important research tools because they focus readers on key vocabulary

FOCUS THE LEARNING

Labels on photographs and illustrations draw readers' attention to content-based vocabulary and increase content retention. Writers of nonfiction need to learn how to use labels as research tools and incorporate them into their own writing as well.

Model

STEP 1: Demonstrate how to use sticky notes to add labels to a photograph or illustration. Use the photograph on the Resources CD-ROM or one of your own.

Possible Think-Aloud: *As I look at this photograph of an enormous farm tractor, I realize that my research would be even easier if I placed labels right on the picture. That will help me think about the ideas in the picture and the important words I need to collect in my research. On my first sticky note, I will write: "Strong engine." That label will remind me that a huge tractor like this needs a big, strong engine to plow fields and plant crops.*

TURN &TALK *I have lots of sticky notes, and you have lots of ideas. Think together about labels that I could place on this photograph. With your great ideas, we will be able to place lots of labels on this illustration.*

Exhaust pipe

Cab for the driver

Knobby tires

Strong engine

Sample Modeled Writing

STEP 2: Have partners use sticky notes to add labels to leveled nonfiction selections or other resources that are lacking in labels.

Possible Think-Aloud: *You have a lot of great ideas. I am going to start with Taylor's observation about the tires. Those are really interesting tires with big knobs for traction in mud. As a researcher, I need to notice details like that. Watch as I create a label, "knobby tires." Good researchers think about important ideas and the words they want to use in their writing.*

TURN &TALK *It looks like there is room for more labels that reflect our research about this tractor. What else should we add? Think together.*

Analyze

STEP 3: Reread and reflect.

Possible Think-Aloud: *The labels we have added to this photograph are important. They remind us of details that we will want to place in our writing. Listen as I touch each label and retell what I have learned from this photograph. Retelling with labels is a great way to get my research ideas ready to write on paper. Think together, why is it helpful for us to add labels to illustrations and photographs when we are researching and getting ready to write?*

Sum It Up

We know how to use sticky notes and add labels to photographs and other visuals. We also know that as researchers, we have to pay attention to the details and the information that are within each photograph. Now, as writers, you need to use the words that are in your labels as part of your writing. That is what great nonfiction writers remember to do.

VARIATIONS

For Less Experienced Writers: Have partners work together to add labels to photographs in leveled nonfiction selections, thinking together about important ideas in each photograph and labels that would capture the most important words. Provide an opportunity for them to share their labels with another partner pair.

For More Experienced Writers: Have experienced writers turn labels into sentences. For example, they could take the label "knobby tires" and turn it into "Knobby tires help farm tractors to pull heavy loads through muddy fields."

LINKS TO CD-ROM: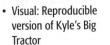
• Visual: Reproducible version of Kyle's Big Tractor

Use *I Remember!* to Summarize Information

WHEN TO USE IT: To help researchers retain content and prepare to present their learning in writing

FOCUS THE LEARNING

When researchers remember to digest small amounts of content and then to pause and think about what they have learned, they remember more.

Model

STEP 1: Before the lesson, place sticky notes in *Snowflake Bentley* by Jacqueline Briggs Martin at intervals such as pages 5, 9, and so on. Model the *"I Remember!"* strategy.

Possible Think-Aloud: *I am going to read up to this first sticky note in* Snowflake Bentley *by Jacqueline Briggs Martin. When I finish reading, I am going to do a retell starting with the phrase,* "I Remember." (After reading the first five pages.) *I am going to be quiet for a minute and think about Snowflake Bentley. It helps to think before I summarize.* "I remember *that Snowflake Bentley loved snow more than anything. He lived in Vermont where it snows 120 inches a year."* Did you notice that I started my retell with* "I remember"? *As researchers, we need to learn information and then retell it in our heads so we know what to write. The* "I Remember!" *strategy helps us think about what we learned so we can retell or summarize the information.*

TURN &TALK *Think about my retell. Is there any other information I should have included from these pages about Snowflake Bentley?*

STEP 2: Continue reading and pausing frequently for students to apply the *"I Remember!"* strategy.

I remember that Snowflake Bentley lived in Vermont and grew up loving snow more than anything. He learned a lot about snowflakes and their patterns, but they always melted before he could finish drawing them.

Sample Modeled Writing

Possible Think-Aloud: *I am going to read up to the next sticky note in the book and do one more* "I Remember." *Then it will be time to starting writing what I remember.* (After oral retell.) *Now it is time to turn my learning into writing. I will begin my writing about Snowflake Bentley with* "I remember!" *just as I did when I was retelling. My first sentence will be* "<u>I remember</u> *that Snowflake . . ."* *This is fun. The* "I Remember!" *strategy helps me get my ideas ready for writing!*

TURN &TALK *Think about Snowflake Bentley and share an* "I Remember!" *with your partner. Your* "I Remember!" *thinking will help us get ready to add more to my writing about Snowflake Bentley.*

Analyze

STEP 3: Reread and reflect.

Possible Think-Aloud: *Let's reread my writing about Snowflake Bentley and think about our research. Have we told the important ideas? Does this retell make sense? Are our facts accurate?*

Sum It Up

Researchers can use the *"I Remember!"* strategy to help themselves remember important content. It is important to read a short amount and then stop and think about what you just read. Researchers, with help from the *"I Remember!"* strategy, you can read, think, and then write!

VARIATIONS

For Less Experienced Writers: Provide more experience with listening to content and using the *"I Remember!"* strategy to orally retell. These writers also benefit from transferring the content they are retaining into a sketch or drawing.

For More Experienced Writers: Challenge experienced writers to determine importance as they remember and focus on the most important ideas for their retell. This will carry over into writing in the form of main ideas and focused details.

LINKS TO CD-ROM:
• Strategy: *I Remember!*

Sketch to Stretch: Visual Summary

WHEN TO USE IT: To help researchers capture important images and words in a visual format

When researchers consolidate their learning in sketches and labels, they activate multisensory learning and increase their ability to retain content. The result is a larger reservoir of information on which they can base their writing.

Model

Before the lesson, select a book on frogs or another relevant topic to support your think-aloud.

STEP 1: Model how to read a bit and then pause to sketch and add labels that summarize understanding.

Possible Think-Aloud: *As I read this book on frogs, I am going to pause frequently to make sketches that help me remember what I am learning. This strategy is called "Sketch to Stretch" and is a very helpful tool for writers. (After reading a few pages.) My first sketch will be of the eggs. I want to show that they are clear jelly on the outside and are clustered together in groups, called spawn. Notice my labels: "tadpole," "egg," and "spawn." Those are words I will want to use in my writing, too.*

TURN &TALK *Think together. If you were going to do a sketch to stretch about this passage, what would you draw? What labels would you add to your sketch?*

STEP 2: Think aloud as you continue reading, sketching, and labeling.

Possible Think-Aloud: *As we continue to read and research, I am realizing how very helpful a sketch to stretch can be. Each time I make a sketch, I really need to think about what I am learning. We just read about how a tadpole starts with gills and then grows lungs so it can live on land. In my sketch I need to show gills on a tadpole and lungs for a frog. That is important.*

Analyze

STEP 3: Reread and reflect.

Possible Think-Aloud: *Let's reread my sketches and my drawings. I have a lot of research and information right in my sketches. As I touch each sketch, I want to think about what I could write using this sketch to remind me of my research.*

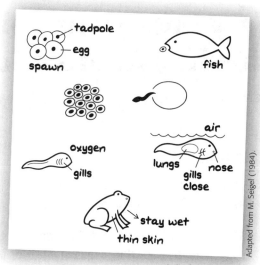

Sample Modeled Writing

Adapted from M. Seigel (1984).

As I touch the sketch of the egg, for example, I am thinking that I could write about the clear jelly that surrounds the egg and how the jelly of the eggs sticks together to create frog spawn. Sketch to stretch helps me put my ideas into writing.

TURN &TALK *Put your heads together and identify sentences that you would write if you had made these sketches.*

Sum It Up

Sketch to stretch is a helpful tool for researchers. We read a bit, pause to think, then draw, and add labels. When our sketches are finished, we can use them to help launch our writing! I know I can count on seeing you use this strategy as you research and begin your drafts.

VARIATIONS

For Less Experienced Writers: Begin with just sketches to capture important information, having learners tell you about their sketches and the information contained within each one.

For More Experienced Writers: Have writers create their sketches on separate pieces of paper; then have them use each sketch to launch a page for a book.

LINKS TO CD-ROM: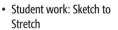
• Student work: Sketch to Stretch

Use the Very Important Points (VIP) Strategy for Key Information

WHEN TO USE IT: To assist learners in determining importance as they read and research for writing

FOCUS THE LEARNING

Young learners can quickly become overwhelmed by detail as they read nonfiction. The Very Important Points (VIP) strategy helps them by limiting the number of details they can mark as important within a given passage.

Model

Prepare for this lesson by printing "Walking on the Moon" from the Resources CD-ROM and gathering scissors and sticky notes.

STEP 1: Show how to cut sticky notes into thin strips and place them as markers for important ideas in a text or in an illustration.

Possible Think-Aloud: *As I read this passage called "Walking on the Moon," I am going to place these strips of sticky note material on words and pictures that I think are very important. I am only going to allow myself to use four strips because I need to pick the MOST important things. First, I want to put a VIP on the spacesuit in the picture. That is important because people would die on the moon without a space suit. There is no oxygen on the moon, so astronauts have to wear the suit to keep oxygen and pressure safely around them. As I look at the title, I think I need a VIP on the word "moon." That will remind me that this is about the moon.*

TURN &TALK *I have used up two of my four VIPs already. Do you think I have made good choices? Why? We have to be careful with VIPs because we can't mark everything!*

STEP 2: Continue reading and identifying VIPs.

Possible Think-Aloud: *As I look at the first two sentences, I am going to put a VIP on the phrase "no gravity." It is important to remember that you would float away if you didn't have heavy weights. Get ready. I am going to read sentence 3, and it will be your job to decide if there is a VIP to mark in that sentence.*

TURN &TALK *Writers, think about this sentence. Is there a VIP in it or not? Be ready to support your opinion.*

Analyze

STEP 3: Reread and reflect.

Possible Think-Aloud:
We have marked four VIPs. Now, as researchers and writers, we need to turn those VIPs into sentences. I can use the VIP about the space suit and the VIP for "moon" in the title to create a sentence. "When astronauts go walking on the moon, they need to wear space suits."
Partners, think together. If you were to turn our VIPs into sentences, what would those sentences be?

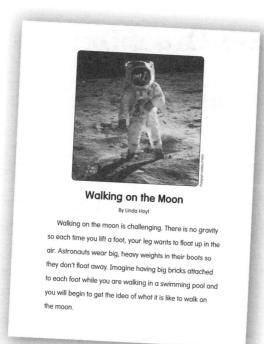

Walking on the Moon
By Linda Hoyt

Walking on the moon is challenging. There is no gravity so each time you lift a foot, your leg wants to float up in the air. Astronauts wear big, heavy weights in their boots so they don't float away. Imagine having big bricks attached to each foot while you are walking in a swimming pool and you will begin to get the idea of what it is like to walk on the moon.

Sum It Up

Researchers and writers can use the VIP strategy to mark the most important points they find in books. Once they select VIPs, writers can turn ideas into terrific nonfiction writing! I am going to place scissors and sticky notes in the research center so you can use the VIP strategy to help you research and prepare for some great writing!

VARIATIONS

For Less Experienced Writers: Encourage less experienced writers to place a VIP at their "favorite" places in a book. They will quickly identify with things that interest or appeal to them and can later transition to the idea of highly important versus less important content.

For More Experienced Writers: Ask writers to justify their thinking as they select VIPs. Why did you mark this point versus another one? Why is this important as you think about your writing? Is there anything that might be more important to the main idea of this writing?

LINKS TO CD-ROM:
- Shared Reading: Walking on the Moon

Use a Pocket Organizer

WHEN TO USE IT: When writers are ready to engage in independent research from multiple sources

FOCUS THE LEARNING

Young writers quickly learn to organize facts if you provide them with a pocket organizer, created from a file folder and envelopes that are labeled with categories such as habitat, food, and description.

Model

Prepare for this lesson by printing "Made for a Frozen World" on the Resources CD-ROM and creating a pocket organizer as per the photo in the modeled writing.

STEP 1: Show students how you read and collect words and phrases or create small drawings and then store your facts in a pocket organizer.

Possible Think-Aloud: *As I read "Made for a Frozen World," I am going to collect facts on these small pieces of paper and put them into my pocket organizer.* (Read two sections.) *I am thinking about the fat on the bear. I will write "3 inches of fat" on this piece of paper. That is about the width of four fingers on an adult hand. So I will draw four fingers of a hand. That will help me remember the thickness of the fat on a polar bear. Now I can put my fact in the pocket that says description. Did you notice how I only wrote a few words and drew a little picture?* (Add additional facts to the organizer and then read two more sections, adding facts into pockets as you go. Try to include "hollow shaft," "air," and "clear"; then place them in a pocket titled, "fur.")

Sample Modeled Writing

Each hair on a polar bear is <u>clear</u> and has a <u>hollow shaft</u> filled with <u>air</u>.

TURN &TALK *Think about the facts I selected. Are those the facts you would have chosen? If your facts are different, which pocket on the pocket organizer might be the best place to put the facts?*

STEP 2: Remove the contents of one pocket in the organizer, and show students how you use the contents to help you create a draft about one subtopic.

Possible Think-Aloud: *I am going to begin writing about the facts that are in the pocket on "fur." In this pocket, I have the words "hollow shaft," "air," and "clear." As I turn these into a sentence, I could say: "Each hair on a polar bear is clear and has a hollow shaft filled with air." Did you notice how I used the words in the pocket organizer to help me make a sentence? Let's try this with another pocket. Let's work on the pocket labeled "description." The words inside of this pocket are _____.*

TURN &TALK *Put your heads together and construct a sentence using these words. As you design your sentences, I am going to put up another piece of paper so we can start writing page 2.*

Analyze

STEP 3: Reread and reflect.

Possible Think-Aloud: *Get ready. I am going to take the facts out of another pocket, and it will be your turn to think together and come up with sentences that use my facts.*

Sum It Up

Pocket organizers are a great way to collect facts as we research. Once we have the facts organized in a pocket, it is easy to turn them into sentences. I often like to think of each pocket as a separate page in a book and create an illustration to go with the contents of each pocket. Researching and writing with a pocket organizer are fun, and it helps you keep your facts organized!

VARIATIONS

For Less Experienced Writers: Focus on drawings as vehicles for collecting facts. Then, gather drawings into categories within the pocket organizer. Have partners use their drawings to retell the contents of their pockets for one another.

For More Experienced Writers: Stretch experienced writers by ensuring that they use multiple sources for the contents of each pocket. To keep track of the sources they use, they might staple a page to the back of the organizer and write down the sources they used for their research.

LINKS TO CD-ROM:
• Shared Reading: Made for a Frozen World

Using a Research Notebook

WHEN TO USE IT: To help writers organize information

FOCUS THE LEARNING

Young writers can easily be overwhelmed by facts if they don't have a system of organizing their data as they collect it. A research notebook dedicates one page to each subtopic, acting as a multipage graphic organizer.

Model

In advance of the lesson, cut 8 x 11 sheets of paper in half vertically.

STEP 1: Demonstrate how to assemble a research notebook.

Possible Think-Aloud: *When I am researching and gathering information for my writing, it really helps to use a research notebook. I am going to carefully stack 10 pieces of this narrow paper and then staple the pages together so I have a research notebook for my research on earthworms. Next, I can think about topics that I want to research on earthworms and place one topic on each page.*

TURN &TALK *Think together. What are some questions you think we should research as we study earthworms?*

STEP 2: Identify subtopics and write one on each page.

Possible Think-Aloud: *My next step is to think of things I want to learn about worms. I know I want to learn about what worms eat. Watch as I write, "What Worms Eat" on page 1. On page 2, I will write, "Where Worms Live." Research notebooks help writers get organized. Now, when I find out what worms eat, I can write the answer right on page 1. When I find information about where they live, that can go right on page 2. It will make writing so easy!*

What Worms Eat

Where Worms Live

Why Worms are Helpful

Sample Modeled Writing

TURN &TALK *Identify more topics that I should learn about as I study earthworms. I want to put headings on more of these pages so I can start researching.*

Analyze

STEP 3: Reread and reflect.

Possible Think-Aloud:
I brought along this book on worms so I could get started researching and putting facts into my research notebook. The first page in my book is about the segments on the worm's body. That is

important, so I will want to write it in my research notebook. I don't want to put this fact on pages 1 or 2; those pages are about where they live and what they eat. I can't put it on page 3 either; that is about why earthworms are helpful. I need a new heading. Watch as I write on page 4, "The Worm's Body." That is the perfect page to write a fact about the segments, the little sections that make up their long bodies. As I read the next page, get ready to decide where I should write the next fact.

Sum It Up

Research notebooks are helpful tools that give us a way to organize our facts and get ready to write. To make a research notebook, you staple slender pages together and then place a heading on each page so you know just where to put your information.

Planning

Thinking, Organizing, and Preparing to Write

The planning phase of writing is one that should be rich in reading, language use, and art. This is a time when writers explore their own understandings, gather their thoughts, and prepare to commit words to paper. When the planning portion of process writing is given adequate time and attention, writers express themselves more fully and present writing that is thoughtfully constructed and layered in rich detail.

LESSON	K	1	2	RELATED LESSONS
1 Draw Pictures Before You Write	●	●	●	*Drafting:* Lesson 1, Write About Your Pictures *Research:* Lesson 7, Sketch to Stretch: Visual Summary
2 Talk Before You Write	●	●	●	*Planning:* Lesson 1, Draw Pictures Before You Write *Planning:* Lesson 3, Create a Labeled Diagram *Planning:* Lesson 4, Map Out Your Writing with Informational Pictures *Research:* Lesson 1, Identify Facts in a Visual
3 Create a Labeled Diagram	●	●	●	*Research:* Lesson 5, Place Labels on Illustrations *Text Features:* Lesson 5, Diagrams with Labels
4 Map Out Your Writing with Informational Pictures	●	●	●	*Organization:* Lesson 3, Plan the Beginning and End . . . Then the Middle *Organization:* Lesson 9, Multiple Pages Are Used: Page Breaks Support Units of Meaning
5 Planning Page Layout and Paper Selection		●	●	*Text Features:* Lessons 2–10
6 Gather Information with the Key Word Strategy	●	●	●	*Research:* Lesson 1, Identify Facts in a Visual *Research:* Lesson 2, Locate and Use Important Words and Phrases: Alphabox *Research:* Lesson 5, Place Labels on Illustrations *Text Features:* Lesson 6, Bold Words

Other Lessons to Create

You might also want to teach writers how to
- look at books and magazines to get ideas for writing,
- collect interesting facts they might write about, or
- make a storyboard of their book, labeling the content of each page (see Planning section of the Resources CD-ROM).

Draw Pictures Before You Write

WHEN TO USE IT: To focus writers on their message and content before they begin to draft text

FOCUS THE LEARNING

Young writers benefit from taking time to draw detailed illustrations that focus their thinking and to organize the language that will support their message.

Model

STEP 1: Demonstrate how to create an illustration that is rich in detail.

Possible Think-Aloud: *I have decided to write about the time I was working in my yard and a snake scared me. I will close my eyes and try to get a picture in my mind. The sun was shining, and I was really enjoying myself, when suddenly a snake raced right in front of me. That was like watching a movie in my head. I could really see the action and remember how scared I was! Watch as I plan my writing by drawing. I need to think about what happened and be sure that my picture tells exactly what happened. I remember that the snake's head was much bigger than its body. I also remember that the snake's body had marks all along it. Those details are important. Adding details to my drawing will help me think of what I want to write.*

TURN &TALK *Look closely at my picture. What can you learn about my experience with the snake by just looking at the picture? What details should I add to my picture so my message is clear even without any words?*

STEP 2: Add additional detail to the illustration, thinking aloud as you draw.

Possible Think-Aloud: *I notice that my picture is missing some important details about my experience. I forgot to show the grass and the rake I was using. My picture doesn't show that the sun was shining or that there was some tall grass that the snake slithered into after he scared me.*

Sample Modeled Writing

TURN &TALK *Help me elaborate and think of details I can add to my illustration. Great writing needs to start with great details!*

Analyze

STEP 3: Reread and reflect.

Possible Think-Aloud: *I thought of another detail. Even though I was really frightened, I noticed that the snake had a red stripe running down its back. The snake had a dark green color on the rest of its body, and it had reddish eyes. Those are important details, so I need to add them to my illustration.* (Add details to illustration.) *My illustration is getting better and better since I added more detail. But my picture doesn't show that I screamed and started to run away. A reader wouldn't understand what happened without that part. I am going to start a second picture and show that I ran away.*

TURN &TALK *Writers need to draw with lots of detail and think about their message. Think together; retell my experience with the snake using details in the picture to help you retell exactly what happened to me.*

Sum It Up

Writers take time to plan before writing so when they write words, the message can be really terrific. One of the best ways to plan is to draw. Get a picture in your mind, close your eyes, and think about details. Then, add as many of those details to your picture as you can before you begin to write words. Writers, you know what to do—let's draw!

VARIATIONS

For Less Experienced Writers: Guide less experienced writers in planning and drawing about a moment that you have personally shared with them so you have firsthand knowledge and can guide them in adding details to their visual.

For More Experienced Writers: Emphasize sketches rather than detailed drawings. Show these writers how a few quick sketches can help them "retell" their message and get ready to write.

LINKS TO CD-ROM:
- Graphic Organizer: Getting Ready for School
- Checklist: Pre-Writing Checklist: Getting Ready to Write

Talk Before You Write

WHEN TO USE IT: When emergent writers need a bit of momentum to begin writing

Emergent writers always have stories to "tell" and need to be reminded that talking about illustrations can help them to solidify their thinking as they prepare to write.

Model

STEP 1: Prepare to write by creating an illustration.

Possible Think-Aloud: *I created this illustration to show what I have learned about a spider's legs. One of the best ways I can get my writing ideas ready is to talk about my picture. Listen carefully: "I have drawn eight legs. If you look closely, you will notice that I had to draw a LOT of knees. Did you know that a spider has six knees on each leg?" Talking really helped. Did you notice that I asked you a question? I said, "Did you know . . . ?" The words I said are also a great way to start my writing. Talking about my picture helped me get my words ready.*

TURN &TALK *Think together about what you just heard me say. Identify something else you heard me say that would be good to include in my writing.*

STEP 2: Begin to write using words and phrases that you included while telling about your illustration.

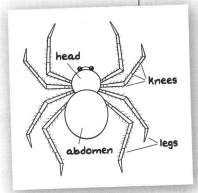

Sample Modeled Writing

Spiders

Did you know that spiders have six knees on each leg? Since spiders have eight legs, that makes 48 knees in all!

Did you know that the hairs on the leg of a spider act like your nose? Those hairs help the spider to smell things! The hairs pick up vibrations and smells.

Possible Think-Aloud: *Talking about my picture helped me as a writer, so I am going to do it again. Get ready and listen carefully.* (Refer to your illustration.) *"Did you know that the hair on the leg of a spider acts like your nose? The hairs pick up vibrations and help the spider to smell! Isn't that a cool fact?" I started with a question again, and I think that sounded pretty good. I am going to use the question I used when I was talking and say, "Did you know that the hairs . . ." When I was talking, I also said that the hairs pick up vibrations. That would be a good fact for my writing as well. Watch as I add, "The hairs pick up . . ." Talking before writing helps me think of great sentences.*

TURN &TALK *Analyze my illustration and talk about what you see. Tell each other about my drawing. Listen for words you could also use in your writing.*

Analyze

STEP 3: Reread and reflect.

Possible Think-Aloud: *As I look at my illustration, I notice that I drew a head and an abdomen, but I haven't talked about that at all yet. As a writer, I know I need to talk first and then write. Partners, think together. What could I say about the head and the abdomen of the spider? What could I include in my writing? Talking and writing are great partners.*

Sum It Up

Writers, one of the best ways we can plan for our writing is to talk about the pictures we have drawn. When we tell others about our learning, we get our words and ideas ready so we can be better writers. Before you begin writing today, I am going to ask you to find a partner and take time to talk about your illustration. After you tell about your picture, use words from your talking to make your writing the best it can be.

VARIATIONS

For Less Experienced Writers: For emergent writers, begin by having them tell about a photograph or illustration in a familiar book, and take dictation as they talk. Write down the words as they say them, and show them how the words they say can turn into writing.

For More Experienced Writers: Have students line up several illustrations in the order in which they would like them to appear in their writing; then have them talk about the writing that will support each illustration.

LINKS TO CD-ROM:
• Reflection: Talk Before You Write

Create a Labeled Diagram

WHEN TO USE IT: To ensure that academic vocabulary related to the content being learned is utilized in oral language and writing

Academic vocabulary is essential to content area understanding. When illustrations are enriched with clear labeling, the academic vocabulary has visual support and is more likely to be retained in long-term memory. Labeled drawings also scaffold integration of key vocabulary into writing, as young writers can easily draw language from their diagrams as they construct their sentences.

Model

You will need to have a resource on chickens or another favorite animal to reference in this lesson. If you want to display a model in addition to your modeled writing, you will find one on the Resources CD-ROM.

STEP 1: Model how to create a diagram with labels before sentences are constructed.

Possible Think-Aloud: *Today I am going to create a diagram that includes labels with important words about raising baby chickens. To help me do this, I am going use this book on chickens so I am sure that my facts are accurate. Writers need to get their facts right! I will start by making a diagram of a chick. I see in this picture a chick that has a beak, tail feathers, and a wing. Watch as I add labels for those important parts on my diagram.*

TURN & TALK *Look at my diagram of the chick. Select other labels that would help us remember the parts of the chicken. What labels do you think I should add?*

STEP 2: Add elements to the diagram such as seeds, a cage, and a heat lamp. Then, insert appropriate labels.

Possible Think-Aloud: *The chicken diagram is looking good. We have labels for lots of the chicken's body parts. Now we need to think about the resources we*

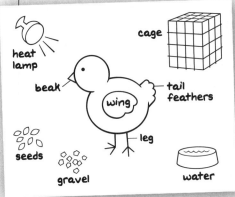

Sample Modeled Writing

need to take good care of a chick. I know we need to have a cage and a heat lamp so the baby stays warm. Watch as I draw those in the diagram. I will be sure to add labels because labels help us remember important information within the diagram. I will also want to use those words when I start writing my sentences.

TURN &TALK *Writers, analyze my labeled diagram. Identify any other elements that should be in this diagram, and think about labels. Do I have everything here that is needed to care for a baby chick?*

Analyze

STEP 3: Reread and analyze.

Possible Think-Aloud: *I am going to read some portions of the book on baby chicks. While I read, think hard about my diagram and my labels. Have I included the most important ideas? Are my labels important words that I will want to use when I write? When I am done reading, be ready to talk with your partner about ways to make my labeled diagram even better.*

Sum It Up

Writers of nonfiction have a lot to remember, and a labeled diagram can help. When we create a diagram and include labels, we are reminded of the important words we need to use when sharing our learning. A labeled diagram will also help you write better sentences because you can use the words in the diagram when you are writing your sentences!

VARIATIONS

For Less Experienced Writers: Provide an enlarged nonfiction photo, and have writers add sticky notes to create labels right on the photo. Then, model how to use the words in the labels to create sentences. (See the Resources CD-ROM for a printable example.)

For More Experienced Writers: Meet with writers in small groups to scaffold writing that includes the labels from their drawing. Show them how the labels in the drawing can become boldface text within their sentences to help a reader notice important words and ideas.

LINKS TO CD-ROM:
- Visual: Animal photo
- Visual: Labeled animal photo

Map Out Your Writing with Informational Pictures

WHEN TO USE IT: To help writers understand that a series of pictures can help them map out the content they plan to cover

FOCUS THE LEARNING

Young writers of nonfiction benefit from scaffolds that help them organize their writing into topics. When they take time to create sketches that relate to their topic but share a different bit of information, they are building a conceptual framework that will result in writing that is organized and focused. These sketches may suggest change, such as the life cycle of a butterfly. They could also be focused on different categories of information on an animal: diet, habitat, physical description, and so on. Or each drawing could relate to a single fact that the writer has learned about the topic.

Model

STEP 1: Post five large pieces of paper. On each piece of paper, create an illustration and a heading for one fact.

Possible Think-Aloud: *I think spiders are really interesting creatures. Watch as I use three pieces of paper to plan my writing about spiders. Mapping out my writing with several pictures will help me to create a book that I can put together. My first fact is that spiders have eight legs. On page 1, I will draw the spider and make sure all eight legs are showing. I am going to add a heading. Notice that I put the heading at the top of the page. It says, "Fact 1: 8 legs." On page 2, I am going to write about the eyes, so I need to make a drawing that shows eight eyes. Notice how I add a label, eyes, so it is very clear to my reader. My heading on page 2 will say: "Fact 2: 8 eyes."*

TURN &TALK *I am ready to think about page 3. Put your heads together and identify spider facts that you think would be good to place on pages 3, 4, and 5.*

STEP 2: Continue mapping out pages with one fact and one drawing per page.

Possible Think-Aloud: *I heard several of you mention that the spider web is important, so I will focus on the web on page 3. Did you know that the web is sticky? This causes flies and other insects to stick when they land on it. That is an important fact. I will draw a web to remind myself that when I add writing to the page, I want to write about the sticky web. Mapping out writing with several pages and lots of pictures is a great way to show the facts that I have learned.*

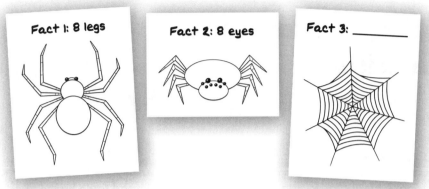

Fact 1: 8 legs

Fact 2: 8 eyes

Fact 3: _____

Sample Modeled Writing

TURN &TALK *I am ready to add the heading above my illustration. Think together. What would be a good heading for this page? (Continue modeling the addition of facts on pages 4 and 5.)*

Analyze

STEP 3: Reread and reflect.

Possible Think-Aloud: *I have mapped out my writing using pictures. Next, we need to reread the pictures and think about sentences that we can add to each page. For page 1, I remember that spiders have eight legs. I will write, "Spiders have eight skinny legs." I added "skinny" because that tells my reader even more information. Writers, read the picture on page 2 and think together. What should I write on that page?*

Sum It Up

Real books have more than one page, so nonfiction writers need to use lots of pages when they write. When you plan out your writing with pictures, it is easy to have lots of interesting pages and pictures that will make your readers want to read on and on. I am placing stacks of paper in the center of each of your tables. I can hardly wait to see the facts you select as you map out your writing with pictures!

VARIATIONS

For Less Experienced Writers: Guide these writers to name two or three facts and then just focus on illustrating one fact per page—no heading. Then, give them an opportunity to tell a partner about their facts before going back and beginning to insert text.

For More Experienced Writers: Encourage the development of several sentences per page so that ideas are fully developed. You may want to scaffold this richer language by modeling in a small group. Writers at this level may benefit from *Revising:* Lesson 9, Recasting a Single Page as a Book.

LINKS TO CD-ROM:
- Graphic Organizer: How to Make a Paper Snowflake
- Graphic Organizer: Storyboard

Planning Page Layout and Paper Selection

WHEN TO USE IT: When encouraging writers to branch out and try various paper sizes and page layouts for their nonfiction writing

FOCUS THE LEARNING

Nonfiction books present text and visuals in a wide variety of ways. Sometimes the visuals are at the top of the page, but often they are set along a margin, across the center of a two-page spread, or carefully framed by text boxes. Writers of nonfiction can become students of nonfiction page layouts by noticing and comparing layouts in a variety of big books and other resources. They should also notice that books are *not* all the same size but come in a variety of sizes.

Model

STEP 1: Display an array of nonfiction big books and trade books of varying sizes and with different styles of page layouts. Have several sizes of paper, lined and unlined, as well. Examples of various layouts can also be found on the Resources CD-ROM.

Possible Think-Aloud: *Nonfiction writers need to think about their facts and also about what a page will look like. Where will the illustrations go? Where will the words be placed? Look at this book. It has the picture right in the middle of the page, and the words are in little boxes. Here is another book that has lots of pictures arranged on the page, and then there is a bit of writing with each picture. The page layout in each of these is really different. Let's examine some more page layouts and see what we notice about ways to arrange pictures and words on a page.*

TURN &TALK *Look closely at the pages I have up here. Which ones do you like the look of? What do you like about each one? What might you want to try in your own writing?*

STEP 2: Model how to place an illustration in the center of a page, and then place small text boxes around the central visual.

Possible Think-Aloud: *Looking at the page layouts in these books really helped me. Now I am going to plan a piece of writing and think about the facts as well as the layout. I want the biggest picture to be in the middle of the page. I know that nonfiction sometimes looks like that. I also want a smaller picture set to the side. I will place that one at the top on the right. A lot of the books we looked at put the words in text boxes in different places on the page. I like the look of that, so I will draw the boxes and think about how it looks. Notice that I am not trying to write sentences yet. I am planning the space and thinking about where my facts will go and how the page will look.*

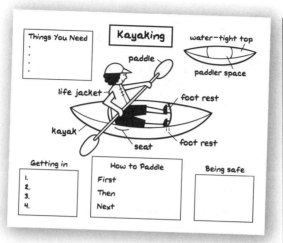

Sample Modeled Writing

TURN &TALK *What suggestions do you have for my page layout? Look at the examples again and see if they give you an idea for something I could use as I think about the layout of this page.*

Analyze

STEP 3: Reread and reflect.

Possible Think-Aloud: *Writers, we forgot something important! Look at the sizes of these books. There are small books and big books. There is even a book that is tall and narrow. We need to think about the size of the paper we use as well. That will make a big difference when we plan the layout of a page. I am feeling good that I selected large paper with no lines because that gave me room to write and insert my text boxes. Let's look at these other sizes of paper and think together. Would any of these be better or more interesting choices for my layout about kayaking?*

Sum It Up

Nonfiction writers need to think about facts and information, but they also need to think about page layout and the size of paper that they will use for their writing. Books in the library use a lot of interesting layouts and sizes, and so can we. I have laid out a variety of paper sizes for you to consider. I can't wait to see what you plan for size and layout for your writing.

VARIATIONS

For Less Experienced Writers: Display only one or two layout options and two sizes of paper. Encourage students to reach beyond the format of a picture at the top and words at the bottom to try at least one variation in layout or sizing of paper.

For More Experienced Writers: Engage these writers in active analysis of the page layout of several books and varying formats while in a small-group setting. Encourage them to compare and contrast what they see in the layouts and then examine their writing folders to consider new ways in which they could present their own work.

LINKS TO CD-ROM:
• Teacher Tool: Sample Page Layouts

Gather Information with the Key Word Strategy

WHEN TO USE IT: When writers would benefit from identifying key academic vocabulary to include in their writing

FOCUS THE LEARNING

Writers of nonfiction must be able to extract key words from resources and then utilize the words in their writing. Key words are those that are essential to understanding a concept. As an example: To understand the life cycle of a frog, words like "egg" and "tadpole" are key words.

Model

STEP 1: Read aloud from a passage on frogs or a topic of your choice. Identify key words and write them on large sticky notes to post next to the text.

Possible Think-Aloud: *On page 1 of this book, I am noticing that the frog eggs are in a clear jelly that seems to be holding the eggs together. I am going to choose two key words from this page, "eggs" and "jelly." Watch as I write each of these words on a separate sticky note and place it to the side of the book. On page 2, I can see tiny tadpoles developing inside the eggs. I am going to choose "tadpole" as a key word on this page. It is really important to remember that tadpoles come from eggs. I have three key words so far: "eggs," "jelly," and "tadpole." Watch and listen as I hold up my key words, one at a time, and use them to tell what I have learned. "Frogs lay **eggs** that stick together with a clear **jelly**. A **tadpole** hatches from the egg."*

TURN &TALK *Think together. What are you noticing about the words I am selecting? What should you remember to do when identifying key words?*

STEP 2: Continue reading and identifying key words, writing each one on an individual sticky note. Pause to retell, using the key words.

Frogs lay **eggs** that stick together with a clear **jelly**.

A **tadpole** hatches from the **egg** and starts to **eat** and **swim**.

Sample Modeled Writing

Possible Think-Aloud: (Continue reading aloud.) *There are a lot of words on this page, so I have to think hard to identify the key words. I can only pick the words that are the most important. This page is mostly about how the tadpoles eat to stay alive and swim to avoid animals that want to eat them. I am going to select "eat" as one key word because I know they won't stay alive without eating. I will write "eat" on a sticky note.*

TURN &TALK *I think we can select at least one more key word from this page about eating and swimming. Think together. What key word or words would you select?*

Analyze

STEP 3: Reread and reflect.

Possible Think-Aloud: *I have collected a lot of key words. Now I am going to arrange them in the order that I think will best help me tell about my learning. Then, I will be ready for "eat" and "swim" because frogs can't do that until they are out of the egg. Think together about the rest of these words. Where do you think they should go? Now that my key words are in order, listen to me retell what I have learned. If you hear me use a key word, put your finger on your nose and I will know that you noticed!* (After the retell.) *Now I am ready to start writing. I have my key words ready so I can remember to include them in my writing.*

Sum It Up

Key words are words that are really important. Nonfiction writers can collect them on sticky notes and then use them in telling about their learning. As you begin today, I will be watching to see which key words you select and how you use them in talking and writing.

VARIATIONS

For Less Experienced Writers: Have these writers place their key words right onto the pages of a book to support them as they retell and plan for writing. You may want to take dictation for them and show them how you insert their key words into the writing.

For More Experienced Writers: Stretch experienced writers to identify key words that are inferences. For example, on a page about the muscles in the leg of the frog, a key word might be "powerful," which is an inference that can be made about the movement of the frog.

LINKS TO CD-ROM:
- Student Writing: Kindergarten Key Words
- Student Writing: Grade 1 Investigation
- Student Writing: Grade 2 Investigation

Drafting

Getting Ideas on Paper

Drafting is the time when we pour our hearts into getting a message onto paper. This is a time when nonfiction writers engage in intense intellectual activity. They are likely to be checking their resources for facts, spending time reflecting and thinking, writing a bit, rereading, and then writing some more. This is also a time when writing is and should be a bit messy, as writers must compose quickly to capture fleeting thoughts and secure language to the page.

LESSON	K	1	2	RELATED LESSONS
1 Write About Your Pictures	●	●	●	*Planning:* Lessons 1–4 *Research:* Lesson 7, Sketch to Stretch: Visual Summary

2 Stretching Words . . .
    Listening to Sounds
	●	●		See Conventions
				Spelling Consciousness: Lesson 2, Stretching Words . . .
				    Writing Sounds You Know

3 Using a Picture Alphabet Card	●	●		*Spelling Consciousness:* Lesson 4, Strategic Spellers Use a Variety of Resources
4 Count the Words in a Message	●	●		*Revising:* Lesson 2, Adding Words with a Caret *Revising:* Lesson 8, Deleting Extra Words
5 Use Mostly Lowercase Letters	●	●		*Capitalization:* Lessons 1–4
6 Scratching Out . . . Changing Your Mind	●	●	●	*Revising:* Lesson 2, Adding Words with a Caret *Revising:* Lesson 5, Adding Ideas by Cutting and Taping

7 Turning Notes into Sentences		●	●	*Research:* Lesson 6, Use *I Remember!* to Summarize
				    Information
				Sentence Fluency: Lesson 4, Varying Sentence Beginnings
				    with Prepositional Phrases

Other Lessons to Create

You might also want to teach writers how to

- use classroom resources to find words to write (see *Spelling Consciousness:* Lesson 4, Strategic Spellers Use a Variety of Resources),
- write quickly so they don't forget their idea, or
- use a portable word wall (see Editing section of the Resources CD-ROM).

Write About Your Pictures

WHEN TO USE IT: To support writers in gathering their thoughts and focusing their message

When writers springboard from an illustration to the creation of text, they are reminded that illustrations carry a great deal of meaning and that their writing and their illustrations should work together. It can be very helpful to have students talk about their illustrations during drafting and then begin to write down the sentences they used to tell about their picture.

Model

Present a labeled diagram prepared in advance.

STEP 1: Create a sentence that describes the illustration, integrating the labels from the diagram in the sentences.

Possible Think-Aloud: *This is a diagram I created when I was reading about baby chickens. Because I drew first and captured my learning in the picture, my ideas are ready for writing. Do you notice how I included labels for water, seeds, and gravel in my diagram? That reminds me that baby chickens need water, seeds, and tiny bits of gravel to eat. That will make a perfect first sentence. Watch as I write, "Baby chicks need . . ." When I write about my picture, the writing flows smoothly.*

TURN &TALK *Think together. Look at my illustration and think of sentences that tell about my picture. Try to use some of the labels you see in my picture.*

STEP 2: Construct a second sentence about the picture, utilizing labels from the diagram as boldface words in the sentence.

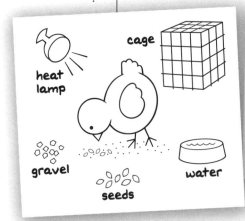

Baby chickens need **water, seeds,** and tiny bits of **gravel** to eat. Because they are so small, chicks need to have a **heat lamp** to keep the **cage** nice and warm. Peep! Peep! Peep! They grow and change each day.

Sample Modeled Writing

Possible Think-Aloud: *Writing about my picture helped a lot with sentence one. I have lots of ideas to write about as long as I keep looking at my illustration. I am thinking about the heat lamp in the diagram. Baby chicks need to be warm since they are so small. Looking at the picture reminds me that I need to tell why the heat lamp is important. Watch as I write my next sentence: "Because they are so small, chicks need to have a heat lamp to keep the cage nice and warm." Did you notice that I started with the word "because"? That is a helpful word that I thought of when I was looking at the picture. The chicks need that heat lamp because they will get cold without it.*

TURN &TALK *Look at my picture; then turn your thinking about the picture into a sentence. Think together and get ready to share your sentences.*

Analyze

STEP 3: Reread and reflect.

Possible Think-Aloud: *Listen as I reread my writing. Analyze to see if I included enough of the important ideas that you see in my illustration. Do I need to add more sentences, or does my writing cover the most important ideas?*

Sum It Up

Writers, we can write about our pictures to help ourselves create really terrific sentences. When you are drafting, look at your picture and the labels you created. Think about the topic and then get ready to write. As you begin writing today, take time to look closely at your picture. Think about the important ideas that you drew, and then turn your ideas into sentences!

VARIATIONS

For Less Experienced Writers: Begin by focusing on oral retelling of content and dictation. As emergent writers tell you about their pictures, you can show them how their words, turned into print, can be read by others.

For More Experienced Writers: Encourage experienced writers to add labels that are phrases when they create illustrations and diagrams. Then, as they draft, the phrases will naturally be infused into their sentences, creating a richer, more descriptive text.

Stretching Words . . . Listening to Sounds

WHEN TO USE IT: To help writers use the sounds they know and keep writing

FOCUS THE LEARNING

To free writers to concentrate on their messages, it is important to help them become comfortable writing the sounds they know and leaving concerns about spelling for later.

Model

It would be great to preface this lesson by blowing real bubbles for the students to observe.

STEP 1: Stretch each word out very slowly, emphasizing individual phonemes. Then, write the sounds that are easily heard, explaining to the students that you are writing the sounds you can hear, even though you know that some of the words are not perfectly spelled.

Possible Think-Aloud: *Writers, we are going to practice stretching out words and listening to the sounds as I write about bubbles. My sentence is, "Bubbles float and shimmer with color." Watch how I say each word very slowly. That helps me to hear the sounds in the word. My first word is "bubbles." (Say it very slowly: "/b/ . . . /u/ . . . /b/ . . . /l/ . . . /s/.") I hear the letters b, u, b, l, s. (As you write, be sure to emphasize beginning and ending sounds as those are the easiest to hear.) When I write the sounds I hear, it helps me write my ideas more quickly so I don't forget what I am trying to say.*

TURN &TALK *What did you notice about the way I stretched out the word "bubbles"? Did I get most of the sounds? My next word is "float." Say it together and think about the sounds you can hear. What letters would you write for "float"?*

STEP 2: Continue drafting, saying each word slowly and showing students how to listen for the sounds. You may even want to target one word in which you show how to write the beginning sound and then draw a line for the rest of the word.

Bubls flot and sh_____r with culr. Tha r delicat bols of fun!

(Bubbles float and shimmer with color. They are delicate balls of fun!)

Sample Modeled Writing

Possible Think-Aloud: *So far I have written, "Bubbles float and . . . " My next word is shimmer. I hear /sh/ at the beginning of the word, and I hear /r/ at the end, so I am going to draw a line for the middle of the word to remind myself to check on the spelling after I am finished writing. It is important to remember that writers stretch out words and write the letters they hear. They don't have to spell every word perfectly at first.*

Analyze

STEP 3: Reread and reflect.

Possible Think-Aloud: *Let's reread. Look closely at my writing and the sounds I used. As we stretch these words out one more time, listen carefully and see if you can think of any other letters that might help us write these words. Think together. What will you remember about stretching out words and using the sounds you can hear?*

Sum It Up

When we are drafting, it is important to get our ideas down quickly so we don't forget what we have to say. So this is not the time to wait for the teacher to come and spell words. This is a time when writers need to use the sounds they know so they don't forget their message. I know I can count on you to stretch your words out slowly and write the sounds that you can hear.

VARIATIONS

For Less Experienced Writers: Gather your least experienced writers into a small group, and assist them in stretching out words, using whiteboards to record the sounds they hear. You might also consider providing them with an alphabet strip such as the one on the Resources CD-ROM to facilitate linking of sounds and their symbols.

For More Experienced Writers: Help these writers clap out the syllables in words and write the sounds they hear in each syllable. This will help them to make better approximations of spelling and increase writing fluency.

LINKS TO CD-ROM:
- Teacher Tool: Alphabet Strips

Using a Picture Alphabet Card

WHEN TO USE IT: To help writers learn to use a reference tool for sound-symbol correspondence

FOCUS THE LEARNING

Emergent writers are often able to articulate sounds they hear without knowing the visual symbol for the sound. It is very common, for example, for a young writer to know that "house" starts with the sound /h/ but not remember the letter name or the shape of the letter that produces that particular sound. For this writer, a picture alphabet card can be a very helpful tool.

Hippos love water. They have sensitive skin, so they stay in water to keep cool and comfortable.

Sample Modeled Writing

Model

You will want to print and distribute the picture alphabet card on the Resources CD-ROM before this lesson.

STEP 1: Say each word slowly, emphasizing the initial sound. Then, skim the picture alphabet card to find a word that has the same beginning sound.

Possible Think-Aloud: *Writers, I am going to write about hippos. They stay in the water to keep their skin cool. I want to say, "Hippos love water." My first word is "hippos." I hear /h/. Watch how I use my picture alphabet card to find a picture of something that starts like hippo. I am looking for a letter that says /h/. Here is a picture of a ball. Ball starts with /b/. That isn't the same sound I hear in hippo. I need to keep looking. Here is a house. "House" . . . "hippo." That's it. They start the same way! I can use the letter "h" for the first sound in hippo. Remember my sentence, "Hippos love water." My next word is love. We all know how to write "love," so we don't need the picture alphabet card for that. All together, let's spell "love" as I write the word.*

TURN &TALK *My next word is "water." It starts with the sound /w/. Think together and use your picture alphabet cards to see if you can find a picture that starts with the sound like "water." It needs to start with the /w/ sound. Put your finger on your nose when you and your partner identify a picture that starts like "water."*

STEP 2: Continue drafting and modeling how to think about sounds, use letters you already know, and then refer to the picture alphabet card for additional support.

Possible Think-Aloud: *We are doing really well on my second sentence. You knew how to write "they and have," so we didn't need to use the picture alphabet card. Now we are ready for "sensitive." What a wonderful big word! Say it slowly with me, "sen-si-tive." I know the letter for the sound /s/. I will write an "s" to begin. The next sound I hear is /e/.*

TURN &TALK *Look at your picture alphabet card. Do you see a picture that begins with /e/? Share your thinking about the sounds I need in sensitive.*

Analyze

STEP 3: Reread and reflect.

Possible Think-Aloud: *Let's reread and see if we can think of more that we want to say about hippos. Partners, look closely at my writing and the sounds I used. I only used the picture alphabet card a few times, but when I did, it really helped me. If you were going to teach someone how to use a picture alphabet card, what would you tell them to do? How could you help them to remember that we don't use the card on every word? We use it only when we really need it.*

Sum It Up

Picture alphabet cards are helpful tools that we can use at times when we need a bit of help in remembering the letters that go with the sounds we are trying to write. If you place your picture alphabet card in your writing folder, it will be waiting for you whenever you need it. As we begin writing today, be sure to keep your card in a handy place.

VARIATIONS

For Less Experienced Writers: Present the picture alphabet card in a small-group setting so you can more effectively coach the writers in locating letters and sounds on the card. Learners at this age have fun making a game of "Find the Letter."

For More Experienced Writers: Remind more experienced writers that the picture alphabet card can help them with middle and ending sounds in words. These sounds are more difficult to discriminate through the auditory system, so the card may help writers to round out incomplete spellings.

LINKS TO CD-ROM:

- Teacher Tool: Picture Alphabet Card
- Teacher Tool: Portable Word Walls

Count the Words in a Message

WHEN TO USE IT: To help writers develop one-to-one correspondence between spoken and written words

FOCUS THE LEARNING

Young writers can be quite expansive as they verbally share information. When they begin to write their messages, however, the process of dissecting the sounds in each word takes so much concentration that they often omit key words in their message.

Model

STEP 1: Say a sentence slowly, holding up one finger for each word. Say it again, and have the children hold up their fingers as they say each word with you. Then, begin to write, pausing often to count the words on the paper.

Possible Think-Aloud: *I am going to write about the pizza that we had for lunch today. We are really lucky to have cooks who know how to make it taste so great. My first sentence is:* "Our cooks make great pizza." (Say the sentence slowly, holding up one finger for each word.) *Get your fingers ready and help me count the words in my sentence. Our . . . cooks . . . make . . . great . . . pizza. How many words did you count? Watch as I start writing my sentence. I am going to write five words and put a space between each one.* (As you add each word, keep returning to the beginning of the sentence to count words and reread. When you finish the sentence, have the students read it with you and carefully count the words to be sure you end up with five.)

TURN &TALK *What did you notice about the way I counted words in my sentence? If you were going to count words in a sentence, what would you be sure to remember to do?*

STEP 2: Continue adding sentences, pausing often to restate and recount the words in each sentence.

> Pizza
>
> Our cooks make great pizza. I love the stringy cheese on the top. Yum!

Sample Modeled Writing

Possible Think-Aloud: *When we take time to count the words we want to write, it really helps us be sure that all of our words show up on the paper. Get your fingers ready; here comes sentence number 2. "I . . . love . . . the . . . stringy . . . cheese . . . on . . . the . . . top."* Watch me count these words on my fingers, and then get ready to join in!

TURN &TALK *Say the sentence together, and use your fingers to count the words. Put your hand on your head when you think you know how many words are in my sentence.*

Analyze

STEP 3: Reread and reflect.

Possible Think-Aloud: *Let's reread. Does it make sense? Do I have all the words I need so a reader can understand what I am saying? How did counting the words help me make better sentences?*

Sum It Up

Writers, when we are drafting, it helps a lot to say a sentence slowly and count the words before writing. Once you know how many words you are going to write, it is easy to write and then check to see how you did. Remember: Say the sentence slowly and hold up one finger for each word. As you write, keep counting and see if you end up with the right number of words. I know I will see lots of you counting words as we begin to write today.

VARIATIONS

For Less Experienced Writers: Confer with individual writers who are having difficulty counting words in messages. Show them how you can count the words in a familiar reading selection. Help them practice in the reading selection; then, using a sentence strip, have them try it with a sentence of their own creation.

For More Experienced Writers: More experienced writers may not need this strategy every time they write. They can be encouraged to gradually shift this tool to revision when they are checking to be sure that their messages are complete.

Use Mostly Lowercase Letters

WHEN TO USE IT: To help emergent writers understand that capital letters are saved for specific purposes

FOCUS THE LEARNING

Many emergent writers enter school writing in capital letters. It is important to transition them to writing in mostly lowercase letters so they understand that capital letters are used for specific purposes.

Model

STEP 1: Think aloud and model writing in lowercase, except for specific purposes.

Possible Think-Aloud: *I am going to write about making soup, but first I need to think about capital letters and lowercase letters. Here is a rule I try to remember: Most words are written in ALL lowercase letters. Capital letters are saved for special reasons like the beginning of a sentence or a person's name. As I start my first sentence, I get to use a capital letter for the first word. Watch as I write: First, open the can and . . . Did you notice the capital letter, F, that I used to begin the sentence? Watch as I write the rest of the sentence. Notice how all the rest of the letters are lowercase. Writers use a capital at the beginning of the sentence, and then most other letters are lowercase.*

TURN &TALK *Think together about when I used lowercase letters and when I used a capital letter. Did I ever put a capital letter in the middle of the word? Did I ever put one at the end of a word?*

STEP 2: Continue thinking aloud and modeling limited use of capital letters.

Making Soup

First, open the can and pour the soup into a pan. Next, add water or milk. Then, you warm it with help from a parent. Finally, you get to eat!

Sample Modeled Writing

Possible Think-Aloud: *My second sentence is, "Next, add water or milk." I know I need to start with a capital letter because all sentences need that. But, I am wondering if I need any other capital letters? There aren't any names in this sentence so I only get to use one capital letter, N, at the beginning of "next." Watch as I write and notice how I am using lowercase letters.*

TURN &TALK *My third sentence is, "Then, you warm it . . ." Think together. How many capital letters do I get to use in this sentence?*

Analyze

STEP 3: Reread and reflect.

Possible Think-Aloud: *Let's reread my directions for soup. I have asked a partner to stand here and hold up one finger for each capital letter in my writing. When we are finished reading, we can count and see how many capital letters I used. Ready, let's read.*

Sum It Up

Writers write most words in lowercase letters. They use capital letters for special purposes like the beginning of a sentence or a name.

VARIATIONS

For Less Experienced Writers: Provide sentence strips with lowercase letters to lay in front of these learners as they write. That will keep their attention on lowercase forms and shapes, guiding them as they craft their words. A printable lowercase strip is on the Resources CD-ROM.

For More Experienced Writers: When writers understand that writing is mostly lowercase, begin building a working list of reasons to use capital letters. This could easily be posted as a chart and added to as lessons on capital letters are provided.

Scratching Out . . .
Changing Your Mind

WHEN TO USE IT: To help writers realize that erasing is not a helpful strategy when drafting, as it often creates smudges that are difficult to read

FOCUS THE LEARNING

Crossing out words and developing a sense of comfort with "sloppy copy" help writers maintain their writing fluency and encourage careful word choice and exploration of spelling options during drafting. Some educators believe in this so strongly that they cut the erasers off the ends of pencils or have learners write with markers so they cannot erase.

Model

STEP 1: Model how to cross words out and insert new thinking.

Possible Think-Aloud: *I am writing a letter to Mrs. McCall, our principal, to thank her for reading to us yesterday. This is a draft, so I will write quickly and get my ideas on the page. Then, I can recopy it and make it look really nice before I give it to her. I will start with "Thank you for coming to red to us." Oops. That doesn't look quite right. I think that I should have written, "read to us." Watch as I draw a line through red and write "read" above it. During drafting, don't erase; just cross things out and write in your new idea.* (Write sentence two using "good.") *I am thinking that the word good in sentence two isn't very exciting. The book on caterpillars was spectacular. I really liked it a lot.*

TURN &TALK *Put your heads together and think of a word that would be better than "good." How else could we describe the book that she read to us? We will pick out the best word we can think of and cross out good. We can do better than that!*

STEP 2: Continue drafting, crossing out words, and modeling how to write new thinking above or beside the original words.

Dear Mrs. McCall,

read
Thank you for coming to ~~red~~ to us.

spectacular
The book on caterpillars was ~~good~~.

We couldn't wait
~~We had fun.~~ to get started writing!

The Writers of Room 21

Sample Modeled Writing

Possible Think-Aloud: *Sentence three is "We had fun." That is okay, but not great. We did have fun, but it is more important that the book on caterpillars gave us some great ideas for thinking, and the writing you did about caterpillars was terrific. I am going to cross out that whole sentence. It isn't very good. We need a sentence that shows her how excited we were and that also lets her know that we wrote about caterpillars after she left.*

TURN &TALK *We crossed out "We had fun." Put your heads together and formulate a sentence that shows Mrs. McCall our excitement as writers!*

Analyze

STEP 3: Reread and reflect.

Possible Think-Aloud: *Let's reread the letter and see how it sounds. Remember that as we read, we want to read our latest thinking and skip right over those old words that we crossed out. (After rereading.) I have noticed something else that I want to cross out and change. The period at the end of the last sentence doesn't show how excited we were to start writing about caterpillars. I think we need an exclamation point instead. I am going to cross out the period and put in an exclamation point. Let's reread that sentence with gusto and see how it sounds.*

Sum It Up

When we draft, we cross out words, letters, and even punctuation. This is a time to use great words and ideas. It is important to remember that we often think of the best words, the best spellings, and the best punctuation after we have already written something down. That's okay. We know how to cross out and insert our new thinking. No erasers for us!

VARIATIONS

For Less Experienced Writers: Engage writers in an interactive writing experience in which they share the pen as text is created on a chart. With shared thinking and coaching, these writers can reread, rethink, and cross out to insert new ideas, new spellings, and enhance punctuation.

For More Experienced Writers: During individual conferences, challenge writers to be sure that their drafts have some cross-outs, insertions, and modifications that are visible. If drafts are completely clean with no cross-outs and adjustments, writers are not likely to have challenged themselves to reach deeply enough into interesting sentence structures, vocabulary alternatives, and punctuation options.

LINKS TO CD-ROM:
• Checklist: Sloppy Copy Checklist

Turning Notes into Sentences

WHEN TO USE IT: When writers need support in expanding words and phrases into sentences and paragraphs

FOCUS THE LEARNING

As nonfiction writers transition from research to drafting, often they are faced with collections of words and phrases that need to be expanded linguistically. At this phase, they need assistance in thinking beyond the isolated words and focusing on the concepts and understandings behind the words they have collected.

Model

STEP 1: Prepare a group of sticky notes with each one featuring a single word or phrase. Model how to cluster them into categories that make sense.

Possible Think-Aloud: *When I read about caterpillars, I used sticky notes and collected words and phrases that I thought would be good to use in my writing. Now I am ready to start drafting, so I need to organize my sticky notes. I want to group them together in a way that will help me write great sentences. I am going to put "egg, hatches, and eats eggshell" together in a group, because these words tell about when the caterpillar hatches. That is important in the life cycle of a caterpillar. Now I need to think of a sentence, or even two, for these words. How about "A caterpillar comes from an 'egg.' It eats its 'eggshell' when it 'hatches.'" Listen as I try a different way: "When a caterpillar 'hatches' from its 'egg,' it eats its 'eggshell' because it is so hungry."*

TURN &TALK *I want my draft to be interesting, so I will try to use these words and phrases in several ways. It helps to test the sentences out loud before I write them down. Think together, and construct a sentence or two that uses my sticky notes about the egg and hatching.*

egg

hatches

never sleeps

eats and eats

shed its skin

butterfly

eats eggshell

Sample Modeled Writing

STEP 2: Continue clustering sticky notes and testing sentences that reflect the concepts.

Possible Think-Aloud: *I am ready to look at the next group of sticky notes. I want to think about which words might fit together and which ones can be turned into sentences of their own. I am going to put "butterfly" off to the side, because I know that is the last step in the life cycle. As I think about these other sticky notes, I am thinking that "never sleeps" needs to be a sentence of its own. Did you know that a caterpillar never sleeps? It just keeps eating. I will write, "It never sleeps!" That really makes it stand out.*

When a caterpillar <u>hatches</u> from its <u>egg</u>, it <u>eats</u> its <u>eggshell</u> because it is so hungry. It <u>never sleeps</u>! It just <u>eats and eats</u> and then has to <u>shed its skin</u> because the skin is too tight.

Sample Modeled Writing

TURN &TALK *Think together about "eats and eats" and "shed its skin." Design sentences for those sticky notes.*

Analyze

STEP 3: Reread and reflect.

Possible Think-Aloud: *Let's reread and see how this sounds. As we reread, I am going to draw a line under the words that were on the sticky notes so I can see where I placed them in my draft. Ready, let's read.*

Sum It Up

When we create drafts of our writing, we often need to build sentences from words and phrases that we gathered during our research. It helps to practice saying the sentences in different ways to see what sounds better. If the sentence sounds good when you say it out loud, it is likely to sound great to a reader who gets to read your work! Turning words into sentences is what good writing is all about. As we get started writing, I know I can count on you to practice your sentences before writing them in your draft.

VARIATIONS

For Less Experienced Writers: Begin by creating a single sentence for each word or phrase collected while researching. The sentences will likely be short and concise. This scaffolds less experienced writers as they develop an understanding of how to expand language and describe concepts.

For More Experienced Writers: As these writers turn notes into sentences, encourage the use of descriptors to add richness to the writing. Try adding adjectives, adverbs, and descriptors to their sticky notes, and see how those additions change the sentences they insert into their drafts.

Revising

Polishing the Message

Revision is the time when writers challenge themselves to reach deeper and put themselves into the role of a reader. This is a time when they wonder about the clarity of the message and challenge themselves to reach for more interesting words and sentence structures, making their message the best it can be.

LESSON	K	1	2	RELATED LESSONS
1 Revising to Add Details	●	●	●	*Ideas:* Lesson 4, Infuse Interesting Details *Word Choice:* Lesson 3, Select Words that Show Order or Sequence
2 Adding Words with a Caret	●	●	●	*Word Choice:* Lesson 6, Add Action: Group *'ing'* Words Together *Organization:* Lesson 5, Details Support Main Idea
3 Revising a Lead to Make It Stronger	●	●	●	*Organization:* Lesson 6, Create an Inviting Lead *Voice and Audience:* Lesson 11, Draw Your Reader into the Setting
4 Sentence Combining		●	●	*Sentence Structure:* Lesson 3, Compound Sentences
5 Adding Ideas by Cutting and Taping		●	●	
6 Revising to Add Variety to Sentence Beginnings		●	●	*Revising:* Lesson 4, Sentence Combining *Sentence Fluency:* Lesson 3, Varied Sentence Beginnings
7 Checking the Closing	●	●	●	*Voice and Audience:* Lesson 7, At the End, Reveal Your Thoughts, Feelings, and Opinions *Organization:* Lesson 7, Craft a Satisfying Ending
8 Deleting Extra Words	●	●	●	
9 Recasting a Single Page as a Book	●	●	●	*Planning:* Lesson 4, Map Out Your Writing with Informational Pictures *Organization:* Lesson 9, Multiple Pages Are Used: Page Breaks Support Units of Meaning
10 Tuning Up Sensory Images		●	●	*Word Choice:* Lesson 1, Use Descriptive Words and Phrases *Word Choice:* Lesson 2, Target Powerful Action Verbs
11 Stick to the Main Idea		●	●	*Organization:* Lesson 1, Main Idea Maintained Throughout *Drafting:* Lesson 1, Write About Your Pictures
12 Using a Revision Checklist		●	●	

Other Lessons to Create

You might also want to teach writers how to

- revise their work with a partner,
- add text features during revision (see *Text Features:* Lessons 4–10), or
- prepare for a revision conference with the teacher.

Revising to Add Details

WHEN TO USE IT: When writing is too general and lacks detail

FOCUS THE LEARNING

Young children love to include authentic details when they tell stories but are known to reduce sentence length and inclusion of details when they shift to writing. It is important for young writers to understand that specific, accurate details add richness and texture to writing and illustrations.

Model

STEP 1: Read the first draft of your writing, and think aloud about the content. Is there enough information that the reader could draw a picture about the content? Show students how you decide how to add details that will improve the writing.

Possible Think-Aloud: *I am rereading these sentences about frogs, and I realize that if I wanted to draw a picture, I would have a problem. It says a frog's tongue is sticky, but it doesn't explain why the tongue is sticky or how the frog catches bugs. The writing doesn't have enough details to help readers get a picture in their minds. I am going to revise and add details. That will improve my writing.*

TURN &TALK *Partners, act out the way a frog uses his long, sticky tongue to catch a bug. Then think together to consider details we could add to tell more about how a frog catches bugs.*

STEP 2: Continue revising, adding carets and additional details.

long, that is really fast
A frog has a ∧ sticky tongue ∧.

by shooting out that long tongue
It catches bugs ∧.

A frog has a long, sticky tongue that is really fast. It catches bugs by shooting out that long tongue.

Sample Modeled Writing

Possible Think-Aloud: *I am going to use some of your ideas as I revise to add details. I am going to use Amanda and Jake's idea and add "long" before the word sticky. That is an important detail about the tongue. I am going to use Emilio and DeShawna's thinking and insert "that is very fast." Did you notice that I am not recopying the sentence? When I revise for details, I can just slip in extra words.*

Analyze

STEP 3: Reread and reflect.

Possible Think-Aloud: *Let's reread. Look closely at my writing and the details I added. What do you think of my writing now? How did the details help?*

Sum It Up

As writers, we need to be sure that we are including enough details that a reader can get a picture of what we are trying to say. One of the best ways to check ourselves is to reread and then revise to add details. As you reread your work today, I know that I will see you rereading and adding details to be sure that you have provided enough information for your reader. Let's write!

VARIATIONS

For Less Experienced Writers: Focus on adding details to illustrations and "telling" how the illustration was revised to add important details for a reader. You might also consider placing a very basic sentence in a pocket chart and asking writers to help you revise the sentence to add details.

For More Experienced Writers: Challenge partners to a listening and questioning experience. Have Partner A read to Partner B while Partner B tries to get a mental picture of what is being described. Partner B then gets to ask Partner A questions about the content as they examine the writing for opportunities to revise to add details. Have partners switch roles and repeat.

LINKS TO CD-ROM:
• Visual: Detailed photograph

Adding Words with a Caret

WHEN TO USE IT: To help writers indicate where words are to be inserted

FOCUS THE LEARNING

All writers need to revise in order to make their writing more clear, more accurate, or more interesting. When writers learn to use a caret to insert missing or important words, revision becomes less daunting.

Model

STEP 1: Display a short section of writing, where you have skipped lines. Demonstrate how to reread the writing carefully and use a caret to add words that improve the writing.

Possible Think-Aloud: *I know that, as a writer, one important job is to reread my writing and ask myself if there is anything I can add to make my writing better. Here is a section of my piece about zebras. Watch as I think about which words I can add.*

The second sentence says, "Some scientists think the stripes may confuse predators." I think I can add the word "hungry" before the word "predators." That would make my writing more interesting. Notice how I use a caret (^) as I slip in the new word.

TURN &TALK *Writers, look closely at the next sentence in my writing. Think together about what word or words would make the writing more interesting.*

STEP 2: Demonstrate how to use a caret to add the words.

Zebras have black and white stripes, but scientists aren't sure why.

Some scientists think the stripes may confuse ^ predators.
                                              hungry

Others think that the stripes keep ^ flies from bothering the zebras.
                                    pesky

Sample Modeled Writing

Possible Think-Aloud: *Let's add the word hungry before predators. I'll use a caret and write the word hungry above. The next sentence says, "Others think that the stripes keep flies from bothering the zebras." I'll add the word* pesky *before the word flies. I love that word, and I think my reader will, too. Adding the words was easy when I used a caret!*

Analyze

STEP 3: Reread and reflect.

Possible Think-Aloud: *Let's reread the new sentences I made. Do you think the sentences are improved? Did the added words make the sentences more interesting?*

Sum It Up

Writers, when we revise, a caret can help us to include words that we might want to add to make our writing more clear or more interesting. Now that you know how to use a caret, I'm sure I'll be seeing a lot of them in your writing! Let's start revising!

VARIATIONS

For Less Experienced Writers: Gather writers in a small group, and provide more guided practice with a common text. Coach and assist as they revise a short section in their own piece of writing.

For More Experienced Writers: Provide opportunities for peer coaching as writers work together to reread and revise.

Revising a Lead to Make It Stronger

WHEN TO USE IT: To add interest to story openings

FOCUS THE LEARNING

Over a period of a week or two, pause for a few minutes at the end of each nonfiction read-aloud to wonder with your students about the lead–the first sentence or two–in the book you just read. Encourage your students to consider leads that they think are great and make them want to read more. Collect great leads on sentence strips, and post them in visible places to support your writers.

Model

In advance of the lesson, create a chart with the first draft of the lead as shown in Step 2.

STEP 1: Reread the first draft of your writing, and think aloud about the lead. Consider: Is the lead inviting? Does it make us want to read more?

Possible Think-Aloud: *As I reread this piece on the old swing, I am thinking about the leads we have been collecting from our read-alouds. I know that a good lead should be like a magnet that pulls a reader into the rest of the selection. I am thinking about the sounds that the old swing makes. It goes "creak," when I pull the swing back, and it goes "swish," when I swing forward. My lead could say, "Creak-swish! Creak-swish!"*

TURN &TALK *Partners, think together. What do you think of a lead that uses sounds? Would that be like a magnet that makes you want to read more and find out what makes the sounds? Can you think of another lead that might be better?*

STEP 2: Continue revising by changing the original lead.

First draft:
I love the swing that hangs from the tree in the backyard. It is old and rusty and makes a lot of noise.

Sample Modeled Writing

Revised draft:
Creak-swish! Creak-swish! I love the swing that hangs from the tree in the backyard. It is old and rusty and makes a lot of noise. Creak-swish. Creak-swish.

Possible Think-Aloud: *I am going to select "creak-swish!" as my lead. Sound words make great leads, and "creak-swish" definitely makes me want to read more. Watch as I revise and insert my new lead.*

Analyze

STEP 3: Reread and reflect.

Possible Think-Aloud: *Let's reread together and make those sound words really come alive! Think together. Is my writing better with this new lead? Did this revision improve my writing? Why is this lead more interesting than starting with "I love"?*

Sum It Up

Today we learned that when we revise, we can also rewrite. We can make our leads like magnets that make a reader want to dive in and read more. As you begin writing today, take a moment to check on one of your leads. See if you can think of any ways that you can revise your lead to make it more interesting to a reader.

VARIATIONS

For Less Experienced Writers: Provide an opportunity for writers to use sticky notes and insert new leads into nonfiction leveled readers that are highly familiar. Once the new leads are inserted, have learners read the books to several people and tell why they think each new lead is better than the one in the book.

For More Experienced Writers: Demonstrate using a question as a lead, and talk about the impact this kind of lead has on a reader. You might also consider *Voice and Audience: Lesson 2, Speak Directly to Your Reader,* as this format can produce highly enticing leads.

LINKS TO CD-ROM: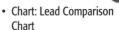
• Chart: Lead Comparison Chart

Sentence Combining

WHEN TO USE IT: When students write in short, choppy sentences

FOCUS THE LEARNING

When writers learn to link short sentences together, they increase their control over creating writing that sounds like natural language. Sentence combining has a very strong research base that supports its use, but it is important to remember that one lesson isn't enough. This is a skill that needs to be encouraged and supported over many lessons and many topics as writers mature.

Model

In advance of the lesson, post the short sentences of draft one in a pocket chart. Using scissors, show how you can cut and move words around to combine two short sentences into one that is longer and more interesting.

STEP 1: Combine two short sentences.

Possible Think-Aloud: *I am going to combine sentence one and sentence two into one sentence that is a bit longer and more interesting. Watch as I insert the word "and" after teeth. I will also take the scissors and replace the period after teeth with a comma. This new sentence says: Bears have big teeth, and they have long nails on their paws. This is a combination of sentence one and sentence two. I turned two short sentences into one longer sentence that tells my reader a lot more.*

TURN &TALK *What did you notice as I combined those sentences? Identify the steps I followed to create one longer sentence out of two shorter ones.*

STEP 2: Cut and rearrange the next two sentences to combine them.

First draft:

Bears have big teeth. They have long nails on their paws. Bears need to build up fat. They eat berries, insects, fish, and even honey. Bears eat a lot in the summer. Bears sleep in the winter.

Sample Modeled Writing

Revised draft:

Bears have big teeth, and they have long nails on their paws. Bears need to build up fat, so they eat berries, insects, fish, and even honey. Bears eat a lot in the summer, so they can sleep through the winter.

Sample Modeled Writing

Possible Think-Aloud: *The next two sentences are about eating. Bears need to build up fat. They eat . . . and, but, or, and so, are all good words for combining sentences. I already used "and," so this time, watch how I insert the word "so." My new longer sentence now reads, Bears need to build up fat, SO they can eat berries . . . . Did you notice that I also added a comma where the period used to be? To combine short sentences, you need to change the period to a comma and then select a connecting word: and, but, so, and or. Sentence combining is fun, and it makes my writing sound better!*

Analyze

STEP 3: Reread and reflect.

Possible Think-Aloud: *Let's reread together and think about the way our newly combined sentences sound when we read aloud. (After rereading.) I am noticing that our new longer sentences sound more like talking. We speak in long sentences, so sentence combining can make our writing sound more like talking. Think together. What do you need to remember about combining sentences?*

Sum It Up

Sentence combining is an important skill for writers. When we revise, it is important to be on the lookout for short sentences that can be combined into longer, more interesting sentences. Sentence combining is fun, so I know I will see you combine sentences as you revise. That's what good writers do!

VARIATIONS

For Less Experienced Writers: Using a pocket chart, begin by combining two short sentences with conjunctions such as and, but, or, so. Less experienced writers can easily remove a period and insert a conjunction and a comma to create a compound sentence. An example: Frogs can jump. They leap long distances. Combined sentence: Frogs can jump, *and* they leap long distances.

For More Experienced Writers: Begin a list of different ways to combine sentences, and post it as a chart to assist writers during drafting and revising. Be sure to help your writers notice the use of a comma.

LINKS TO CD-ROM:

• Thinking Challenge: Combining Sentences

Adding Ideas by Cutting and Taping

WHEN TO USE IT: To help writers revise without rewriting the entire piece

FOCUS THE LEARNING

The more children learn about their topic, the more information they may wish to add. When children learn how to revise by cutting and taping, the task becomes more manageable.

Model

In advance of the lesson, have paper, scissors, and tape on hand.

STEP 1: Show how to cut apart a prepared piece of writing and insert new paper to make room for more writing.

Possible Think-Aloud: *Let me show you a smart way to make room to add facts about my topic. I'll use scissors to cut my original piece of writing, and then I use tape to insert a new piece of new paper right in the middle. Now that I have room, I can write "such as rodents, small birds, and lizards." I will write the new words in a bright color so you can see the new words I am adding.*

TURN &TALK *Writers, what do you think of my cool way to revise for adding ideas and information? How might cutting and taping help you with your writing?*

STEP 2: Insert another new piece of paper, and revise the next sentence.

First draft:

Sun bears eat a lot of different things.
The sun bear can use its tongue to slurp up insects.

Sample Modeled Writing

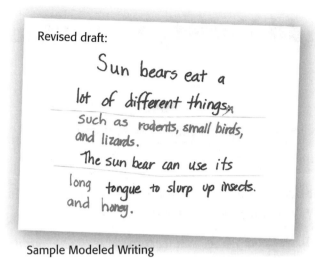

Revised draft:

Sun bears eat a
lot of different things,
Such as rodents, small birds,
and lizards.
The sun bear can use its
long tongue to slurp up insects.
and honey.

Sample Modeled Writing

Possible Think-Aloud: *Writers, the next sentence is about how the sun bear can use its tongue to eat insects. I think I can add more information about that, too. Watch again to see how I cut my paper after the word "its" and tape on a new strip of paper. I have room to revise and add "long tongue to slurp up insects and honey." Revising this way is fun and really boosts my writing!*

Analyze

STEP 3: Reread and reflect.

Possible Think-Aloud: *Let's reread my writing and think together. Is there any other new information that will help make my piece more clear or interesting? I have paper, scissors, and tape so I am ready for more ideas!*

Sum It Up

Writers, when we revise, cutting and taping to make room for new information are an easy way to make our writing better. Now that you know this smart way to add bits of writing, I'm ready to admire you as you give it a try!

VARIATIONS

For Less Experienced Writers: For early experiences with cutting and taping to revise, work with writers individually or in a small group so you can coach their thinking as they decide where to cut and insert additional information.

For More Experienced Writers: Challenge writers to work with a partner to use cut-and-paste revision as a way to incorporate information they gain from a new book on the same topic.

LINKS TO CD-ROM:
• Visual: Cut and Paste Revision

Revising to Add Variety to Sentence Beginnings

WHEN TO USE IT: When students are using the same word to begin each sentence

FOCUS THE LEARNING

Young writers are often so focused on writing down facts about their topic that they pay little attention to how each sentence begins. Our goal is to encourage them to examine each sentence beginning for variety.

Model

STEP 1: Demonstrate how to read the first word of each sentence and tally the number of times it is used.

Possible Think-Aloud: *We've been learning how to read our writing carefully and think about how it sounds. I am working on a piece about grasshoppers. Listen as I read my piece. Pay close attention to the first word in each sentence. I'm going to use this sheet to help me think about my sentence beginnings. I'll write the first word of each sentence on the lines. If I have used a word more than once, I'll add a tally mark next to that word.*

TURN &TALK *Partners, what did you notice about my piece? What are you thinking? Have I used lots of different words to begin my sentences?*

STEP 2: Demonstrate how to use a tally sheet to begin to revise.

Possible Think-Aloud: *I think I have a problem. Many of my sentences start with the same word, "grasshoppers." I need to revise. I think I can combine my second and third sentences, and that might help. Let's try that. For the next sentence, I need to come up with a different way to begin. I think I'll try, "Most*

First draft:

Great Grasshoppers!

There are 18,000 kinds of grasshoppers. Grasshoppers have five eyes. Grasshoppers have no ears. Grasshoppers eat plants. Grasshoppers can live in all kinds of habitats. Grasshoppers can rub their wings to make music.

Sample Modeled Writing

Revised draft:

Great Grasshoppers!

Did you know that there are 18,000 kinds of grasshoppers? Grasshoppers have five eyes, but no ears. Most grasshoppers eat plants. They can live in all kinds of different habitats, and most of them can rub their wings together to make music.

Sample Modeled Writing

grasshoppers eat plants." That would add some variety! Notice how I just put a line through "grasshoppers" and slip the word "most" right in.

Analyze

STEP 3: Reread and reflect.

Possible Think-Aloud: *Let's read my writing now. Do my sentence beginnings have a little variety now? Do you think revising this way improved my piece? Using the tally sheet helped me discover the problem with this draft, and it led me to revise.*

Sum It Up

Today we learned that one way we can improve the way our writing sounds is to use different words to begin our sentences. I showed you one tool that writers can use to examine each sentence and improve the whole piece. Today as you look at your own writing, try our new tool and see what you think. I will look forward to reading your revisions. Who's ready to begin?

VARIATIONS

For Less Experienced Writers: Provide more guided practice in identifying the first word in the sentence and finding alternatives for repeated words. Teach different pronouns that can be used to identify the subject of each sentence.

For More Experienced Writers: Challenge students to examine a piece of writing from a published writer. Discuss ways in which the author utilizes several different techniques to begin sentences. Encourage students to try some of the sentence beginnings that the author has used.

LINKS TO CD-ROM:
- Checklist: Beginning Words Tally Sheet

Checking the Closing

WHEN TO USE IT: To add interest and a sense of closure to story endings

FOCUS THE LEARNING

Over a period of a week or two, read aloud several examples of great endings from a variety of nonfiction texts. Collect powerful endings on a chart, and post it in a visible place to support your writers.

Model

STEP 1: Reread a prepared first draft, and think about the ending. Consider options for improving the closing.

Possible Think-Aloud: *As I reread my piece on garden helpers, I am thinking about the powerful endings we've been collecting from books. I know that I need to come up with an ending that will wrap it all up. "The End" is okay, but I think I can do better. I think that my ending could tell my reader to think twice before squishing bugs in their gardens.*

TURN &TALK *Partners, what do you think about speaking directly to the reader in my closing? Should I tell my reader not to squish bugs? What words might I use to say that to my reader?*

STEP 2: Continue revising by changing the original ending.

Possible Think-Aloud: *Anna and Julio, can you come up here and talk to the class? Tell them that you don't want them to squish bugs. We are going to listen carefully and then revise this writing so it sounds like the way Anna and Julio talked to us. Perfect! Watch as I write Anna and Julio's words and talk directly to my reader—just like they talked to you.*

First draft:

Earthworms can help your garden by making the soil rich and healthy. Even spiders can be a big help! They catch small plant-eating bugs in their sticky webs. The End

Sample Modeled Writing

New ending:
So don't squish bugs!

Analyze

STEP 3: Reread and reflect.

Possible Think-Aloud: *Let's reread my writing and think together. Do you like this new ending? Did this revision help my reader to feel as though my piece is finished? Why do you think this ending is better than just writing "The End"?*

Sum It Up

Writers, we know that endings are important. They are your last chance to make an impression on your reader. From now on, you'll know how to take time with your endings and write them carefully. As you look at your own writing today, take a moment to focus on your ending. See if you can think of any ways that you can revise your ending and even speak directly to your reader!

VARIATIONS

For Less Experienced Writers: With a shared text that is familiar, coach students as pairs come up with new endings for the selection. Encourage pairs to share the new ending with the group.

For More Experienced Writers: Encourage students to try out a few different endings. Once they have a few written, have them read the endings to a partner and choose the one that works best.

Deleting Extra Words

WHEN TO USE IT: When students have added unnecessary words

FOCUS THE LEARNING

Young writers need not waste precious minutes erasing. The goal is to teach them an easy way to delete unnecessary words.

Model

STEP 1: Display a short section of writing where you have inserted some extra and unnecessary words. Demonstrate how to reread and cross out extra words.

Possible Think-Aloud: *I know that as I writer, I sometimes get going so fast on my writing that I accidentally add some extra words that don't belong. As I read my second sentence, I see that the word "the" doesn't belong. It doesn't make sense! Watch as I draw a line through that extra word. This is much better than using an eraser.*

TURN &TALK *Partners, do you see any other words that don't belong? Think together and see if there are any other words I should draw a line through.*

STEP 2: Demonstrate how to delete extra words by making a line through the words.

Possible Think-Aloud: *Watch me again as I use a line to show which words need to come out. I put a line through the word "the" in the second sentence. In the third sentence, I need to draw more lines. This doesn't make sense. I will draw a line through "get" in the third sentence.*

Did you know that snakes shed their skins? One reason they do ~~the~~ this is because they grow too big and they need a bigger skin! Shedding the skin helps to get ~~get~~ rid of the nasty bugs that have made themselves at home in their skin.

Sample Modeled Writing

Analyze

STEP 3: Reread and reflect.

Possible Think-Aloud: *Let's look at my piece of writing now. Did it help now that I've taken out the extra words? Revising to remove words was easy when I put a line through them! No erasers for me!*

Sum It Up

Today we learned something that more experienced writers do. Now we know that when we revise, we need to check for extra words that don't belong. When we find them, we can simply put a line through those extra words—no erasing! As you look at your own writing today, take some time to reread carefully and see if you can revise to delete some extra words. Let's begin!

VARIATIONS

For Less Experienced Writers: Confer one-on-one with students and help them to reread their writing. Model once again how to put a line through any unwanted word. Coach them as they reread and check for clarity.

For More Experienced Writers: Provide opportunities for peer coaching as writers work together to reread and delete extra words.

Recasting a Single Page as a Book

WHEN TO USE IT: To help writers understand that writing can be spread out over several pages

FOCUS THE LEARNING

For many young writers, inserting carets and adding information are helpful strategies when they are just adding a word or two. They are quickly challenged, however, when they decide they want to reorganize their work, add substantial amounts of information, or completely rewrite a section. When you teach writers to courageously use scissors to cut early drafts apart, they are thrilled to discover that a short piece of writing can quickly bloom into a book!

Model

To prepare for this lesson, create a piece of writing in advance or plan to reuse a modeled writing from a previous lesson. You will also need scissors, tape, and several pieces of extra chart paper.

STEP 1: Read the first draft of your writing, and think aloud about the content. Suggest that it would be good to stretch the writing over several pages so you could add details and more pictures.

Possible Think-Aloud: *As I reread this draft about hummingbirds, I realize that there aren't enough details. I tell that hummingbirds are tiny, but I don't say how tiny. Watch as I take my scissors and move that sentence to the top of a new piece of paper. Now I have more room to add details about size and more illustrations, too. This one sentence will turn into a whole page about the size of hummingbirds!*

My second sentence is really short, "They migrate." This is a new topic, so it needs a new page of its own. Watch how I cut this out and paste it onto page 2 of my book. My book now has two pages!

TURN &TALK *Partners, think together. Should the third sentence about wings be on a page of its own, or should I put it with the sentences on pages 1 and 2? Where do you think it belongs? Talk about WHY you think I should put it in a particular place.*

(Prepare a chart of the first draft in advance.)

First draft:

Hummingbirds are tiny birds. They migrate. Their wings move really fast.

Notice that the revised draft is now three pages long.

Sample Modeled Writing

Sample Modeled Writing

STEP 2: Continue revising.

Possible Think-Aloud: *This is exciting. With this revision, I have a three-page book and lots of room to add information and illustrations. It said in my book that a hummingbird weighs about as much as a penny. On page 1, I am going to add a diagram that shows a tiny little hummingbird and a penny. After I add my diagram, I am going to add sentences to tell more about how really small a hummingbird can be. Revising this into a book so that I have room for my ideas is really fun.*

Analyze

STEP 3: Reread and reflect.

Possible Think-Aloud: *Let's reread my three-page book. Each page now has an illustration, a page number, and even more information. If you were going to teach others how to turn a short piece of writing into a book, what would you tell them to do?*

Sum It Up

Writers, since you know how to turn short pieces of writing into books, I am going to place extra paper, glue sticks, and staplers in our writing center. That way you can do what I just did and give yourselves room to add illustrations and ideas. You can make books that are going to be very much like the books we enjoy reading. Being an author is even more fun when your writing looks like a book!

VARIATIONS

For Less Experienced Writers: Create a big book: Bring these writers into a guided writing group and model the process again with new starter sentences. Have partner pairs place one sentence on a large sheet of paper; then have them work together to add sentences and illustrations. Bind the pages together with a cover so it can be shared with the class as a new big book for everyone to enjoy.

For More Experienced Writers: Before they begin drafting, have them plan their writing as a multiple-page book. They can plan their pages by drawing a bit on each page, creating a storyboard, or placing a sticky note on each page with key words they want to include on the page.

LINKS TO CD-ROM:
- Student Writing: Wolves Big Book

Tuning Up Sensory Images

WHEN TO USE IT: When writing is too vague and lacks vivid images

FOCUS THE LEARNING

All young writers need to learn how to create vivid images for their readers. This lesson is designed to help students understand how utilizing all five senses can enhance a piece of nonfiction writing.

Model

Prepare a chart of the first draft in advance. Skip lines so there is room for revision.

STEP 1: Read the first draft of your writing, and think aloud about the topic. Show students how you wonder about adding some descriptions that involve the senses.

Possible Think-Aloud: *I am rereading my sentences about rain, and I'm asking myself, "Have I included words that show my reader how rain feels, tastes, smells, and sounds?" I have some information about rain, but the writing doesn't really help the reader get a clear picture in his or her mind. I am going to revise and add some words that give more description. That will really boost my writing!*

TURN &TALK *Partners, think together and come up with some words that describe how rain sounds, looks, feels, and smells. Get a picture in your mind of running in the rain. What words could I add to my writing that would help a reader share your mental picture?*

First draft:
Rain falls from the sky.

Revised draft:
Pitter, patter. Pitter, patter. As the soft rain falls, the fresh smell and sparkling drops splash right off my coat.

Sample Modeled Writing

STEP 2: Continue revising.

Possible Think-Aloud: *I heard some great ideas for words that I could add to boost my writing. Carson and Olivia suggested that I could add the words "Pitter, patter." I think I could add those words to the beginning of my piece. David and Anna were talking about how rain can feel soft. I could add the word "soft," too. As writers, we need to use words that help our readers get a picture in their minds.*

Analyze

STEP 3: Reread and reflect.

Possible Think-Aloud: *Let's reread. What do we think of the writing now? I think my favorite parts are the words that show sound, "pitter, patter." I also like the part about "sparkling drops." I can really picture shiny drops of water bouncing off the arm of my new coat. Think together. Did this revision help us get a clear mental picture of the rain? How did adding words about smells, sounds, and things we see improve the writing?*

Sum It Up

As writers, we need to be sure we think about the picture we are helping a reader to create in his or her mind. It is important to write in ways that help readers get a clear mental picture. Writers, I know I can count on you to help your readers visualize. As you write, use your senses and help your reader to "see" what you see and "hear" what you hear.

VARIATIONS

For Less Experienced Writers: Coach writers as they work in pairs to list words that describe how an orange looks, smells, feels, and tastes. Assist them as they craft descriptive writing with sensory imaging.

For More Experienced Writers: Challenge partners to listen with an ear for sensory images and clear mental pictures. Have Partner A read his or her writing to Partner B while Partner B tries get a clear mental picture. Partner B can then coach Partner A in revising the piece to improve sensory images. Have partners switch and repeat.

Stick to the Main Idea

WHEN TO USE IT: When the main idea is unclear or when unrelated ideas distract the reader

FOCUS THE LEARNING

Less experienced writers will sometimes start out focused, but as they continue to write, they may lose track of the main idea. The goal is to teach students how to reread and ensure that a central focus or main idea is maintained throughout the writing.

Model

STEP 1: Post the sentences of draft 1 in a pocket chart. Turn over one sentence at a time, asking students whether the piece has stayed focused up to this point.

Possible Think-Aloud: *This writing is about my backyard, so as I revise, I need to be sure that all of my sentences tell about my yard. If these sentences give you a mental picture of me in my yard, then you know I have stuck to my topic. Sentence one says, "My backyard is . . ." If I close my eyes and picture this, I see myself in my yard with a big smile. That sentence fits with my topic, doesn't it? Close your eyes and get ready to visualize. Sentence two says . . .*

TURN & TALK *Share the mental picture you got from sentence two. Are you able to picture my yard and the things that are in it? Did I stick to my topic?*

STEP 2: Continue revising.

My Backyard

My backyard is a place where I feel really happy. I really enjoy having my lawn chairs, flower beds, and garden all in one place. On hot summer days, I love to sit under the tall apple tree and read. ~~Once, I baked an apple pie and served it to my family.~~

Sample Modeled Writing

Possible Think-Aloud: (Read to the end, uncovering one sentence at a time and asking students to visualize the yard.) *Uh-oh. I think I have a problem. My last sentence gave us all a visualization that wasn't about my yard. It was about the apple pie! I need to either remove that sentence or fix it so that it tells about my yard. Writers need to stick to their topic, and my last sentence didn't do that.*

Analyze

STEP 3: Reread and reflect.

Possible Think-Aloud: *I think we made the right decision to delete the last sentence. Some other time I can write about how much fun it is to make apple pie. That is a different topic and doesn't belong in my writing today. Let's reread together one last time and see what we think about the writing now. Does the writing stay on track now? Did I stick to my topic? Think together. How does sticking to a topic help a reader?*

Sum It Up

Today we learned how to reread our writing with the goal of making sure that our writing stays on topic. When you look at your writing today, be sure to remove any sentences that get off track.

VARIATIONS

For Less Experienced Writers: In partners or small groups, have students read their writing sentence by sentence. Ask listeners to visualize after each sentence and decide if their mental picture fits the main idea. Discuss the piece as a group, and see if the group can come up with a title that tells about the main idea of the piece.

For More Experienced Writers: Have students use the same sentence-by-sentence and title strategies to revise their piece. Then, have students write an explanation of the changes they made and how the changes improved their writing.

Using a Revision Checklist

WHEN TO USE IT: When writers are ready to be more independent as they revise

FOCUS THE LEARNING

Revision Checklists remind writers of things they have learned. It is essential to use Revision Checklists that list only those elements you have modeled and supported through direct instruction.

Model

STEP 1: Give each writer a Revision Checklist and model its use.

Possible Think-Aloud: *Writers, I am going to use a Revision Checklist as I revise. It will help me make sure that my writing is the best it can be. The first point on my checklist says: "Reread and touch each word." That helps me make sure that my words say exactly what I want them to say. Watch me as I do that, and then place a check mark next to that item on the checklist.*

TURN &TALK *Partners, look at your Revision Checklists together. What is the next item on the list? Think about what I should do next to revise my writing.*

STEP 2: Reread for another revision point.

Possible Think-Aloud: *The next thing on my Revision Checklist is adding extra words if I need them.* (After rereading.) *Look at the sentence that starts with "The buttery . . ." This doesn't make sense. I need a word that tells what the buttery smell does. Does it drift, float, or race? I will use a caret and insert "floats." Watch as I add a √ next to "add missing words" on the checklist.*

Popping Popcorn

By Mrs. Boswell

Pop! Pop! Pop! The buttery smell through the whole house. Soon, everyone is gathered in the kitchen. Is the popcorn ready yet?

Sample Modeled Writing

Analyze

STEP 3: Reread and reflect.

Possible Think-Aloud: *We have reread this piece of writing several times now. When we take the time to reread and think about our writing, our work just keeps getting better and better. What do you think of this checklist? Are there other things we could add that would help us as we revise?*

Sum It Up

Today we have learned how a Revision Checklist can help when we are ready to revise. I'll put several Revision Checklists in the writing corner so that you can select one that is right for the kind of writing you are doing. When you are ready to revise, you now have another tool that can help you make sure your writing is all you want it to be.

VARIATIONS

For Less Experienced Writers: Together with the class, create a Revision Checklist that includes words and pictures. Refer to this checklist as you revise your piece of writing. Work with writers in a small group to choose just one or two items on which to focus.

For More Experienced Writers: Once writers become comfortable with using a Revision Checklist, work with a small group to create new Revision Checklists that are appropriate for different genres.

LINKS TO CD-ROM:
- Checklist: Revision Checklist A
- Checklist: Revision Checklist B
- Checklist: Revision Checklist C

Editing

Being Polite to Your Reader

Editing should not be seen as a function of correctness or that step you "have" to take before publishing. Instead, it should be a joyful infusion of possibility in which artistic punctuation, jaw-dropping grammar, and carefully spelled words add the final touch of elegance to a piece of writing.

LESSON	K	1	2	RELATED LESSONS
1 Word Boundaries: Keep Letters in a Word Close Together	●	●		
2 Reread and Touch Each Word	●	●		*Drafting:* Lesson 4, Count the Words in a Message
3 Focused Edits: Reread for Each Editing Point	●	●	●	*Editing:* Lesson 6, Using an Editing Checklist
4 Reread to Add Letters to Words	●	●	●	*Drafting:* Lesson 2, Stretching Words . . . Listening to Sounds *Drafting:* Lesson 3, Using a Picture Alphabet Card
5 Using Spelling Consciousness While Editing	●	●	●	
6 Using an Editing Checklist	●	●	●	
7 How to Peer Edit	●	●	●	
8 Using Familiar Resources to Help You Edit	●	●	●	

Other Lessons to Create

You might also want to teach writers how to

- take extra care with handwriting on a final draft (see *Presenting:* Lesson 1, Handwriting Is Neat and Legible),
- check end punctuation of every sentence, or
- read a draft aloud to edit for grammar.

Word Boundaries: Keep Letters in a Word Close Together

WHEN TO USE IT: When students need support in creating clear boundaries between their words

Many emergent writers struggle to create word boundaries that make the beginning and ending of each word clear to a reader. Understanding of word boundaries is a developmental step that launches readers and writers forward as literacy learners.

Model

STEP 1: Use a whiteboard to model both correct and incorrect spacing of letters and word boundaries.

Possible Think-Aloud: *Words are made up of letters, so when I write, I need to think about the sounds in each word. But I also need to think about spacing. I need to help anyone who reads my work to see which letters go together to make a word. Writers need to be really sure there are big spaces between each word and that letters inside a word are close to each other.*

Watch as I write, "Cats can be loving . . ." Notice how I cluster the letters in "cats" closely together and leave a big space before the word "can" That shows where each word stops and starts.

Write *"Catscanbe"* with no spaces.

TURN &TALK *Partners, what do you think of "Catscanbe"? What do I need to think about to make sure everyone can read my writing?*

STEP 2: Continue writing a second sentence on the whiteboard or a chart, involving the students in helping to make decisions about spacing and clustering of letters within words.

Cats can be loving and friendly pets. They have silky fur and purr softly when they are happy.

Sample Modeled Writing

Possible Think-Aloud: *My next sentence is, "They have silky fur and purr softly when they are happy." For this sentence, we will be sharing the pen and thinking together about spaces. Put your hand on your left shoulder if you would like to write the word "They" and show us how to cluster the letters together so we know it is a word. Touch your right ear if you would like to show us the perfect amount of space to leave before we write the next word.* (Continue to the end of the sentence, interactively engaging students in helping you model spacing.)

TURN &TALK *Partners, explain what you have seen me doing with spacing. What did you notice? What do I need to think about to make sure that a reader can read my writing?*

Analyze

STEP 3: Analyze and reflect.

Possible Think-Aloud: *Writers, letters in a word need to be right next to each other so we can tell that they belong together. We also need spaces between words so we can tell where each word ends and a new one begins. Think together. If you were going to teach someone about spaces, what would you be sure to tell them?*

Sum It Up

Spaces between words help readers know where one word stops and the next one starts. Writers, I know I can count on you to really think about spaces when you are writing so your readers will know exactly what you have to say!

VARIATIONS

For Less Experienced Writers: Some inexperienced writers benefit from having a spacing "helper." You can make them by painting tongue depressors a bright color and adding movable eyes. These spacing helpers are fun to use and a great motivator for adding spaces between words.

For More Experienced Writers: See *Presenting: Lesson 3, Page Layout Includes Effective Use of Margins.* This lesson will expand their thinking about spacing to utilizing the full width of a page before making a return sweep to a new line of text.

LINKS TO CD-ROM:
• Teacher Tool: Spacing Buddy

Reread and Touch Each Word

WHEN TO USE IT: When writers retell rather than carefully reread the words they have written

FOCUS THE LEARNING

It is very common for emergent writers to glance at their writing and then "tell" what they meant to write. This behavior shows a strong link to a message but diverts writers from realizing that every word they say must actually appear on the paper. To help emergent writers develop an awareness that each word must actually appear on the page, they should touch each word while editing. This focuses the eye on the page and helps the writers confirm that the words they are touching have the letters and sounds associated with the words they are "saying." Touching the words will help your emergent writers craft written sentences that more closely match oral production.

Model

STEP 1: Prepare the modeled writing in advance, and deliberately leave out a few key words that you can discover as you reread to edit.

Possible Think-Aloud: *I am ready to edit to be sure that all my words are actually on the paper. This is an important job that editors need to do. To edit, I am going to touch each word as I say it to be sure the word on the paper is the same word I am saying. Listen to me say my sentence: We planted seeds in little pots. Now I need to touch each word to be sure it is on the paper. (Touch We.) We starts with /w/. That is the right beginning sound for "we." Good. (Touch planted.) Planted starts with a /p/. That looks good, too. My next word should be "seeds," so when I touch the word, I will expect to see an "s." Oops. I see the letter "i." I forgot to write "seeds." I need to use a caret and insert "seeds." Touching each word helped me notice that a word was missing.*

TURN &TALK *Partners, list the steps I just followed to edit. What did I do to make sure that every word in my message was actually on the paper?*

STEP 2: Continue touching and cross-checking the words.

Possible Think-Aloud: *Before I reread and touch each word in sentence two, I want to remind myself of the steps. First, I say the sentence that I want on the paper. Then, I touch the words one at a time. When I touch a word, I check to see if it starts with the letter that matches the word I am saying. If I discover a missing word, then I need to insert it. Get ready. Watch as I touch the word in sentence two. (Begin reading and touching.) Oh, no! It says "sunlight into plants." That isn't what I meant. I want this to say,*

Before editing:

Planting Seeds

We planted in little pots.

They will need water and sunlight into plants.

After editing:

Planting Seeds

We planted ∧ seeds in little pots.

They will need water and sunlight ∧ to grow into plants.

Sample Modeled Writing

"They will need water and sunlight TO GROW into plants." I am so glad that I was rereading and touching every word.

TURN &TALK *Think together. To edit this, what should I do?*

Analyze

STEP 3: Reread and reflect.

Possible Think-Aloud: *Editing is important work. When I touch each word as I reread, that helps me to notice if I have forgotten one of my words. I am going back to the beginning to reread this one more time. I want to be sure that all the words are there. Why don't you read this with me and help me to check my editing?*

Sum It Up

Remember that writers get their ideas on paper first. Then, after writing, they reread and touch each word to make sure they didn't leave out any words. Authors know that they want their talking and the words on the page to match. I know I will be seeing you edit by rereading and touching each word.

VARIATIONS

For Less Experienced Writers: During one-on-one conferences, support writers in touching individual words. You may want to assess and be sure that they understand word boundaries. A lack of understanding in that area can greatly affect their ability to reread and edit.

For More Experienced Writers: Link this lesson to *Planning:* Lesson 4, Count the Words in a Message, to scaffold more experienced writers in predicting the number of words they expect to see in each sentence and then counting to see if all words are present.

LINKS TO CD-ROM
- Teacher Tool: Editing Helper

Focused Edits:
Reread for Each Editing Point

WHEN TO USE IT: When focusing students on the importance of rereading several times during editing, once for each editing point

Writing experts often assert that rereading is the heartbeat of good writing. We reread to maintain our focus and add details, we reread to revise and enhance our work, we reread to edit and fine-tune the surface features of our writing. The problem for most writers is that rereading to edit requires total concentration on the surface features of writing. This is best accomplished when writers reread with a single purpose in mind, then reread again with a new focus, until all editing concerns are addressed, one at a time.

Model

STEP 1: Prepare the modeled writing in advance, and demonstrate how to reread with a single focus. Then, explain that you are changing your focus, and read the entire piece again for a new editing purpose.

Possible Think-Aloud: *Today I am going to model how to do a focused edit. That means I need to reread for just one editing point and then reread again for another. In this piece about the tarantula, I am going to start by checking for spaces between words. I am not going to think about spelling or anything else . . . just spaces. Watch as I read it and touch my finger to the space between each word. We need spaces so we can tell where one word stops and the next one begins. When you read for just one editing point, that is called a focused edit.*

I am ready to reread again. This time I am going to reread and check for periods. I want to be sure that every sentence has its own period. Are you noticing that each time I reread, I am only focusing on one thing?

TURN &TALK *Think together about a focused edit. What are the steps you need to follow?*

STEP 2: Reread for a third editing point.

Possible Think-Aloud: *I am not done editing yet. I haven't checked for capital letters. I will return to the beginning, because that is what you do when you use focused editing. There are two sentences, so I need to be sure that they both start with a capital letter. I also want to check and see if there are any names that should be*

A Really Big Spider

The buggest spidr in the world
is the tarantula. when its eight
legs are stretchd out, it can
measure tenn inches across

Sample Modeled Writing

capitalized. In sentence one, I see that "The" started with a capital letter. That looks good. Oops. Look at sentence two. I forgot the capital letter at the beginning of the sentence. Watch as I edit and fix that problem. I don't see any names, so I am finished with capital letters. Since I was just looking for one thing, the focused edit helped me to do a careful job.

TURN &TALK *Think together. The next focused edit is for periods. Get ready to reread and see how I did in placing periods at the end of each sentence.*

Analyze

STEP 3: Reread and reflect.

Possible Think-Aloud: *We reread a lot. Thanks to focused edits, I only checked for one thing each time I read, and it helped me to notice things I might have missed. I have one thing left to check. I have one more focused edit, and I need your help. It is time to do a focused edit for spelling. This time I will touch each word and look carefully at the letters to edit my spelling.* (Engage writers in rereading and adjusting spelling on misspelled words.)

Sum It Up

We have reread this piece a lot. That is what happens in a focused edit. You reread once for each editing point. If you were going to teach someone how to do a focused edit, what would you tell them to do?

VARIATIONS

For Less Experienced Writers: Provide a poster with some simple editing points, such as put your name on the paper, put the date on the paper, and check for spaces. In a small-group format, guide writers as they use the poster to cue them during the focused edit.

For More Experienced Writers: Utilize editing checklists such as those provided in *Editing: Lesson 6, Using an Editing Checklist,* and have writers utilize focused edits for each point on the checklist (see Resources CD-ROM).

Reread to Add Letters to Words

WHEN TO USE IT: When writers are ready to focus closely on word parts and spelling

FOCUS THE LEARNING

When writers edit, they need to slow down and really pay attention to individual letters, noticing spelling, and opportunities to add more letters to words.

Model

STEP 1: Think aloud about adding letters to your writing.

Possible Think-Aloud: (Prepare a piece of writing in advance in which you have used temporary spelling.) *We know writers stretch out words and write the sounds they know. But did you know that rereading can help you think of even more letters to add? My first sentence is "Fall is my favorite season." When I look at "favit," I hear /or/ in the middle of that word. But I didn't write any sounds for /or/. I am going to add an "o" and an "r" so my word will have more of the sounds I can hear. I can add letters to "sezn," too. The middle sound in season is /eeeee/, so I know I need another vowel. One "e" says /eh/, not /ee/. Rereading is helping me add letters!*

TURN &TALK *Talk about my writing. Can you think of any more letters that we might add to make my writing even better?*

STEP 2: Continue rereading and adding letters to your piece.

Possible Think-Aloud: *In the second sentence, I want to focus first on the word "crunchy." I can see that there isn't a vowel in that word, and every word needs a vowel. Let's say "crunchy" very slowly. What sounds do you hear in the middle? (Pause to listen.) I agree! I hear /u/ in the middle, so I will add the letter "u."*

Fl is my favit sezn. I lv the brit and crnch levs.

Translation:
Fall is my favorite season. I love the bright and crunchy leaves.

Sample Modeled Writing

TURN &TALK *Think together. Crunchy ends with a long /e/ sound. We know other words that say "e" at the end: baby, party, funny, happy. What letters should I add for the ending of "crunchy"?*

Analyze

STEP 3: Reread and reflect.

Possible Think-Aloud: *We have added a lot of letters to this message, and now it is much easier to read. Let's read it one more time together and see if we can think of any other places where we can add letters.*

Sum It Up

Writers, rereading and stretching out words can help us add letters so our words are more complete. That is important because we want our readers to know what we have to say! I know I can count on you to remember that during editing, one of our important jobs is to reread and add letters to our words.

VARIATIONS

For Less Experienced Writers: Gather less experienced writers into a small group so they are close to you. Engage them in helping you to add letters to a message, sharing the pen, and becoming your partner in the addition of letters and sounds. Remind these writers that the process is the same when they edit their own writing.

For More Experienced Writers: Select a familiar big book, and use slim strips of sticky notes to mask off beginning sounds and word endings from selected words. Have the children read the text with you and try to identify the missing letters. Then, have them take a piece of their own writing and try to add more letters.

LINKS TO CD-ROM:
• Thinking Challenge: Caterpillar Story

Using Spelling Consciousness While Editing

WHEN TO USE IT: To heighten awareness of spellings within messages

FOCUS THE LEARNING

While we never want to divert emergent writers from their central message, a sense of spelling consciousness can serve them well as they prepare to share their writing with others.

Model

STEP 1: Explain that writers need to pay attention to spelling when others are going to read their writing.

Possible Think-Aloud: *As I edit today, I am going to focus on "spelling consciousness." That means that during editing, I need to notice when words don't look quite right. As I reread my writing, I will touch each word and decide if it looks right to me. If it doesn't, then I will draw a line under the word to remind myself that I want to check the spelling of this word. (Read the modeled writing, touching each word as you read.) I am noticing some words that I need to check. I think that "wintr" and "bloo softlee" all need attention. Watch as I draw a line under each of those words.*

TURN &TALK *Think together. Are there any other words that I should have underlined?*

STEP 2: Model the correct spelling of words ending in -er.

Possible Think-Aloud: *I am going to think about winter first. I know that an /r/ sound at the end of a word is usually made by /er/, so I will rewrite winter with "er" at the end on this extra piece of paper and see how it looks. I know that shorter and longer have "er." I bet this will be the same. How does it look with the /er/ ending?*

Does that look better to you? Miguel, here is a book on winter. Will you hold it up as we check to see if our spelling is better with the /er/ ending? We did it! Now let's change the spelling in my original writing to "w-i-n-t-e-r."

I am the wind. I howl in wintr and bloo softlee through the leafes in summer. I am the wind. Whoosh.

Sample Modeled Writing

TURN &TALK *Look at my writing and use your spelling consciousness. Are there any other words that don't look quite right to you? Think together.*

Analyze

STEP 3: Continue thinking aloud about possible spelling patterns that would help you with bloo softlee (blow softly).

Possible Think-Aloud: *We used our spelling consciousness to think about winter and we did really well. Now let's try "bloo softlee." I know that blow rhymes with mow, row and crow. Those all have an /ow/ at the end. Simi, could you come up here and use our extra piece of paper and write blow with an /ow/ at the end? When you work at using spelling consciousness, it helps to write words out to see which one looks right. When Simi is finished, we can compare bloo and blow. While we think, Emerson will get our directions on blowing bubbles so we can use them to check ourselves. Writers, we have been using our spelling consciousness to think about spelling as we edit. Here is a Spelling Checklist that you can use as you apply your spelling consciousness while editing. (See Resources CD-ROM.)*

Sum It Up

When we edit, we need to use spelling consciousness and decide if words look right or not. It also helps to write out different spellings on a separate sheet of paper. That helps you focus on what looks right. Finally, it's smart to use a resource and check yourself to see how you did. Our Spelling Checklists will remind us of the things we do when we use spelling consciousness.

VARIATIONS

For Less Experienced Writers: Focus writers on underlining words that do not look right. Learning to recognize misspelled words is an important developmental step. Don't be in a hurry to bring less experienced writers to "correctness."

For More Experienced Writers: Remind writers that each syllable should have a vowel. As they identify words that need spelling attention, have them count syllables in the words and ensure that there are enough vowels.

LINKS TO CD-ROM:
- Checklist: Spelling Cosciousness: Checklist A
- Checklist: Spelling Consciousness: Checklist B
- Checklist: Spelling Consciousness: Checklist C
- Checklist: Spelling Consciousness: Checklist D

Using an Editing Checklist

WHEN TO USE IT: When writers are ready to be more independent as they edit

FOCUS THE LEARNING

It is important to remember that Editing Checklists do not teach. They simply remind writers of those things they already know how to do. As a result, it is essential to utilize Editing Checklists that list only those elements you have extensively modeled and supported through direct instruction.

Model

STEP 1: Provide each writer with a copy of an Editing Checklist that is carefully matched to the developmental level and previous editing experiences of your writers. See Resources CD-ROM for examples.

Possible Think-Aloud: *Editors, I am going to use an Editing Checklist as I check my writing. This will help me to be sure that my writing is ready to share with others. The first item on my checklist says: "Write my name on my paper." That is important. I need to be sure that my name is on the paper so everyone knows that I am the author. My name is there, so I can place a √ next to that sentence on the Editing Checklist. (Model placing the √.) Next, it says: "Leave spaces between words." Watch as I reread very slowly and put my fingers in the spaces between words. Editors need to be very careful to check for spacing. Now watch as I place a check next to the spacing sentence on the checklist.*

TURN &TALK *Look at your Editing Checklists together. Find another item on the list, and think about what I should do to check my writing for the next editing point.*

STEP 2: Reread for an additional editing point.

Possible Think-Aloud: *The next item on the list is about ending each sentence with punctuation. I am going to use your*

Spiders

By Mrs. Hoyt

Did you know that spiders have eight legs? These agile predators weave sticky webs where flies, bees, and other insects can quickly become tangled and become a spider's dinner.

Sample Modeled Writing

advice and reread to check the ending of each sentence. I am looking for periods, question marks, and exclamation points. I see that in sentence one I used a question mark and that in sentence two I used a period. I feel proud to see that all sentences don't have the same ending punctuation.

TURN &TALK *Another item on the editing list is to check for capital letters. You are in charge, so read carefully. Decide if I placed the capital letters in the right places. Think together.*

Analyze

STEP 3: Reread and reflect.

Possible Think-Aloud: *We have reread several times as we edited and have used this Editing Checklist to help us identify focus points. I am wondering, however, what you think of this list. Does this list cover the elements that you most need when you are editing? Are there any changes you would like to make to create a checklist that will be helpful to you?*

Sum It Up

Editing Checklists are helpful tools that remind us what to look for when we are editing. I am going to place several Editing Checklists in the writing center so you can select the checklist that fits the kind of writing you are editing. Now, when you are ready to edit, you have another tool that can help you make your writing the best it can be!

VARIATIONS

For Less Experienced Writers: Rather than using individual Editing Checklists, create an editing poster that combines words and pictures, and post it in a highly visible place. Show your emergent writers how you refer to the poster and check to be sure you have included your name, spaces between words, and so on. It would be ideal to create the poster with the students and add elements to it as they gradually gain proficiency in writing.

For More Experienced Writers: Increase the complexity of the Editing Checklists that students are applying to their writing. It is helpful to match the checklists to demonstrations and focus lessons that have built expertise for your writers.

LINKS TO CD-ROM:
- Checklist: Editing Checklist A
- Checklist: Editing Checklist B
- Checklist: Editing Checklist C
- Checklist: Editing Checklist D

How to Peer Edit

WHEN TO USE IT: To encourage partners to think together and lift each other to higher levels of proficiency in editing

FOCUS THE LEARNING

When writers work with a partner to co-edit writing, they help each other to notice details. Peer editing has the added benefit of having partners teach one another.

Model

STEP 1: Before the lesson, post a checklist for peer editing and a piece of writing that has a few errors in spelling, punctuation, or other elements that are appropriate to your students. Both should be on chart paper so they are highly visible to the learners. Identify an editing partner—a student, the principal, or another teacher—before the lesson begins. Each partner will need a highlighter in a different color.

Possible Think-Aloud: *My partner and I are going to use a Peer Editing Checklist to help us as we edit my writing. The first item on this checklist is spelling. Watch as we both use our highlighters to place dots next to words that we want to check. "Partner, please tell me about the words you marked. What did you notice about the spelling?" Writers, did you notice that I asked my partner to share her thinking? Now that we have shared our thinking about spelling, it is time to look at resources to check the words. "Partner, I am thinking we can find some of these words in the book we read on ants. Where else do you think we should look?"*

TURN &TALK *Writers, peer editing is a partnership where two people work together to edit a piece of writing. What did you notice about the way we worked together with our highlighters and about the way we talked to each other?*

STEP 2: Continue modeling the conversation and peer editing for another element.

Possible Think-Aloud: *Now we are ready to look at punctuation— periods, exclamation points, and question marks. I am going to use my fingers to make a window around the punctuation at the*

Bissee Inseckts

Do you like aunts. An aunt is a tine inseckt that livs in a burroe. It has feelrs on its head and six legs.

Sample Modeled Writing

end of each sentence. *"Partner, do you agree that a period is the best punctuation for this sentence? Do you have any suggestions for me?"*

TURN &TALK *Analyze the way my editing partner and I are thinking together. What do you notice? What are we doing that makes us good editing partners?*

Analyze

STEP 3: Reread and reflect.

Possible Think-Aloud: *My partner and I are going to reread my writing one more time and double-check the Peer Editing Checklist. If we see something we still need to check, we will place a dot with a highlighter. If we agree that we have done everything we can, we will both sign at the bottom. Our signatures show that we are partners and we worked on the editing together.* (Partners read and highlight.) *"Partner, I see that you placed a dot above this. What is your thinking about that? How can I make it better?"*

Sum It Up

Peer editing is fun. It is a chance to work with someone else to make your editing the best it can be. When you are ready to edit, select an editing partner, and one of the Peer Editing Checklists. I think you will find that two editors can notice much more than one of us could manage on our own.

LINKS TO CD-ROM:
- Checklist: Peer Editing Checklist I
- Checklist: Peer Editing Checklist II
- Interactive Assessment: A Celebration
- Interactive Assessment Example

Using Familiar Resources to Help You Edit

WHEN TO USE IT: To help writers realize that charts, big books, word walls, and nonfiction selections are tools that assist them in editing

FOCUS THE LEARNING

Young writers have an ever-widening repertoire of familiar charts, songs, resources, and tools. A key to effective editing is to help them realize that they can utilize these well-known selections as references when they are editing.

Model

STEP 1: Model how to use familiar texts and tools to check spelling.

Possible Think-Aloud: (You will need copies of *Snowflake Bentley*, *Where the Wild Things Are*, and *Lilly's Purple Plastic Purse*. Students will need copies of the Portable Word Walls from the Resources CD-ROM.) *As I edit my writing, I am going to use some of the tools in our room to help me edit. In my first sentence, I underlined "wilde" and "snow" because I think I need to check the spelling. I know we have a copy of* Where the Wild Things Are, *so I can use that book to check the spelling for "wild." That is a great tool. I also know I find "snow" in* Snowflake Bentley, *another one of our favorite books. Watch as I compare my spelling to the spelling in these great books and then edit my work. Familiar books are great resources to help us edit.*

TURN &TALK *Think together. What are some other places where you could look to check my spelling?*

STEP 2: Model using a resource to check punctuation.

Possible Think-Aloud: *I am thinking about the word trees. This doesn't mean a lot of trees. This means my very favorite tree that grows by my window. This is saying the branches belong to the tree, so I think I need to use an apostrophe. I know that in* Lilly's Purple Plastic Purse, *the author wanted us to know that*

Storm

On a <u>wilde</u> winter day, <u>snow</u> clouds playe in the sky. Wind rattles the windows and snaps my favorite trees branches. What a storm!

Sample Modeled Writing

the purse belonged to Lilly, so he wrote, "Lilly's purse." Notice the apostrophe. Who can come and fix my writing so it uses an apostrophe to show the branch belongs to the tree?

TURN &TALK *Think together. I am wondering about the word "playe" in my writing. I am thinking that we should find a classroom resource to use in checking that word. What resource do you think would help us? Think together and find a resource that will help us to check that word.*

Analyze

STEP 3: Reread and reflect.

Possible Think-Aloud: *Writers reread a lot when they are editing. When I reread this time, I am going to use my Portable Word Wall and see how many words in my writing that I can check with this tool. I think "on" is correct, but I will check to be sure. Watch as I find the section for "O" and slide my finger down to "on." O-N. That's right! Partners, use your Portable Word Walls and check "playe." How did I do? What other words can you check for me?*

Sum It Up

Writers, we have a lot of resources to use when we edit. We can use familiar books, charts, and even songs! We can also use a classroom word wall, a Portable Word Wall, or an Alphabox. We have a lot of tools to help us be great editors, so I know I can count on you to have lots of tools close by when you are editing.

VARIATIONS

For Less Experienced Writers: Focus on just one tool at a time to scaffold these writers in moving toward independence.

For More Experienced Writers: Have experienced writers keep track of the tools they used while editing and write a reflection focused on the tools that they thought were most helpful as they engaged in editing. These writers may also benefit from lessons on homophones and other tricky words. See *Spelling Consciousness:* Lesson 5, Navigating Homophones.

LINKS TO CD-ROM:
- Teacher Tool: Portable Word Wall Grades K–1
- Teacher Tool: Portable Word Wall Grades 1–2

Presenting

Preparing Our Work for Others

Presenting is like the icing on a cake or the moment of the final performance at a recital. It is the final touch that lifts a work to a higher level and makes it memorable. Presenting work to others is a subject to be taken seriously, as careful handwriting, spelling, conventions, spacing, and visuals are an expectation of future schooling and the workplace. When presenting is not given the attention it deserves, barriers are formed between writers and readers, affecting comprehension and appreciation of the work.

LESSON	K	1	2	RELATED LESSONS
1 Handwriting Is Neat and Legible	●	●	●	*Drafting:* Lesson 5, Use Mostly Lowercase Letters
2 Illustrations Are Detailed and Add Information	●	●	●	*Organization:* Lesson 2, Pictures and Words Work Together *Planning:* Lesson 3, Create a Labeled Diagram
3 Page Layout Includes Effective Use of Margins	●	●		*Planning:* Lesson 5, Planning Page Layout and Paper Selection
4 Careful Spacing Between Words Clarifies Word Boundaries	●	●		*Editing:* Lesson 1, Word Boundaries: Keep Letters in a Word Close Together
5 In Final Drafts Most Words Are Spelled Correctly		●	●	*Spelling Consciousness:* Lesson 3, Strategic Spellers Pay Attention to Syllables *Spelling Consciousness:* Lesson 5, Navigating Homophones
6 About the Author	●	●	●	

Other Lessons to Create

You might also want to teach writers how to

- create a dedication for their books, honoring someone important to their writing,
- use different types and sizes of paper to present their work, or
- present their work in different formats (posters, letters, signs, and so on).

Handwriting Is Neat and Legible

WHEN TO USE IT: When students are careless with handwriting or when they are ready to polish a piece before publishing

FOCUS THE LEARNING

There are times when a "sloppy copy" is just fine. However, there are other times when special care should be taken with handwriting. This is especially true when writing is to be read by others. At this point, it should be an expectation that time and effort on handwriting are important facets of written communication.

Model

STEP 1: Display a sentence written with sloppy handwriting. Discuss the problem with the piece.

Possible Think-Aloud: *Writers, I've just begun work on a piece of writing about clouds. I have one sentence written here, but I think I have a problem. I'm not sure if my handwriting is the best it can be. I know that, as a writer, I need to show respect for my reader. One of the ways I do is to take some time and make sure my handwriting is neat and legible, which means it's easy to read.*

TURN &TALK *Talk about my writing so far. What do you think? Do you think my handwriting is neat and legible, or do I have some work to do?*

STEP 2: Model how to write neatly.

Possible Think-Aloud: *Many of you think I have some work to do, and I agree! I'm going to continue writing about clouds, but watch me as I take a little extra time to make sure my handwriting is neat. I want my next sentence to say, "They are sometimes white because they reflect the light of the sun." My first word is "They." I'm going to write the letters slowly and carefully, really paying attention to how the letters look.* (Continue writing the next two sentences.)

A cloud is made up of tiny droplets of Ice and Water. They are sometimes white because they reflect the light of the sun. Clouds can become gray if they become thick or if they float very high.

Sample Modeled Writing

TURN &TALK *Analyze my handwriting. What am I doing that makes it easier to read?*

Analyze

STEP 3: Reread and reflect.

Possible Think-Aloud: *Let's read my sentences so far. Wow! I notice a real difference between my first sentence and the next two sentences. When I slowed down and worked hard to make my handwriting neat, it improved my writing. Now it will be easier to read. I know that my reader will appreciate that.*

Sum It Up

Today we learned that one of our important jobs is to make sure our handwriting is neat and legible. When we do that, it shows respect for our reader and makes our piece easy to read. Today as you begin to write, take some time to think about your handwriting and try to make it the best it can be.

VARIATIONS

For Less Experienced Writers: Emergent writers are often focused on stretching out words and getting each letter down. As you confer with students, take some time to correct improper form early, and provide multiple ways to practice correct letter formation.

For More Experienced Writers: Lead a discussion about when handwriting matters and when it doesn't. Create a Quality Level Chart. Quality Level 1: The writing only needs to be able to be read by the author. Quality Level 2: Someone else will need to be able to read it. Quality Level 3: Published work.

Illustrations Are Detailed and Add Information

WHEN TO USE IT: When illustrations lack details

FOCUS THE LEARNING

A picture is worth a thousand words, especially when you are creating a nonfiction piece in which illustrations often teach. We want students to take care when crafting their illustrations.

Model

STEP 1: Display an illustration of the water cycle that has a very limited amount of detail.

Possible Think-Aloud: *When writers create a piece of nonfiction writing, the illustrations are an important part. The illustrations need to be full of interesting details designed to teach a reader about the topic. I am looking at an illustration here that could go with my piece about rain. I realize that it doesn't have many details. A reader would have a hard time understanding my message. Nonfiction illustrations should be loaded with facts.*

TURN &TALK *Think together. What are some facts about rain that I could add to my illustration to give it lots of details?*

STEP 2: Model adding details to the illustration.

Possible Think-Aloud: *I am ready to get serious about details in my picture. I need to show that the cloud is heavy with condensation, so I am going to darken the cloud and fill it full of drops. I also want to show that the temperature is above freezing, so I will add a little thermometer to the side.*

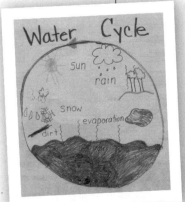

Rain is water that falls to the earth in drops. It forms when clouds have too much condensation. If the temperature is above freezing, the condensation comes down as rain. If it is colder than that, then there is snow.

Sample Modeled Writing

TURN &TALK *Let's add more facts to this illustration. What else should I include so my picture tells a lot about rain? Let's add details.*

Analyze

STEP 3: Reread and reflect.

Possible Think-Aloud: *Watch as I reread my picture to count the details. I feel so much better about this illustration because now it is filled with facts. I counted six facts in my picture! My ideas are ready. Watch as I begin to write, "Rain is . . ."*

Sum It Up

Today we talked about the importance of illustrations that have rich detail and real facts. When you look through your own writing today, see if you can find a place to add a detailed illustration. If you've already added illustrations, look back at them and ask yourself if they have enough detail and facts.

VARIATIONS

For Less Experienced Writers: Challenge writers to draw a picture of something in the classroom, encouraging them to add details that would help others to identify it.

For More Experienced Writers: Display several quality illustrations from nonfiction books. Ask partners to examine the illustrations and write down facts that they can learn from each of the illustrations.

Page Layout Includes Effective Use of Margins

WHEN TO USE IT: When students are not writing all the way across the page

FOCUS THE LEARNING

Emergent writers need to see how proficient writers use space on the page by extending lines of writing across the full width of the page or by wrapping text around or beside an illustration.

Model

STEP 1: Craft a short piece of writing, thinking aloud as you pay attention to the margins on the page.

Possible Think-Aloud: *Today I want to show you how writers use the whole page when they write. Watch me as I think about writing all the way across the page. I'm going to start my piece by writing, "I love going to the beach!" I'll start with "I love." Am I ready to go down to the next line? No, I want to keep writing on this line until I get all the way over to the margin on the right.*

TURN &TALK *Partners, talk together about how you know when it's time to go to the next line with your writing.*

STEP 2: Continue writing, thinking aloud about utilizing the entire page.

Possible Think-Aloud: *Next, I'll write, "When I first arrive, I take off my shoes and head for the salty surf." Raise your hand when you think I've arrived at a place where I should move my writing down and start the next line. Great job! I want to write all the way across the page and start the next line only when I've done that.*

I love going to the beach! When I first arrive, I take off my shoes and head for the salty surf. I love the feel of the sand and warm water between my toes.

Sample Modeled Writing

TURN &TALK *If we were going to create a rule about when to move to the next line, what would we want to say?*

Analyze

STEP 3: Reread and reflect.

Possible Think-Aloud: *Let's look at my piece now. Do you see the spaces to the right and left of my words? Those spaces are called margins. The margins are there to help organize my words and to make my writing easy to read. When you look at any of the books in our book corner, you'll notice that each book has margins and that writing and pictures fill most of the space.*

Sum It Up

Today I showed you how I think about writing all the way across the page. When I do that, my writing is much easier to read. Today, as you begin your writing, think about using the whole page and writing all the way across it. Think about how your margins will help your reader. Let's get to work!

VARIATIONS

For Less Experienced Writers: Lightly draw margins down the right and left sides of writing paper until students become more comfortable with writing all the way across the page.

For More Experienced Writers: Display an array of nonfiction books in which the illustration is at the side or bottom of the page. Show more experienced writers how creative use of spacing can enable them to position text in new and interesting ways.

Careful Spacing Between Words Clarifies Word Boundaries

WHEN TO USE IT: When writing lacks word boundaries and is difficult to read

FOCUS THE LEARNING

Many emergent writers need support in remembering to leave spaces between words. They need multiple exposures to quality modeling, as well as plenty of independent writing time to master this skill.

Model

STEP 1: Display a sentence in which you have not included spaces between words. Discuss the problem with the sentence.

Possible Think-Aloud: *I have written a sentence about eagles. As I look at this sentence, I think I have a problem. I'm not sure where one word ends and another word begins. That makes it almost impossible to read! Let's take a look at a page from a book in our book corner. Do you see how the author placed a space between each word? He did that so his reader would be able to read the words more easily.*

TURN &TALK *Partners, what do you think I need to do to help my reader know where one word ends and another begins?*

STEP 2: Rewrite the first sentence, thinking aloud about adding a space between the words.

Possible Think-Aloud: *I'm going to write my sentence again, but this time I'm going to stop after each word and concentrate on leaving a space before writing the next word. My first word is "Eagles." I'll write that here. Now I'm going to leave a space. To remind me, I'll put my finger there and then begin the next word, "use." I know it's important to leave a "finger space" between each of my words.* (Continue writing, leaving a space between each word.)

Draft 1:
Eaglesusetheirstrong

Draft 2:
Eagles use their strong and powerful talons to capture prey. Once they catch their dinner, they use their hooked beak to tear the food.

Sample Modeled Writing

TURN &TALK *How will you help yourself remember to leave spaces between words so that others can read your work?*

Analyze

STEP 3: Reread and reflect.

Possible Think-Aloud: *Let's reread my sentence. Wow! Leaving a space between the words helped us read the sentence easily. When we remember to leave a "finger space," it helps our readers know where one word ends and another begins. I know that the more I think about adding a space between words, the more it will become a habit as I'm writing.*

Sum It Up

Today we learned how important it is to leave a space between each word. We saw how hard it was to read the writing when I forgot to leave a space. As you begin writing today, take the time to add a "finger space" between each of your words. Your reader will be glad you did! Let's begin!

VARIATIONS

For Less Experienced Writers: Give each child a chopstick or craft stick with a smiley face on one end. Explain that this is called a "space man" or a "spacing buddy" and that it helps writers remember to leave a space between each word. (See Resources CD-ROM for directions, as per *Editing Lesson 1*.)

For More Experienced Writers: Encourage students to work in pairs to peer edit, looking for appropriate use of word boundaries.

In Final Drafts Most Words Are Spelled Correctly

WHEN TO USE IT: When students are ready to bring a piece to publication

FOCUS THE LEARNING

Once students are ready to share a piece of writing with a larger audience, they are ready to learn that spelling matters at this stage in the writing process.

Model

STEP 1: Display a piece of writing with some misspellings.

Possible Think-Aloud: *I've worked hard on my piece, and now I'm ready to publish. As I prepare to write my final draft, there is something I need to remember. In final drafts, most words are spelled correctly. So I need to read each word carefully to make sure I have spelled most of my words correctly. If I come to a word that I'm not sure about, I'll need to use the resources in our classroom to help me.*

TURN &TALK *Writers, why do you think it is important that most words be spelled correctly in a final draft? Talk together.*

STEP 2: Demonstrate how you reread the piece to check for spelling accuracy.

Beavers have strong teeth and powerful jaws. They use theez to naw sticks and branches. Beavers use the sticks to make homs, called loges.

Sample Modeled Writing

Possible Think-Aloud: *Watch me as I reread each word carefully to check my spelling. I have a word that I'm not sure about. For this word, I think I can look in one of the books I used for my research. Aha, here it is! I was close, but the word "naw" is spelled g-n-a-w. Notice that I don't erase the word, I just cross it out and write the correct spelling above. (Continue with two to three other words.)*

TURN &TALK *Look at my writing carefully. Identify other words that you think we should check.*

Analyze

STEP 3: Reread and reflect.

Possible Think-Aloud: *Let's reread my piece now. I'm glad I took the extra time to make sure that my words are spelled correctly. When a final draft has a lot of words that are misspelled, it distracts the reader. The reader ends up paying attention to the mistakes and loses some important information. I think my piece will be read with ease now.*

Sum It Up

Today we learned that most words should be spelled correctly in final drafts. When writing is presented to others, spelling is important. Careful spelling in final drafts helps the reader focus on your message. As you reread your piece and prepare to write your final draft, take some time to read each and every word carefully. If you aren't sure if it's spelled right, use our classroom resources to check.

VARIATIONS

For Less Experienced Writers: During one-on-one conferences, help writers to underline a few high-frequency words that need to be corrected. Coach them as they use classroom resources to edit.

For More Experienced Writers: Challenge partners to peer edit, reading each other's writing to check for correct spelling, punctuation, and grammar.

LINK TO CD-ROM:
• Chart: Classroom Resources I Can Use to Check My Spelling

About the Author

WHEN TO USE IT: When students have finished a piece for publication

FOCUS THE LEARNING

When you finish reading a well-written book, it's fun and interesting to read about the author. Young students can learn to write a short section about themselves that helps them connect to the reader.

Model

STEP 1: Display an "About the Author" section in several books from your classroom library. Talk about the features, including a photograph, personal information, and so on.

Possible Think-Aloud: *We've been working on polishing our pieces for publication. One thing that writers can add to a piece of published writing is an "About the Author" section. In this section, the author tells a little bit about himself or herself. Let's look at this section in a few of the books from our book corner. Do you notice how the author tells about where he or she lives and what he or she likes to do? I really like seeing a picture of the author as well.*

TURN &TALK *Think together. Have you ever noticed this kind of section in the books you have read? Why do you think the author includes such a section?*

STEP 2: Craft an "About the Author" section. Think aloud about what you will include.

Possible Think-Aloud: *I'm going to follow the same format that we saw in our books as I write my own "About the Author" section. I'll start with my name and tell where I live. I'll write "Linda Hoyt lives in Oregon with her husband, Steve, and her dog Oakely." Notice that I did not write, "I live . . ." I am writing*

About the Author

Linda Hoyt lives in Oregon with her husband, Steve, and her dog Oakely. She enjoys traveling and reading books of all kinds.

Sample Modeled Writing

as though this is about someone else. Next, I'll write a bit about what I enjoy doing. I'll write, "She enjoys traveling and reading books of all kinds." Notice again that I didn't use the word "I." I used "She." If I was a boy, I would have used "He."

TURN &TALK *If you were writing an "About the Author" page for yourself, what would you want to say?*

Analyze

STEP 3: Reread and reflect.

Possible Think-Aloud: *Let's reread my "About the Author" section. How does it sound? Did I include some important and fun information about myself? I like the way it sounds, and I think my reader will, too.*

Sum It Up

Today we learned how to include an "About the Author" section in our published books. When we include this section, it helps our reader get to know us a little better. And it's fun to write! When you go back to your writing today, try to craft your own "About the Author" section.

VARIATIONS

For Less Experienced Writers: Support emergent writers with a template (see Link to Resources CD-ROM).

For More Experienced Writers: Challenge them to add a little more information about themselves while still remaining brief. Encourage them to include their age, school, and favorite subjects.

LINK TO CD-ROM: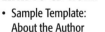
• Sample Template: About the Author

Ideas

The Content and Focus of the Writing

Ideas make up the content of a piece of writing. When the ideas are strong and the content is rich in facts and imagery, nonfiction writing sparkles with possibility. When writers focus on ideas, they quickly learn that narrow topics, rich details, action, and description entice their readers and lift nonfiction writing to greater heights.

LESSON	K	1	2	RELATED LESSONS
1 Creating a Topic List	●	●	●	
2 Write About Pictures	●	●		*Planning:* Lessons 1–4 *Research:* Lesson 1, Identify Facts in a Visual
3 Narrow the Topic	●	●	●	*Planning:* Lesson 4, Map Out Your Writing with Informational Pictures
4 Infuse Interesting Details	●	●	●	*Organization:* Lesson 5, Details Support Main Ideas *Voice and Audience:* Lesson 3, Capture the Interest of Your Reader
5 Add a Little Action		●	●	*Ideas:* Lesson 10, Using Comparisons *Word Choice:* Lesson 6, Add Action: Group *-ing* Words Together
6 Make the Setting Stand Out		●	●	*Revising:* Lesson 10, Tuning Up Sensory Images *Word Choice:* Lesson 10, Transition Words to Add Information or Conclude
7 Teach Your Reader	●	●	●	*Voice and Audience:* Lesson 3, Capture the Interest of Your Reader *Research:* Lesson 8, Use the Very Important Points Strategy (VIP) for Key Information
8 Separating Fact and Opinion	●	●	●	*Research:* Lesson 1, Identify Facts in a Visual *Research:* Lesson 4, Create a Visual That Contains Facts
9 Details Highlight Attributes of Subject	●	●	●	*Revising:* Lesson 1, Revising to Add Details *Ideas:* Lesson 4, Infuse Interesting Details
10 Using Comparisons	●	●	●	
11 Focus on "One"	●	●	●	

Other Lessons to Create

You might also want to teach writers how to

- select topics that interest them,
- read nonfiction books to get ideas, or
- include the facts that they find most interesting.

Creating a Topic List

WHEN TO USE IT: To support writers in selecting topics for their nonfiction writing

Topic selection can be a challenge for some nonfiction writers, so it is often helpful to demonstrate. Do a think-aloud to consider possibilities and make a decision.

Model

STEP 1: Help students understand that to be good writers of nonfiction, they need to spend time reading nonfiction.

Possible Think-Aloud: *To be a good writer of nonfiction, it is important to spend time reading nonfiction resources and magazines. Reading and looking through resources help you to power up with a list of topics that you think are interesting. As I look through these magazines and books, I am going to think out loud and share my ideas about what I am seeing. When I come to something that I might like to write about, I will add it to my list of nonfiction writing topics. I am looking through this magazine, and I see it has great pictures showing many different kinds of rabbits. I like rabbits, so I will add "rabbits" to my topic list. There is another article in here on making pancakes. That could be interesting, but I don't think I want to add pancakes to my topic list. Now this book about koala bears looks terrific. I think koala bears are really interesting. That is definitely a topic to add to my list.* (Continue modeling browsing and identifying possible topics for your topic list.)

TURN &TALK *Are you noticing that I only put some of the topics I am reading about on my list? I don't want to list everything. I write down only the topics that I find interesting enough to spend time reading and writing about them. Think together. What topics would you have on a list? Would any of your topics be the same as mine?*

STEP 2: Make a decision about topic.

Possible Think-Aloud: *I am feeling really good about my list. Now I have a decision to make. Which one is most interesting to me right now? Which one do I want to spend time making into a nonfiction book? That means that I need to read and learn and then put my learning into writing.*

> ### Nonfiction Writing Topics
> Different Kinds of Rabbits
> Koala Bears
> Wilma Rudolph: A Woman of Courage
> *How to Make Ice Cream
> Butterflies and Caterpillars
> The Animals of Yellowstone National Park
> Polar Bears

Sample Modeled Writing

TURN & TALK *Think together. Which topic do you think I will select? After you guess, I will surprise you by placing a star next to the topic I am going to select today.* (After students share their guesses, place a star next to your favorite topic.)

Analyze

STEP 3: Reread and reflect.

Possible Think-Aloud: *It is really helpful to keep a list of nonfiction topics in your writing folder. Then, as you are reading and think of a great topic, you can easily add ideas to the list. When you are ready to begin a new piece of writing, the list may help you decide what to write.*

TURN & TALK *Think together. What are the steps to follow in creating a list of nonfiction writing topics? How do you know which one to choose when it is time for a new topic?*

Sum It Up

When we write nonfiction, we need to commit to our topics and plan to read, learn, and do research. Then, we will know enough to be ready to write. To help ourselves be the best writers we can be, it is a good idea to keep a topic list that you can add to when you get a great idea. With a great topic list in your writing folder, you will find it is easy to start a new topic as you already have great ideas that are ready to use.

VARIATIONS

For Less Experienced Writers: For less experienced writers, start a team or a class topic list by coaching writers as they explore a variety of resources, and then help them to add ideas to a chart of writing topics that can be posted for all to share.

For More Experienced Writers: Assist more experienced writers in challenging themselves to reach for balance in their writing topics. Help them evaluate their topic lists using a form such as the one on the Resources CD-ROM.

LINKS TO CD-ROM:

• Checklist: Evaluating My Topic List

Write About Pictures

WHEN TO USE IT: When students are not strong readers but are ready to collect information and write about a topic or when the text is too difficult, but the pictures provide a wealth of information

FOCUS THE LEARNING

Emergent writers are often intimidated at the thought of reading and researching a topic. When we teach them how to "read" the pictures and write about what they discover, a variety of texts become accessible.

Model

STEP 1: Display a quality picture or photograph. Model how you "read" the pictures, illustrations, or photographs to gather information.

Possible Think-Aloud: *Today I want to show you how you can "read" the pictures, illustrations, and photographs in a book and use the information you find to do some writing. I found this great book about foxes. Watch me as I look carefully at this photograph. Well, right away I can tell that foxes have big, bushy tails. I can also tell that they have pointy ears and that they eat mice, since the fox looks like he is hunting that mouse.*

TURN &TALK *Partners, think together. Is there anything else you can learn from this photo? What else could you say about foxes?*

STEP 2: Craft a short piece of writing based on what you discovered by "reading" the picture.

Possible Think-Aloud: *Now that I've gathered some information from the picture, I can write. Let's see, I noticed the fox's tail and ears, so I'll write a little bit about that. I'll say, "Foxes have big, bushy tails and small, pointy ears." If I look closely, I can see sharp claws on the fox's feet. And it looks like the fox is hunting a mouse. Watch as I write, "They use their sharp claws to catch mice." Notice how I am getting writing ideas right from the picture.*

TURN &TALK *Look closely at the picture. What else could I say about this picture that would be a good addition to my writing? Use the picture to get ideas!*

Foxes have big, bushy tails and small, pointy ears. They use their sharp claws to catch mice. Foxes can live in snowy places.

©Tom Brakefield/Corbis

Sample Modeled Writing

Analyze

STEP 3: Reread and reflect.

Possible Think-Aloud: *I'm amazed at how much information I could gather from a photograph! When I looked closely at this picture, I could find many things to write about. And it was fun! I am going to take one more look at the details of the picture and make sure that I have written most of the important ideas.*

Sum It Up

Pictures are great places to get ideas for writing. As you are researching today, take some time to look carefully at the illustrations and photographs in the books you have found. Use the information you gather from the pictures to help you write about your topic. Let's go, writers!

VARIATIONS

For Less Experienced Writers: Gather writers in a small group. Provide more guided practice by showing the group a detailed photograph and having partners share what they can learn from the photo. Demonstrate how you write using the information you gathered from the picture.

For More Experienced Writers: Provide partners several pictures that work together in sequence. Challenge them to craft the words that go with the pictures.

LINKS TO CD-ROM:
- Visuals: Photo from modeled writing
- Visuals: Additional images

Narrow the Topic

WHEN TO USE IT: When writing is broad and too general, or when writers are overwhelmed by the amount of information in their research

FOCUS THE LEARNING

Once students begin researching, they often realize that their topic is much larger than they had anticipated. The goal of this lesson is to support students as they narrow the topic to one that is more manageable.

Model

STEP 1: Demonstrate how you choose a topic and then quickly realize that it needs to be narrowed.

Possible Think-Aloud: *I have chosen to write about bears, and I spent some time yesterday researching about them. I wrote some of my facts down on this chart. I could write about all eight species of bears, but I think I need to narrow my topic. If I try to write about all these different kinds of bears, my book will be too big! That means that I will choose just **one** kind of bear to write about. Writers often do that. As they begin researching, they discover that their topic is too big, so they narrow the topic.*

TURN &TALK *Think together. Why do you think it would be important to narrow my topic? Why do you think writers do that?*

STEP 2: Think aloud as you narrow your topic and begin to research about your new topic.

Possible Think-Aloud: *As I look at my facts, I notice that I have some facts about brown bears here. As I was reading, I found myself interested in the brown bear. I think I'll write about those bears in particular. That will make my writing more manageable, and my reader won't be overwhelmed either. Now I'm ready to research again, but this time I'm ONLY going to be looking for information on brown bears.*

TURN &TALK *Identify some important questions that I should consider as I research brown bears. What should I be wondering? What information might be interesting to a reader?*

FACTS ABOUT BEARS

There are eight species.

1. Black bear
2. Sun bear
3. Asiatic black bear
4. Grizzly bear
5. Brown bear
6. Polar bear
7. Spectacled bear
8. Panda bear

Brown bears are predators, and they are very fast.
Brown bears dig dens for hibernation.

Sample Modeled Writing

Analyze

STEP 3: Reread and reflect.

Possible Think-Aloud: *Did you notice that, at first, I had a topic that was really big? If I tried to write about all those different kinds of bears, my book would have been HUGE, and it would have taken me all year to write it. Now that I have narrowed my topic to the brown bear, I can be more focused when I'm researching. I think my writing will be more focused, too. Having a narrow topic will help me be a better writer.*

Sum It Up

Today we learned that writers often start out with a broad topic, but then they narrow the topic to something that is more manageable. As you begin working today, think about your topic. Is it too big? Could your topic be narrowed? When you narrow your topic, you'll be able to focus more on the quality of your writing, and you won't be overwhelmed by too many facts. Let's get started!

VARIATIONS

For Less Experienced Writers: Encourage students to complete a web graphic organizer on their topic. (See Link to Resources CD-ROM.) Then, demonstrate how you can take one section of the web and write about that.

For More Experienced Writers: Explain that good writers have the ability to focus on a specific topic. Give students several examples of topics, and have them choose the topic that would be more specific, narrow, and interesting. (See Link to Resources CD-ROM.)

LINKS TO CD-ROM:
- Graphic Organizer: Narrowing the Topic
- Thinking Challenge: Which Topic Is More Specific (and Interesting)?

Infuse Interesting Details

WHEN TO USE IT: When writing is dull and lacks rich and interesting details

Students often fall into the trap of thinking that nonfiction writing consists of dry and lifeless facts. Our goal is to teach them to add the interesting details that will make their piece a joy to read.

Model

STEP 1: Display two pieces of writing. One should be lifeless and dull, and the other should be infused with interesting details.

Possible Think-Aloud: *Today I want to show you one thing that writers do to make their writing more fun to read. I have two pieces about pandas. As I read both of them, think about which one you find more interesting.*

TURN &TALK *Which piece of writing did you prefer? What is it about the piece that makes it more interesting? Talk together.*

STEP 2: Discuss what it is that the author does to make the piece more interesting.

Possible Think-Aloud: *Many of you said that you preferred Sample B. I agree! It's a much more interesting piece that is fun to read. Did you notice what I did to make the piece better? As I was writing this piece, I was thinking about the interesting details I could add.*

Sample A

Pandas eat bamboo shoots and leaves. That's why they live in bamboo forests. They don't drink much water.

Sample B

Sitting upright, like a human sitting on the floor, the panda munches on juicy bamboo. The bamboo has so much water in it that the panda doesn't need to drink a lot of extra water.

Sample Modeled Writing

When I added the interesting details, it made a big difference, didn't it? I especially like the part about sitting upright like a human. This is a detail that we can visualize, so I know that will help my reader.

TURN &TALK *Identify the detail that you think helped make sample B a better piece of writing.*

Analyze

STEP 3: Reread and reflect.

Possible Think-Aloud: *Let's reread my piece again. I really worked hard to infuse interesting details in this piece, and I think it shows. We know that if we want our writing to be read, it needs to be filled with the interesting details that make the reader want to read on. As we read, be thinking about other details we could add to this piece about pandas.*

Sum It Up

Today we saw the importance of adding interesting details to our writing. When we do that, it makes our writing much more enjoyable. Today, as you write, think about the interesting details that you can add to boost your writing. Your reader will be glad you did!

VARIATIONS

For Less Experienced Writers: Show students how you use a Note Taker Graphic Organizer to collect interesting facts and details. (See Link to Resources CD-ROM for *Voice and Audience:* Lesson 3.) Model how to use the facts and details to craft a piece of writing.

For More Experienced Writers: Provide students with a dull and lifeless draft that needs some interesting details added. Challenge partners to revise the piece and share the revisions with the rest of the class.

Add a Little Action

WHEN TO USE IT: When writing is dry and lifeless

One of the best ways to boost nonfiction writing is to borrow the techniques that are often used in fiction. One technique is to add an action scene.

Model

STEP 1: Model how to visualize a scene and focus on the action.

Possible Think-Aloud: *Writers, today I want to show you how writers make their writing come to life for their readers. One way they do that is to add a little action. I am planning to write about eagles, but I want to open with some action so my reader can visualize the eagle in action. Listen as I close my eyes and visualize the eagle in flight. I can "see" the eagle slowly circling. I notice that he doesn't flap his wings much. He holds them out wide and glides in slow circles over the water. I can't see his eyes, but I know he is watching for a fish to catch. Suddenly the eagle dives toward the water. Could you picture that eagle? Could you see the "action" as he searched and then plunged toward the water?*

TURN &TALK *If you were going to write about the actions of the eagle, what would you describe? What would you want your reader to know?*

STEP 2: Model writing about the action of the moment.

Possible Think-Aloud: *Visualizing really helped me to picture the action in my mind and then to use the action in my writing. I am going to visualize again and see if that helps me to add more to the action in this writing. I see the eagle as he plunges toward the water. His wings are still held out straight, and his head is pointed right at the water. He is diving really fast. I also visualize his talons. I know he needs those sharp claws to grab the fish,*

The eagle slowly circles above the clear water, gliding with wings stretched wide. Suddenly he spots a plump fish and . . .

Sample Modeled Writing

so I visualize that he pushes his talons forward so they are ready to hook into the fish.

TURN &TALK *I need to turn the rest of my visualization into action in my writing. What should I say about the eagle's dive toward his prey?*

Analyze

STEP 3: Reread and reflect.

Possible Think-Aloud: *Let's reread and think about the action in the writing. I need to decide if I described it well enough that a reader could get a mental picture of the way the eagle hunted for his food. (After rereading.) What are your thoughts about my action? Do I need to add more description? Were you able to get a picture of the eagle in your mind?*

Sum It Up

Today we learned how to add action to our writing to make it more interesting. Now you know how to look at a list of facts and think about how you can use those facts to create an action-packed scene for your reader. When you go back to your own writing today, challenge yourself to add a little action. Let's go!

VARIATIONS

For Less Experienced Writers: Encourage writers to create a list of actions that go along with their topic. For example, if they are writing about monkeys, they could make a list of verbs such as eat, swing, run, crawl, and call. Dramatizing may also provide support for visualizing actions to infuse into writing.

For More Experienced Writers: Show students how authors include an action scene as a way to begin the piece of writing and hook the reader. Challenge them to try this in their own writing.

Make the Setting Stand Out

WHEN TO USE IT: When writing lacks a setting, or when the setting is vague and dull

FOCUS THE LEARNING

Often writers set the stage by describing the setting in a vivid and colorful way. Writers need to learn to include sensory images to make the setting come to life.

Model

STEP 1: Display a beginning sentence for a piece of writing in which you describe the setting. Think aloud as you consider how to make the setting stand out.

Possible Think-Aloud: *I'm writing a piece about the morning I went walking at the beach. I want to set the scene for my reader. I've written one sentence that says, "It was a beautiful morning." That's okay, but I think I can do a better job of describing the setting. Sometimes it helps to close my eyes and try and picture just what that morning was like. I'll try to remember how it looked, sounded, and smelled. When I close my eyes and think about smells at the ocean, I think of moist, salty-smelling air. When I think about sounds, I hear the call of seagulls and the crash as the waves roll toward the shore.*

TURN &TALK *Take a moment and try this. Close your eyes and picture a beautiful morning on the beach. Tell your partner what you see, hear, and smell.*

STEP 2: Add sentences to emphasize sensory images.

Possible Think-Aloud: *As I pictured what the morning was like, I remembered that the sun was bright and the waves were white and foamy. There were a lot of round pebbles on the beach, and I loved watching the waves roll over them. Watch me as I add some of those things to my writing to set the scene.*

It was a beautiful morning. The bright sun shone on the sand as white waves washed over smooth round pebbles. The smell of fresh, salty water was in the air.

Sample Modeled Writing

First, I'll say, "The bright sun shone on the sand as white waves washed over smooth, round pebbles." (Continue with another describing sentence.)

TURN &TALK *Close your eyes and visualize. Can you picture the setting? If you were going to draw a picture of this, what would you draw? Share your thinking with your partner.*

Analyze

STEP 3: Reread and reflect.

Possible Think-Aloud: *Let's reread my piece so far. Reading this again made me realize that I forgot to mention the breeze. It wasn't just that the air smelled salty; there was a light little breeze that kicked up bits of sand and swirled them around. That was really fun to see. Watch as I add that detail to this description of the setting.* (After writing.) *Think together. Did I set the scene for my reader? Does my setting stand out? If you were the reader of this piece, would you be able to picture the beach?*

Sum It Up

Today I showed you how I close my eyes and think about the setting before I write about it. I showed you how I think about what I could smell, hear, and see. When you include those things, your setting will stand out. When your setting stands out, it helps to create a picture in your reader's mind, which makes your writing more interesting to read. As you begin writing today, try adding some descriptions to your setting. Let's write!

VARIATIONS

For Less Experienced Writers: Engage students in a guided writing experience. Work together to set the scene for a shared experience, such as a fire drill or a field trip. Use student suggestions to craft an opening paragraph that describes the scene.

For More Experienced Writers: Encourage students to try a graphic organizer to support them as they write about the setting. (See Resources CD-ROM.)

LINKS TO CD-ROM:
• Graphic Organizer: Sensory Image

Teach Your Reader Something New

WHEN TO USE IT: When writing lacks originality and interest

FOCUS THE LEARNING

Most of us read nonfiction texts to learn something new. When we work with nonfiction writers, we need to support them as they think about how to add new and interesting facts to their writing.

Model

STEP 1: In advance of the lesson, create a chart with facts about your topic. Think aloud as you write and consider facts that will teach the reader something new.

Possible Think-Aloud: *I'm working on a piece about zebras. As I begin to write, I'm thinking about my readers. What could I add that would teach them something new? I've collected a few facts on this chart. As I read my facts, I'm thinking I could write a bit about how no two zebras have the same pattern of stripes. That might be new and interesting information to my reader. It was new to me! I'll start by saying, "Everyone knows that zebras have stripes." Now I want to surprise my reader, so I will say, "But did you know that no two zebras have the same pattern of stripes?" I like using "Did you know," as that tells my reader that something interesting is coming.*

TURN &TALK *What do you think of the fact I just added? Would that teach my reader something new?*

STEP 2: Add some facts about zebras.

ZEBRA FACTS
· No two have the same stripes.
· Social animals.
· Uses kicks for defense.

Sample Modeled Writing

Everyone knows that zebras have stripes. But did you know that no two zebras have the same pattern of stripes? A zebra's stripes are as individual as our fingerprints! No two are the same!

Possible Think-Aloud: *Surprising and teaching my reader are fun. Now I get to add one more surprise. Get ready. Watch as I write: "A zebra's stripes are as individual as our fingerprints! No two are the same!"*

TURN &TALK *Did you just learn something new? Did I say it in a way that made you want to read more? Think together about teaching a reader something new. Why is this a good idea for nonfiction writers?*

Analyze

STEP 3: Reread and reflect.

Possible Think-Aloud: *Let's read my piece so far. I think I've done a good job using the facts that I've collected to create sentences that would teach my reader something new. It helped me to think about my reader as I was writing. Let's think together as I search in my books about zebras and try to find one more surprising fact to use in teaching my reader something new.*

Sum It Up

As writers, we need to be constantly thinking about our readers. We need to ask ourselves: What could I include that would be new and interesting? What would make my piece more enjoyable to read? It also helps to think about these questions as you are researching about your topic. Be on the lookout for facts that might be new and interesting, and then make sure you include them. Let's get started teaching our readers something new and maybe even surprising!

VARIATIONS

For Less Experienced Writers: Provide more opportunities for modeled writing and guided practice as you craft a piece of writing together within a small-group setting. Think aloud as you select facts that would be new and interesting to a reader.

For More Experienced Writers: Have Partner A read to Partner B. Partner B listens to the piece and identifies new information he or she learned from the piece. Partner B then gets to read his or her piece to Partner A while Partner A identifies learning that is new or surprising.

LINKS TO CD-ROM:
- Thinking Challenge: Analyzing Facts About My Topic

Separating Fact and Opinion

WHEN TO USE IT: To ensure that writers understand the importance of reporting factual information accurately and without bias

FOCUS THE LEARNING

Nonfiction writers need a clear understanding of the difference between a fact and an opinion to ensure that nonfiction writing is, in fact, nonfiction. This is especially important when students are writing descriptions, explanations, procedures, and so on. When writers create persuasion and response, opinions and facts co-exist comfortably. What is important is that the writer is clear about the difference.

Model

STEP 1: Create a list of everyday facts that are familiar to your students, and present them down the left side of a T-chart labeled "Fact" and "My Opinion About It."

Possible Think-Aloud: *A fact is information that is true. For example, it is a fact that spinach is green. It is a fact that spinach is a vegetable. My opinion about spinach is different. An opinion is what I think about it. I personally think spinach is delicious. What do you think about spinach? What is your opinion?* (Give students a moment to talk to each other.) *It is a fact that pizza is sometimes on the menu in the cafeteria. It is a fact that the pizza in the cafeteria has a lot of cheese and usually olives as well.*

TURN &TALK *What is your opinion about pizza? What kind of pizza do you like best?* (After students talk.) *If you said pizza is the best food ever, that is an opinion. If you said pepperoni is the best topping, is that a fact or an opinion? As writers, we need to be very careful because facts and opinions are different.*

STEP 2: Engage the students in naming facts that can be listed on the left side of the chart, and then list opinions about the facts on the right side.

Fact	My Opinion About It
Spinach is a vegetable.	It is delicious.
Pizza is on the menu for lunch.	Pizza is the best food ever.
The yellow pencil is short.	This pencil is too short to use.
The marker is green.	Green is my favorite color.

Sample Modeled Writing

Possible Think-Aloud: *Let's think of some more facts. Look outside at the weather. I can see that it is _____ outside. That is a fact. My opinion about the weather is _____. Watch as I add this information to our fact and opinion chart.*

TURN & TALK *Think together of a fact about the weather today, and I will write it on our chart. After we record a few weather facts, we can share our opinions about the weather.*

Analyze

STEP 3: Reread and reflect.

Possible Think-Aloud: *I am getting ready to write about lop-eared rabbits. I am going to share my information out loud and decide what is fact and what is opinion. Lop-eared rabbits have very long ears that almost touch the ground. That is a fact. I love lop-eared rabbits. They are the best pets. Think together. Are those sentences facts or opinions?*

Sum It Up

Writers of nonfiction need to know the difference between a fact and an opinion. Nonfiction writing is usually based on facts that are written as accurately as possible. When I write, I need to be careful and notice when I add opinions. Adding opinions is okay as long as you know that opinions are not facts.

VARIATIONS

For Less Experienced Writers: Scaffold understanding of fact versus opinion by providing opportunities to examine and taste a variety of foods. Use a fact/opinion chart such as the one in the lesson to record observations (facts) and writer opinions about the items they are tasting.

For More Experienced Writers: Compare and contrast persuasive writing and advertisements with resources that describe with a focus on facts. Help students to notice descriptive words and adjectives or examples of exaggeration.

LINKS TO CD-ROM:
• Thinking Challenge: Fact and Opinion Chart

Details Highlight Attributes of Subject

WHEN TO USE IT: To help writers develop stronger powers of description in their writing

FOCUS THE LEARNING

When writers provide rich descriptions of their subject, readers notice attributes and features that they might miss when descriptions are sketchy and underdeveloped.

Model

STEP 1: Model and think aloud about attributes of a frog; then show writers how to highlight details in writing.

Possible Think-Aloud: *As I write today, I am going to focus on bringing out lots of details about how a frog catches insects. I know that frogs have big, bulgy eyes and long, sticky tongues. I will use those details so my reader understands that these are important attributes of a frog. My first sentence is, "A frog's big, bulgy eyes . . ." Notice that I don't just say they have big eyes. I am using "bulgy" because that helps the reader get a better image of the frog. When we describe, it is important to use really specific words. "Bulgy" is much better than big.*

TURN &TALK *I am going to write about the tongue next. What are some really great words we could use to describe the tongue of a frog?*

STEP 2: Continue modeling and thinking aloud about precise word choices that highlight attributes and improve description.

Catching Insects

A frog's big, bulgy eyes help it to catch food because the eyes allow it to see all around. As the frog watches and patiently waits, it gets its long, sticky tongue ready. When an insect approaches, the tongue flashes out. Snap! Yum.

Possible Think-Aloud: *I am ready to describe how the frog uses its tongue, but first it will be important to explain that the frog has to sit still and watch for insects. I could say, "Frogs sit still," but that doesn't describe the frog very well. I am thinking it would be*

Sample Modeled Writing

good to say that it "patiently waits." That would make it clear that the frog has to sit very still and be patient until its dinner arrives.

TURN &TALK *Think together. What else should I say to describe how the frog catches insects? What can we say that will highlight the frog's attributes and insect-catching skills?*

Analyze

STEP 3: Reread and reflect.

Possible Think-Aloud: *Rereading our writing is really helpful, isn't it? When I reread, I realized that "flicks out its tongue" doesn't clearly describe how fast that tongue needs to be to catch a fly! That tongue has to be speedier than _____ to catch a fly or a grasshopper. Think together. Let's select really precise words that make it clear that the tongue is lightning-fast.*

Sum It Up

Nonfiction writers need to include lots of details and select words that help a reader to really picture the attributes of the subject. "Lightning-fast" tells a lot about the tongue, and "bulgy" helps us to picture the eyes. As you begin writing today, try to focus on bringing out details so that your reader will learn a lot about your subject.

VARIATIONS

For Less Experienced Writers: Use large photographs or visuals from a familiar big book, and coach writers in coming up with lots of descriptors for attributes that are present in the visuals. Help them think of different phrases and words to describe what they see.

For More Experienced Writers: Have partners trade descriptive writing pieces and attempt to draw an illustration based only on what the partner has written. Guide them in having conversations about details that would have helped to highlight attributes of their subject.

Using Comparisons

WHEN TO USE IT: To help writers learn to integrate comparisons into their writing

FOCUS THE LEARNING

When comparisons are included in nonfiction writing selections, a reader has support in making connections between prior knowledge and the information of the passage. These comparisons may appear as a comparison diagram, as a descriptive passage, or as a simile.

Model

STEP 1: Think aloud as you generate comparisons between students in class and other familiar concepts.

Possible Think-Aloud: *Nonfiction writers often use comparisons to help readers connect new learning to things they already know. Let's practice: (Name a student.) _____'s eyes are as dark as chocolate pudding. We all know the color of chocolate pudding. We can compare the chocolate and _____'s beautiful eyes. That was fun. Let's try another one. (Name a student.) _____'s eyes are as blue as the sky on a summer day. Let's try it with an animal.*

TURN &TALK *A cheetah is known to be able to run as fast as 75 miles per hour. So I could say: A cheetah is as speedy as _____. (A car) A whale is as big as _____. (A school bus)*

STEP 2: Model creating comparisons in writing.

Possible Think-Aloud: *I am remembering the book we read about baby sea turtles. It said that the baby was the size of a bottle cap. That is a comparison. Use your fingers to make a circle about the size of a bottle cap. In your mind, compare a baby turtle to that tiny little bottle cap. Comparisons are really helpful. Watch as I write, "A rabbit is as small as a soccer ball." (Display a soccer ball or playground ball.) Imagine you are holding it in your hands. Hold your hands just like you were holding the ball. Now picture*

A baby turtle is as tiny as a bottle cap.
A rabbit is as small as a soccer ball.
A worm is as slow as a snail.
The corn is as high as my knee.

Sample Modeled Writing

a rabbit in your hands, but don't move your hands. What do you notice? What did that comparison help you to understand?

TURN &TALK *Tell your partner about your comparison between the soccer ball and the rabbit. What did the comparison help you to learn?*

Analyze

STEP 3: Reread and reflect.

Possible Think-Aloud: *As we reread our comparisons, I am reminded of the wonderful book* Big Blue Whale *by Nicola Davies. She used comparisons to help us learn about the blue whale. She said, "Reach out and touch the blue whale's skin. It's springy and smooth like a hard-boiled egg, and it's as slippery as wet soap." Those comparisons really helped me to get a picture in my mind!*

Sum It Up

Comparisons help readers connect what they already know to what they are learning, so it is important for nonfiction writers to use lots of comparisons. I am going to challenge you to look closely at your writing today and insert at least one comparison. I know you can do it! I can hardly wait to see what you write.

VARIATIONS

For Less Experienced Writers: Assist emergent writers in comparing familiar classroom items. Examples: A pencil is as long as a marker. The paper towels are as rough as _____. The top of my desk is as smooth as _____.

For More Experienced Writers: Guide more experienced writers in analyzing nonfiction writing that they have already completed, considering opportunities to enrich their thinking with comparisons.

LINKS TO CD-ROM:
• Teacher Tool: Comparisons in Literature

Focus on "One"

WHEN TO USE IT: To help writers move beyond detached, general descriptions

FOCUS THE LEARNING

Young writers often fall into the trap of writing about birds, sea life, or animals in generalized terms. If they focus on a single animal, however, the writing takes on a personal feel that evokes sensory imaging and engages the reader more fully.

Model

STEP 1: Think aloud to focus on an individual animal and its relationship to its setting. Focus on visualizing.

Possible Think-Aloud: *Writers, today I am going to show you how I can focus on an individual animal to make my writing more interesting. I want to write about the deer who lives near my house. I could say things like: "Deer protect their babies. They have babies with spots." But I want to try something different. Today I am going to focus on just one deer and her baby fawn. I start by getting a picture in my mind of one deer and her baby. I visualize the mother's ears perked up, watching to be sure that nothing comes near her fawn. I visualize the baby with his white spots curled up in the tall grass where he is very hard to see. This mother deer is totally focused on her baby, and I want that to be clear in my writing.*

TURN &TALK *Describe the picture in your mind of the mother deer and her baby. Remember we are focusing on just this one deer and her baby.*

STEP 2: Model writing that focuses on an individual animal to bring a sense of connection between the reader and the subject of the writing.

Possible Think-Aloud: *In the picture in my mind, I "see" how her ears stand tall, and she is watching carefully for danger. I picture her tiny fawn curled up in grass that is so tall that he is hardly visible.*

A mother deer stands with her ears perked, listening for danger. Her tiny fawn, still dotted with white spots, is curled up in the tall grass a few feet away. She stretches to tug at tender sprouts, but she is alert and watchful.

Sample Modeled Writing

Watch as I write, A mother deer . . . *Notice that I am writing "A" mother deer. I am not talking about all deer. I am focusing on just one. In my third sentence, I will write,* She stretches . . . *Notice that I am still talking about this one deer. Did you notice that I wrote "She stretches" rather than saying "Deer stretch." That would be too general for this kind of writing.*

TURN &TALK *Analyze my writing. What do you think of this style of nonfiction writing where the focus is on one? How might you use this in your own writing?*

Analyze

STEP 3: Reread and reflect.

Possible Think-Aloud: *Let's reread together. This kind of writing helps readers connect to the subject, doesn't it? If you were going to teach someone else how to write about "just one," what would you tell a nonfiction writer to do?*

Sum It Up

Nonfiction writers can write in ways that are general, but we can be very specific as well. When we write about "just one," we help our readers come in close and look very carefully. It is like focusing a camera and seeing a single animal in detail. As you begin writing today, spend a moment thinking about "just one." Is there a way you could use this in your writing?

VARIATIONS

For Less Experienced Writers: Focus on oral retelling of facts and a focus on "just one." Provide photographs on highly familiar topics, and encourage the writers to orally rehearse messages such as *A tiny seed, softened by water, cracks open. . . . One tiny caterpillar inches through the crack in his shell and feels the warmth of the sun for the first time. . . .*

For More Experienced Writers: Assist these writers in adding details to their focus on "one." They could focus on physical attributes, behavior, setting, and so on. Continue to support them in using personal pronouns, such as he and she, or possessive pronouns, such as his and hers.

LINKS TO CD-ROM:
• Book List: Mentor Books

Organization

Giving Structure to Our Work

The internal structure of a piece of writing gives it stability just as the foundation of a home provides a solid base for the dwelling. Writing with strong organization begins with a clear purpose; then events and descriptions proceed logically. Information is organized into meaningful groupings. An inviting lead and a satisfying ending draw readers smoothly through the writing.

LESSON	K	1	2	RELATED LESSONS
1 Main Idea Maintained Throughout	●	●	●	*Planning:* Lesson 4, Map Out Your Writing with Informational Pictures *Revising:* Lesson 11, Stick to the Main Idea
2 Pictures and Words Work Together	●	●		*Drafting:* Lesson 1, Write About Your Pictures *Text Features:* Lesson 4, Add Captions to Illustrations
3 Plan the Beginning and End . . . Then the Middle	●	●	●	*Organization:* Lesson 6, Creating an Inviting Lead *Organization:* Lesson 7, Craft a Satisfying Ending
4 Use a Logical Sequence	●	●	●	*Planning:* Lesson 4, Map Out Your Writing with Informational Pictures
5 Details Support Main Idea	●	●	●	*Ideas:* Lesson 9, Details Highlight Attributes of Subject *Sentence Fluency:* Lesson 6, The Rule of Three
6 Create an Inviting Lead		●	●	*Word Choice:* Lesson 6, Adding Interest with "-ing" Words *Voice and Audience:* Lesson 3, Capture the Interest of Your Reader
7 Craft a Satisfying Ending		●	●	*Voice and Audience:* Lesson 7, At the End, Reveal Your Thoughts, Feelings, and Opinions
8 Organizing with a Graphic Organizer	●	●	●	Storyboard Resources CD-ROM *Ideas:* Lesson 3, Narrow the Topic *Organization:* Lesson 3, Plan the Beginning and End . . . Then the Middle
9 Multiple Pages Are Used: Page Breaks Support Units of Meaning	●	●	●	*Planning:* Lesson 4, Map Out Your Writing with Informational Pictures
10 Paragraphs		●	●	*Text Features:* Lesson 2, Headings Help Your Reader *Presenting:* Lesson 3, Page Layout Includes Effective Use of Margins
11 Create a Question and Answer Book	●	●	●	
12 Sharing Information as a List Poem	●	●	●	

Other Lessons to Create

You might also want to teach writers how to

- create an alphabet book,
- use a timeline to organize their writing, or
- use a repeating refrain ("And I'll huff, and I'll puff, and I'll blow your house in").

Main Idea Maintained Throughout

WHEN TO USE IT: To help writers stay focused as they craft their writing

FOCUS THE LEARNING

A developing writer might start off strong and focused on a single topic, but as he or she gathers more information, the main idea can become muddled. Writers need to learn how to stay "on topic" as they craft each sentence.

Model

STEP 1: Think aloud as you construct a short piece with a clearly focused title. Show how you are tempted to get off track, but you remember your main idea, think about your title, and work to stay focused.

Possible Think-Aloud: *I know that sometimes when I am writing, it's easy to get off track and start writing about something else that interests me. I'm going to start my section about what sharks eat. Watch me as I write and think about staying focused on what I really want my writing to say. I'll start with the sentences, "Sharks eat all kinds of things. Some eat crabs, small fish, and shrimp."*

TURN & TALK *Partners, think together. Have I stayed focused so far? Are my sentences all about what sharks eat?*

STEP 2:

Possible Think-Aloud: *When I write the word "shrimp," it reminds me that I love to eat shrimp, too. I am tempted to start writing about how much I love to eat my shrimp with lemon and butter. However, I remember that I want this part of my writing to be all about what sharks eat. I'm going to get right back on track and write more about that. I'll add, "Others eat lobsters, squid, and even other sharks!"*

What Sharks Eat

Sharks eat all kinds of things. Some eat crabs, small fish, and shrimp. Others eat lobsters, squid, and even other sharks!

Sample Modeled Writing

TURN &TALK *My topic is "What Sharks Eat." Do you have other ideas of what they eat that would help me stick to my main idea?*

Analyze

STEP 3: Reread and reflect.

Possible Think-Aloud: *Let's reread my writing and think together. Have I stayed focused on my topic? Do all of my sentences tell about what sharks eat? Is my writing clear and focused?*

Sum It Up

Writers, don't be surprised when you're writing and you become tempted to start writing about something else. It happens to all writers from time to time. When it happens, remember to stop and ask yourself, "What did I want this section of my writing to be about? What is my title? Am I still on track?" Then, get right back to writing about your topic. Let's begin!

VARIATIONS

For Less Experienced Writers: Gather writers in a small group, and coach them as they use a graphic organizer to arrange facts about their topic into sections. Show them how this organizer can help them stay focused. Coach them as they begin to write. (See Resources CD-ROM.)

For More Experienced Writers: Challenge partners to listen to their partner's writing. Have Partner A read to Partner B while Partner B tries to listen for any points where the writer has gone off track. Partner B can then coach Partner A in revising the piece. Have partners switch and repeat.

LINKS TO CD-ROM:
- Graphic Organizer: Main Idea and Details

Pictures and Words Work Together

WHEN TO USE IT: When writers are using illustrations and text to create meaning

FOCUS THE LEARNING

Young writers know how to create illustrations that work with the text and enhance the writing.

Model

STEP 1: Read a small section of your writing, and pause to think about an illustration that you could add to enhance the writing.

Possible Think-Aloud: *As a writer of nonfiction, I want to make sure that my pictures and words are working together to make my piece the best it can be. As I reread this section about bees, I want to come up with an illustration that would reinforce my writing. So far my piece says, "Once the honeybee has collected the pollen . . . "*

TURN &TALK *Partners, think together. If you were the author of this section, what illustration might you add? Describe what your illustration would look like. What details would you include?*

STEP 2: Demonstrate how to create a detailed illustration to accompany the text.

Possible Think-Aloud: *Watch as I reread this section about bees and think about an illustration that could go with my words. This section talks about the honeybee storing the pollen in a honeycomb cell. I'm thinking that it might improve my piece to add a picture of a honeycomb cell. That might help my reader understand more about my topic. Watch as I add this visual to the page.*

Once the honeybee has collected the pollen, she returns to her hive. She carefully stores the pollen in a honeycomb cell.

Sample Modeled Writing

TURN &TALK *As writers, we need to always be sure that our pictures and our words go together. How could we help ourselves remember to check and see if everything matches? How can we make sure that we always include pictures and words that work together?*

Analyze

STEP 3: Reread and reflect.

Possible Think-Aloud: *I just noticed something important. My writing tells that pollen is stored in the honeycomb cell, but I didn't include the pollen in my drawing. If I am going to make my pictures and words work together, I need to do that. Writers, let's reread this section again and look closely at my illustrations. Do my illustrations and words work together to help my reader understand more about my topic?*

Sum It Up

We know that, as writers, we can use both words and pictures to make our message clear. When you are careful about how your writing and pictures work together, you really boost your writing! I am looking forward to admiring your work.

VARIATIONS

For Less Experienced Writers: Gather writers together in a small group. Provide illustrations and sections of text that are meant to go together. Challenge the group to see if they can match the illustrations with the appropriate sections of text.

For More Experienced Writers: Gather students in a small group, and show them other kinds of pictures that support text. Challenge them to experiment with diagrams, close-ups, maps, and cutaways.

Plan the Beginning and End . . . Then the Middle

WHEN TO USE IT: When writers do not have a clear beginning, middle, and end to their writing

FOCUS THE LEARNING

Young writers often run out of steam before they can consolidate a satisfying ending to their writing. For these writers, it is helpful to plan the beginning and the end and then come back to the main ideas that comprise the middle.

Model

STEP 1: Explain that writers often plan bookends—the beginning and the end of their writing—before they plan the middle section.

Possible Think-Aloud: *We all know that writing needs to have a beginning, a middle, and an end. Today you are going to learn a little trick that writers sometimes use. They plan the beginning and the end of their writing BEFORE they work on the middle. If I were going to write about going out for pizza, the beginning might be that delicious moment when I take my first big bite! The ending might be when I hold my stomach and think about how full I am.*

TURN &TALK *Think together about the middle portion of my pizza experience. What would make a good main idea for the middle section of my writing? What happened between my first and my last bites of pizza?*

STEP 2: Model writing the beginning and the end on separate sheets of paper.

Possible Think-Aloud: *Let's shift our thinking to caterpillars and butterflies. We know that a butterfly lays an egg, and a caterpillar hatches from the egg. Since I want to write the beginning and the end before I worry about the middle, I will use separate pieces of paper. Here is my beginning, "A butterfly . . ."*

TURN &TALK *Think together. What would make a good end?*

Analyze

STEP 3: Reread and reflect. Work together to create a meaningful middle section.

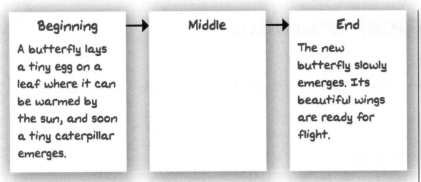

Beginning	Middle	End
A butterfly lays a tiny egg on a leaf where it can be warmed by the sun, and soon a tiny caterpillar emerges.		The new butterfly slowly emerges. Its beautiful wings are ready for flight.

Sample Modeled Writing

Possible Think-Aloud: *We have a beginning and an end. Now we are ready for the middle of this nonfiction writing. I have several pieces of paper ready because the middle section just might take more than one page. Put your heads together and think. What should the middle section tell a reader about the caterpillar?*

Sum It Up

Writers, you have learned an important trick that writers often use. You can think of the beginning and end of your writing and then come back and plan the middle. That way you will always have a satisfying ending for your readers. As you begin writing today, take a moment to think first about the beginning and the end of your writing. They are like important bookends for your work.

VARIATIONS

For Less Experienced Writers: Develop the beginning and end of the writing with sketches rather than words. Then, go back and consider how many sketches will be needed to build up the middle portion of the writing. Once all the sketches are in place, writers can tell the story and prepare to create text to match each picture.

For More Experienced Writers: Lift writing expertise by working on the quality of the beginning and end. For these writers, you may want to consider lessons such as *Organization:* Lesson 6, Creating an Inviting Lead, or *Organization:* Lesson 7, Craft a Satisfying Ending.

LINKS TO CD-ROM:
- Graphic Organizer: Beginning . . . End, Then Middle

Use a Logical Sequence

WHEN TO USE IT: When writing lacks a logical sequence, or when events are written out of order

FOCUS THE LEARNING

Providing the reader with a clear and logical sequence is imperative. Writers need to take the time to read and reread their writing to make sure that it is written in an order that makes sense.

Model

STEP 1: In advance of the lesson, write several sentences on strips. Place the sentences in a pocket chart in random order. Read and think aloud about how to organize them.

Possible Think-Aloud: *I've written some sentences about how a butterfly grows. Let's read the sentences and see if they are in an order that makes sense. I think my first sentence should be about eggs, since I know that butterflies start out as eggs. Watch as I move that sentence to the beginning of my writing.*

TURN &TALK   *What sentence would come next? What would make sense? How do you know?*

STEP 2: Continue to reread and arrange the rest of the strips in a logical sequence.

All butterflies start out as eggs.

When the eggs hatch, small caterpillars emerge.

They grow and grow as they continue to munch on leaves.

Once the caterpillar has grown big enough, it forms a chrysalis.

Soon, it will push its way out of the chrysalis and emerge as a beautiful butterfly!

Sample Modeled Writing

Possible Think-Aloud: *Many of you suggested that the next sentence should be "When the eggs hatch, small caterpillars emerge." I think that makes sense. We used what we knew about our topic to help us decide which sentence would come next, didn't we? Let's reread.* (Continue arranging the rest of the sentences.)

TURN &TALK *What would come next? Think about a logical sequence and the life cycle of a butterfly.*

Analyze

STEP 3: Reread and reflect.

Possible Think-Aloud: *Now that we've arranged our sentences, let's read our writing and see what we think. Is it in an order that makes sense? Will our reader be able to understand what we have written?*

Sum It Up

We all know that our writing needs to flow with a logical sequence that makes sense to a reader. Today I showed you a way to check to see if your sentences are in an order that makes sense. We reread the piece many times and asked ourselves, "What would come next?" Today take some time to look at your piece of writing. Do your sentences make sense, or do you need to do some rearranging? Let's get busy!

VARIATIONS

For Less Experienced Writers: Gather writers in a small group. Together, use a planning sheet to write the steps involved in brushing your teeth. Craft a short piece of writing using the planning sheet. Encourage students to utilize the planning sheet when working on their own writing.

For More Experienced Writers: Model how writers use pictures, diagrams, and captions to show an order of events, such as the life cycle of a plant or animal. Challenge writers to incorporate these features into their writing. The storyboard example on the Resources CD-ROM would be a supportive tool for these writers.

LINKS TO CD ROM:
- Graphic Organizer: Planning Sheet for Sequencing Events
- Graphic Organizer: Life Cycle Planning Sheet

Details Support Main Idea

WHEN TO USE IT: When writing is too general and lacks detail

FOCUS THE LEARNING

Rich details invigorate a piece of writing and make it more appealing. It's important for students to know how to include enhancing details that don't detract from the main idea.

Model

STEP 1: Explain that writers need to think about what details they could add to make their writing the best it could be. Think aloud as you add details to a topic sentence.

Possible Think-Aloud: *Writers, we know that good writing includes lots of rich details. Today I want to show you how those details can support the main idea by telling how, what, when, where, or why. I am working on a piece about how animals can hide. So far, I've written "Animals can hide from predators in many ways." That's a good start, but I think my reader may wonder, "What are the ways they can hide?" I need to add some details.*

TURN &TALK *Partners, put your heads together and see if you can think of all the different ways that animals can hide. What details could I add to support my first sentence?*

STEP 2: Model adding some details to support your topic sentence.

Possible Think-Aloud: *As I listened in on some partners' thinking, I heard great details. Connor and Ben were talking about how some animals can blend into their surroundings. That's a detail that I can add to support my first sentence. Claire and Jen remembered that animals sometimes hide underground. Watch me as I add some of these details to my piece.*

Animals can hide from predators in many ways. Some animals use camouflage to blend into their surroundings. Other animals hide underground in a burrow or den. Some animals simply hide by scurrying under rocks or leaves.

Sample Modeled Writing

TURN &TALK *Think together. What other details would support the main idea of this piece?*

Analyze

STEP 3: Reread and reflect.

Possible Think-Aloud: *Let's take a look at my writing now. Do all of my details go with my first sentence? Do they give my reader more information? When I took the time to really think about the details I could add, it made my writing much better!*

Sum It Up

Writers, today we learned how to add details that support the main idea, or what our piece is mostly about. When you are working on your writing today, think about what details **you** can add to make your writing the best it can be. Turn to your partners, and tell them what you are going to work on today.

VARIATIONS

For Less Experienced Writers: Reread a familiar story such as "The Three Bears," but take out all of the details. Ask students to talk about what is missing and how it affects the story. Confer one-on-one with students to scaffold them as they begin to add details to their writing.

For More Experienced Writers: Gather writers in pairs. Give partners several topic sentences and several details. Challenge students to see if they can match the topic sentences with the supporting details. Discuss the strategies they used to solve the "puzzle."

Create an Inviting Lead

WHEN TO USE IT: When writers need a good lead to draw the reader in

FOCUS THE LEARNING

It takes time, thought, and attention to begin a piece of writing in a way that draws the reader in. The goal is to teach students to take those extra moments to create an inviting beginning.

Model

STEP 1: In advance of the lesson, create a chart displaying the weak leads in Column 1. Consider and discuss: Which beginning is more inviting? Which lead makes us want to read more?

Possible Think-Aloud: *When you begin your piece of writing, it's important to think about how to draw your reader in. You want to create a lead, or beginning, that makes your reader want to read more. Let's take a look at these beginnings and think about making them really inviting. First, let's look at Lead 1 about spiders. It is just okay. It doesn't really pull me in, like a magnet. Watch as I make it better. I am going to start with a question, "Do you think you know everything there is to know about spiders? Think again!"*

TURN &TALK *Compare these two leads, and decide which one is better. What makes it better?*

Column 1	Column 2
Here is my report about spiders.	Do you think you know everything there is to know about spiders? Think again!
One day I was outside, and it started to rain.	Crash! Bang! Boom! I heard thw rainstorm before I felt the first drops of rain.

Sample Modeled Writing

STEP 2: Model how to make a lead about rain more inviting.

Possible Think-Aloud: *That was fun. Let's try it again. Lead 1 on the rainy day is ho-hum, not very exciting. I am going to think about the sounds that I hear in a really big storm. I hear "Crash! Bang! Boom!" Now there's a great way to create an inviting lead—sound words! I am going to write, "Crash! Bang! Boom! I heard the rainstorm before I felt the first drops of rain." I feel much better about that lead. It is exciting. The sound words made it very inviting.*

TURN &TALK *If you were to list the attributes of a great lead, what would be on your list?*

Analyze

STEP 3: Reread and reflect.

Possible Think-Aloud: *We've talked about how authors can use questions and fun sounds to draw their readers in. Let's think together. What are some other ways we could start a piece of nonfiction writing?*

Sum It Up

Writers, today we learned that a strong, interesting lead draws the reader in and makes the reader want to read more. We've learned that there are many ways to do that. Who thinks they can try one of the strategies we've learned about today? I can't wait to read your pieces!

VARIATIONS

For Less Experienced Writers: Provide more guided practice by gathering students in a small group and displaying a short piece of writing on a familiar topic. Challenge partners to create inviting leads. Add them to an ongoing chart displayed in the classroom.

For More Experienced Writers: Provide partners with several ho-hum leads. Challenge them to revise each lead so that it is rich, inviting, and interesting. Add them to an ongoing chart displayed in the classroom.

Craft a Satisfying Ending

WHEN TO USE IT: When writers do not know how to end a piece of writing, or when the writing ends abruptly

FOCUS THE LEARNING

Emergent writers struggle with how to end their writing, hence the often-used "The End!" This lesson is designed to challenge students to take time to craft an ending that will bring closure and satisfaction to the reader.

Model

STEP 1: Read a short section of your writing, pausing before the ending to think aloud about how you can make it effective.

Possible Think-Aloud: *I know that, as a writer, one of my important (and most difficult) jobs is to write an ending that will satisfy my reader and wrap up my piece. It takes some time and hard work to write an ending that works! Watch me as I think about an ending for my piece about building a tree house. I've told the readers all I want to tell them, but I need to find a way to wrap it all up. I know I can do better than, "The End." I want to make the ending sound like a tree house is exciting. How about, "Whatever you do, remember to take the time to sit back, relax, and enjoy your new place to play!"*

TURN &TALK *What do you think of this ending? Is it satisfying? Is it interesting? Does it feel like the end of the writing? Can you think of another way to end this piece?*

First draft:

Finally, add some decoration and style to your tree house. Find some pictures of things you love and display them, or bring in a cozy beanbag chair.

Second draft with ending:

Finally, add some decoration and style to your tree house. Find some pictures of things you love and display them, or bring in a cozy beanbag chair. Whatever you do, remember to take the time to sit back, relax, and enjoy your new place to play!

Sample Modeled Writing

STEP 2: Try several endings and decide which one is most satisfying.

Possible Think-Aloud: *Let's keep thinking about endings. Here is another one that we could try; "Now that the playhouse is finished, call your friends and have a wonderful time!"*

TURN &TALK *Evaluate this ending. How does it compare to my first try? Which one do you like?*

Analyze

STEP 3: Reread and reflect.

Possible Think-Aloud: *I brought several great nonfiction books so we could read the endings.* (Read the ending from each one.) *Reading these endings helped me think about my writing. Let's reread our ending one more time and see if we can think of more ways to make it satisfying. Writers have a lot to think about, but writing endings can be a lot of fun.*

Sum It Up

Today we talked about the importance of a good ending. We know that the ending gives us one more chance to make a good impression on our reader, so we want to make sure we choose our words carefully. As you work on your own writing today, think about how you might wrap it up in a way that is interesting and satisfying. Let's get to work!

VARIATIONS

For Less Experienced Writers: Provide more guided practice with another piece of modeled writing. Confer and coach writers as they work to craft their own endings.

For More Experienced Writers: Invite writers to offer up their pieces for group revision, or have a conversation with the student(s) in front of a small group or the class. Challenge the group to think of some other possible endings.

Organizing with a Graphic Organizer

WHEN TO USE IT: When students need support in planning and organizing their piece

FOCUS THE LEARNING

It's important to remember that a graphic organizer does not teach. Our goal is to show students how it can be one more *tool* to help them as they prepare to write.

Model

STEP 1: Introduce the graphic organizer and your topic.

Possible Think-Aloud: *Writers, I want to show you a tool that authors sometimes use to help them get organized and plan for their writing. It's called a graphic organizer, or a planning page, and there are lots of different kinds. Today I'm working on a piece of writing that is meant to teach my reader how to make a peanut butter and jelly sandwich, so I'm going to use this graphic organizer to help me. First, I need to think about what to do when I make the sandwich.*

TURN &TALK *Partners, think together. What do you do first when you make a peanut butter and jelly sandwich? What does my reader need to know?*

STEP 2: Demonstrate how you use the graphic organizer to organize your thoughts and plan for your writing.

Instructional Writing Graphic Organizer

Writing	Picture
Step 1 Get two slices of your favorite kind of bread	
Step 2 Now get the peanut butter and jelly	Peanut Butter / Jelly
Step 3	
Step 4	
Step 5	

Sample Modeled Writing

Possible Think-Aloud: *I heard you say that the first thing we need to do is take out the bread. The boxes on the left show me where I can write some words, and the boxes on the right are where I can make a quick sketch to remind me of each step. I think I'll add, "Get two slices of your favorite kind of bread" to the first box. I can add more information about that once I begin writing my piece. Watch as I make a quick sketch so I remember what this part is about.*

TURN &TALK *What should come next? What should we write, and what should we draw?*

Analyze

STEP 3: Reread and reflect.

Possible Think-Aloud: *Let's read what I have on my planning page. What might I add next? Do you think using this tool will help me as I begin to write? How might it help me?*

Sum It Up

Today we learned about one kind of tool that writers use to help them organize their thinking and prepare to write. As you begin writing your directions, try using a graphic organizer like we did together and see if it helps you as a writer. Remember to think and plan, using the organizer to get ready, and your writing will be better than ever!

VARIATIONS

For Less Experienced Writers: Bring a small group of writers together and continue modeling and providing guided practice with the graphic organizer that you used in the whole-group lesson. Then, confer and coach them as they use an organizer for their own topics.

For More Experienced Writers: Examine other graphic organizers and how they can be utilized. Challenge writers to try a variety, and have them reflect on which ones were helpful.

LINK TO CD ROM:
- Graphic Organizer
- Graphic Organizer: Instructional Writing Organizer

Multiple Pages Are Used: Page Breaks Support Units of Meaning

WHEN TO USE IT: To help writers transtion to multiple-page books

FOCUS THE LEARNING

When we teach young authors to utilize multiple pages, they stretch themselves to write more and get the satisfaction of knowing they have created an entire book.

Model

STEP 1: Display three sheets of blank paper. Think aloud as you plan for writing.

Possible Think-Aloud: *When authors create informational books, they use lots of pages and they plan each page. I have placed three sheets of paper on this chart because I am going to write at least three pages to make a book about rabbits. Watch as I quickly plan each page. My first page is about burrows. I'll make a drawing of a burrow here. My next two pages are about teeth and groups of rabbits. I'll draw those next. Now I can add page numbers and begin to think about the words I want on each page. It works really well to have everything about a topic on one page. Listen as I "tell" what I plan to say on each page. On page 1, I will write . . . On page 2, I will write . . .*

TURN &TALK *Partners, talk together. How might planning my pages help me get organized and be a better writer?*

PAGE 1

Most rabbits live in burrows and holes in the ground. This keeps them safe from predators.

PAGE 2

A rabbit's teeth never stop growing, but they wear them down by chewing on tree branches and other things.

PAGE 3

A group of rabbits is called a herd. Rabbits like to live with other rabbits.

Sample Modeled Writing

STEP 2: Add text to the pages, thinking aloud about organizing your ideas.

Possible Think-Aloud: *Now that I've taken some time to plan my pages, I'm ready to write. On this first page, I drew a picture of a burrow. On this page, I'll write, "Most rabbits live in burrows . . ."* *So, on my first page, I'll have some information about burrows along with a picture of a burrow. That will help my book be organized and clear. On page 2, I will write, "A rabbit's teeth never stop growing . . ." That reminds me of an important idea! Rabbits don't use their teeth to attack predators. I need to make a decision.*

TURN & TALK *Does this idea fit better on page 1 about predators and burrows or on page 2 about teeth?*

Analyze

STEP 3: Reread and reflect.

Possible Think-Aloud: *Let's read each page of my book about rabbits. Is it organized? Have I written lots of facts about rabbits? Planning my pages helped me to stay organized and helped me write more. Now I have a good start to a whole book.*

Sum It Up

Today I showed you one way to plan and organize the facts about your topic into a book with several pages. I used three pages, but some of you may want to make a book with five, six, or even seven pages. I'll put some blank paper in the writing corner. Try and use the paper to plan for your writing. Let's get started!

VARIATIONS

For Less Experienced Writers: Display a piece of writing that is only words. Demonstrate how you can cut it apart and place each section on a new page.

For More Experienced Writers: Provide another shared experience, demonstrating how you plan each page in terms of sentences, diagrams, bold words, captions, and other text features.

Paragraphs

WHEN TO USE IT: When students are crafting several sentences about a single topic, or when writing seems to go on and on with no breaks

FOCUS THE LEARNING

In this lesson, we show writers a simple way to plan, organize, and record information so that even our youngest students can craft a paragraph.

Model

STEP 1: Explain that writers often place their writing on several pages so that they can easily organize their writing in paragraphs.

Possible Think-Aloud: *Today I want to show you a smart way to organize your writing so that you can write several paragraphs. A paragraph is a group of sentences that all tell about the same thing. I'm writing about how tadpoles turn into frogs. (Display several pieces of paper in a pocket chart.) On this first piece of paper, I'll write about frog eggs. I'll write a number 1 at the top of this page to remind me that this will be my first paragraph.*

TURN &TALK *Writers, if you were going to write this paragraph, what would you include? Think of all that you know about frog eggs. What sentences could we add to this paragraph?*

STEP 2: Model and think aloud as you write the first paragraph and begin writing the second paragraph.

Possible Think-Aloud: *Watch me as I think about that first stage of life for frogs and then write about it. Since I'm writing a paragraph, I'm going to indent a few spaces. That tells my reader that I've begun a new paragraph. (Write the first few sentences about eggs.) Now I can move*

From Tadpole to Frog

    Frogs don't start out as frogs. They actually begin as frog spawn, or eggs. The eggs are laid in the water and are covered with jelly.

    Once the eggs hatch, they become tadpoles. Like fish, tadpoles can swim and breathe underwater through their gills.

Sample Modeled Writing

on to the second page. I know that the next step in the life of frogs is when the eggs hatch into tadpoles. Now I'll indent again and write a paragraph about that topic. Notice that all the ideas in a paragraph are about the same topic.

TURN &TALK *If you were going to write a paragraph, what would you need to remember?*

Analyze

STEP 3: Reread and reflect.

Possible Think-Aloud: *Let's read the paragraphs that we have written so far. How did using a separate page for each paragraph help me as I began to write?*

Sum It Up

Today I showed you something smart that writers can do when they want to write in paragraphs. Now you know how to use several pieces of paper to plan out your writing, and you know how to indent to show your reader that you are beginning a new paragraph. Who thinks they can try this today? Okay, give it a go!

VARIATIONS

For Less Experienced Writers: Coach writers as they work in a small group to continue the piece of writing you modeled with the whole class. Then, confer one-on-one with writers as they begin to write their own pieces.

For More Experienced Writers: Teach writers the acronym T.I.P.S. (Time, Incident or Topic, Place, Speaker) to help them remember when to start a new paragraph. Challenge them to try utilizing paragraphs in other types of writing.

LINKS TO CD-ROM:
• Reference Chart: T.I.P.S. When to Start a New Paragraph.

Create a Question and Answer Book

WHEN TO USE IT: To help students learn to utilize their questions as structural support for nonfiction writing

FOCUS THE LEARNING

When writers of nonfiction have opportunities to create and record questions on topics of interest, interest is naturally piqued and the groundwork is laid for ongoing research. There are many published books written in this format that would serve as powerful mentors to writers. A few examples are: *The Magic School Bus Answers Questions* by Joanna Cole and Melvin Berger; question-and-answer books such as *Do Whales Have Belly Buttons? Do Tarantulas Have Teeth? Do All Spiders Spin Webs?*

Model

STEP 1: Read aloud from a book written in a question-and-answer format such as the titles listed in Focus the Learning.

Possible Think-Aloud: *I really like the way this book is organized. Each two-page layout is organized in the same way. There is a question and then the answer. What a great way to organize a nonfiction book. As readers, we ask questions all the time. This is helping me understand that I can use questions in my nonfiction writing, too.*

TURN &TALK *Discuss the features of this question-and-answer book. What do you notice about the way it is organized? How might you use this structure to write a question-and-answer book of your own?*

STEP 2: Post several sheets of paper, and begin to create a question-and-answer book while the students observe and participate in thinking.

Possible Think-Aloud: *I am going to create a question-and-answer book about our classroom. I think this will be a really helpful tool that we can use when we have visitors or when we get a new student. For my first question, I am going to write: "How many students are in this classroom?" The answer will be: "We have 28 first graders, 16 boys and 12 girls."*

TURN &TALK *Put your heads together. What should we have for our second question?*

Analyze

STEP 3: Reread and reflect.

How many students are in this classroom?

We have 28 first graders. 16 boys and 12 girls.

What happens during independent reading?

Each student has a personal bag of books that includes fiction, nonfiction, and magazines. They read for 30–45 minutes every day.

How do students in this classroom feel about writing?

Students in Room 15 love to write. They write all day long, in every subject area, and also have a daily writer's workshop time. They are especially proud to know how to write in a wide range of text types.

Sample Modeled Writing

VARIATIONS

For Less Experienced Writers: Scaffold less experienced writers by providing a prepared book that already has the questions inserted as headings. Then, all they need to do is create illustrations and writing that support their answers to the questions.

For More Experienced Writers: Challenge more experienced writers to come up with open-ended questions that will need several sentences to answer. Multiple facts should be integrated into each two-page layout.

Possible Think-Aloud: *This question-and-answer book is going to be filled with great information about our classroom. For the next questions, I want to focus on independent reading and writing. Those are both really important to our classroom. Watch as I write, What happens during independent reading? Notice that I start with a question, and then I answer it using sentences. Watch as I write my answer, "Each student has a personal bag . . ." Evaluate my answer. Is there any other information that would have been helpful to include?*

Sum It Up

Question-and-answer books are great ways to organize nonfiction writing. All you have to do is create a list of questions on your topic and then write the answers!

Sharing Information as a List Poem

WHEN TO USE IT: To offer writers another organizational format for sharing their learning

FOCUS THE LEARNING

Nonfiction poetry comes in many formats and organizational patterns, offering writers a wide range of possibilities for communicating about their learning. Best of all, poetry stimulates imagery and style, bringing facts to life in a new and unique way.

Model

STEP 1: Create a list of facts about bubbles.

Possible Think-Aloud: *I brought along some bubble mix for us to consider today as we continue learning about gases. Watch as I take a big breath and blow into this bubble wand. The air from my lungs goes into the bubble and it grows, holding my breath inside! That is pretty cool. On this chart, I will begin listing words that describe bubbles. I will list single words and phrases. First, I will write* "Floating," *because the bubbles float in the air like magic. Next, I will add* "air bubbles," *because the air from my lungs is inside the bubbles. My goal is to gather terrific words and phrases so I can read this as a list poem when I am finished.*

TURN &TALK *Examine my list of words and phrases. What other words and phrases do you think we should add?*

STEP 2: Continue adding words and phrases in combination with blowing additional bubbles for students to observe.

Possible Think-Aloud: *Did you notice the colors in the bubbles? I see pink, yellow, red, and even a bit of blue. I am going to add,* "Filled with colored light" *to my chart. I also want to add* "Glistening." *I love the way the bubbles shine and glisten as they float.*

Bubbles

Floating
Air bubbles
Filled with colored light
Glistening
Shining
Pop!
They're out of sight

Sample Modeled Writing

TURN &TALK *We aren't finished. What other words and phrases should be on our list about bubbles?*

Analyze

STEP 3: Reread and reflect.

Possible Think-Aloud: *Let's reread, and this time, let's read our list like a poem. We need to be dramatic and really make our reading expressive. Poems are terrific ways to organize nonfiction writing.*

Sum It Up

List poems are created by listing facts, words, and phrases and then reading the list like a poem. There are all kinds of ways to share nonfiction information, and now you have one more way to organize your writing to share with others.

VARIATIONS

For Less Experienced Writers: Provide additional hands-on experiences that stimulate descriptive language and guide these writers in generating list poems as they expand their vocabulary. Present the list poems for an audience.

For More Experienced Writers: Encourage writers to stretch and use rich descriptions as they craft their list poems. The power of a list poem can be further heightened by having students create a phrase that stimulates sensory imaging and use it as their ending.

LINKS TO CD-ROM:
- Student Writing: List Poems
- Poem: Understanding a Frog

Text Features

Enhancing Our Messages and Supporting Navigation

Nonfiction text features are helpful adaptations that enhance readability of complex texts and improve the organization of nonfiction selections. Nonfiction text features include navigational tools such as a table of contents, headings, a glossary, page numbers, numbered steps, and an index. They may include attention-directing features such as boldface words, bullets, text boxes, and callouts. Visual organizers of information such as diagrams with labels, charts, graphs, tables, and photographs are text features that are of essential importance to reading and should be featured in most forms of nonfiction writing.

LESSON	K	1	2	RELATED LESSONS
1 Choose a Title that Is Interesting		●	●	*Voice and Audience:* Lesson 5, Pick an Enticing Title *Word Choice:* Lesson 7, Use Onomatopoeia
2 Headings Help Your Reader		●	●	*Capitalization:* Lesson 3, Capitalize Words in a Title
3 Questions Make Great Headings		●	●	*Research:* Lesson 9, Use a Pocket Organizer
4 Add Captions to Illustrations		●	●	
5 Diagrams with Labels	●	●	●	*Planning:* Lesson 3, Create a Labeled Diagram *Research:* Lesson 5, Place Labels on Illustrations
6 Bold Words	●	●	●	
7 Table of Contents		●	●	
8 Insert Page Numbers	●	●	●	
9 Chart/Table/Graph		●	●	
10 Bullets	●	●	●	

Other Lessons to Create

You might also want to teach writers how to

- choose important words and definitions to create a **glossary**,
- write interesting extra information in **text boxes**, or
- make an **index** of the topics in their book.

Choose a Title that Is Interesting

WHEN TO USE IT: When titles are too general

Learners are reminded of the importance of titles every time they go to select a book for independent reading or join the class at the rug for a read-aloud. They know that the title either captures their interest or doesn't. As writers, they need to learn to create several titles, preferably after a selection is finished, before choosing the title that will be most likely to capture the interest of a reader. This lesson is designed to help writers move beyond lifeless labels and create specific titles that add interest and voice to their work.

Model

STEP 1: Display an array of nonfiction selections that are all on the same topic. Guide a conversation about titles. Which ones are great? Which ones could be improved?

Possible Think-Aloud: *I have three books on frogs. Their titles are:* Frogs; Freaky Frogs; *and* A Frog Has a Sticky Tongue. *As I look at these books, they all appeal to me. They have terrific photographs on the covers that make me want to look more closely. However, the titles* Freaky Frogs *and* A Frog Has a Sticky Tongue *cause me to wonder and to want to learn more. Why would a frog be freaky? A sticky tongue? How cool is that?*

TURN &TALK *Look at the titles and think together. What are your opinions of these titles? Which ones would you most want to read? Which titles are the best and why?* (After discussing, repeat the process of considering titles and discussing with one more group of books.)

STEP 2: Create a T-chart (general and specific), and then think aloud about the components of an interesting title.

General	Specific
Spiders	Eight-Legged Climbers
	Web Masters
	Terrific Tarantulas
	Be Nice to Spiders

Sample Modeled Writing

Possible Think-Aloud: *It is interesting that we all preferred titles like* A Frog Has a Sticky Tongue. *That title is really specific, and it makes us want to read the book. As writers, we need to remember that readers like a title that tells something specific about the topic. General titles like* Frogs *are not as appealing. Let's create interesting titles of our own. I have written the topic"Spiders," on a chart. I want to create some titles that are specific and interesting, so I need to think about what makes spiders special. They have eight legs, and they can walk straight up a wall. What would you think of the title* Eight-Legged Climbers? *How about* Eight-Legged Wall Walkers?

TURN &TALK *Think together. Let's make a great list of spider titles.*

Analyze

STEP 3: Reread and reflect.

Possible Think-Aloud: *Have you noticed that it helps to create several titles and then select the one that you think will be the most interesting to a reader? One of the tricks I use when I write is to keep a list of possible titles handy while I am researching and writing. Then, every time I get a great idea for a title, I can add it to the list. When I am finished writing, I have a menu of possible titles so I can be sure that my title won't be just good—it will be great!*

Sum It Up

Titles are important. They help readers decide if they want to read a book. The title is like a sign advertising your writing, so you need titles that are interesting and specific. When creating a terrific title, remember: Be specific. Make the reader wonder. Surprise the reader a bit! As you get ready to write, take a minute to examine some of your titles and see if you can find any that could be improved.

VARIATIONS

For Less Experienced Writers: Cover the titles of leveled books at the "just right" level for these writers. Sticky notes that are doubled will ensure that your students cannot see what is underneath. Then, have partners come up with several possible titles for each book before uncovering the title selected by the author and deciding which titles are better!

For More Experienced Writers: Challenge these writers to come up with bold titles that utilize humor, alliteration, or onomatopoeia. Then, present their titles to a partner to vote on the best and most interesting selection.

LINKS TO CD-ROM:
• Thinking Challenge: Team Title Challenge

Headings Help Your Reader

WHEN TO USE IT: To help writers organize their writing and give readers a focus for reading

FOCUS THE LEARNING

Headings, like mini-titles spaced through a text, keep each section organized and support comprehension. A heading represents a main idea and can be formatted as a word, a phrase, a declarative sentence, or a question.

Model

STEP 1: Show writers the passage "No Wooden Teeth" on the Resources CD-ROM or another passage with clearly laid out headings. (Note: If your students find this topic interesting, they might enjoy *George Washington's Teeth* by Deborah Chandra and Madeleine Comora.)

Possible Think-Aloud: *Let's look at the headings in "No Wooden Teeth," a passage about George Washington, the first president of the United States. Headings are like little titles that appear within a piece of writing. They tell what each section is going to be about. The first heading is "Wooden Teeth?" As a reader, that helps me anticipate the content and be ready to understand what this section is about. I can tell it is about wooden teeth, but the question mark makes me wonder if there is a puzzle here. The next heading is "Constant Pain." That tells me that this section will be about pain. I am noticing that both of these headings are phrases, not single words. Headings can be a single word, but in this passage, they are phrases.* (Read the first two headings and their corresponding texts.)

TURN &TALK *Think together. What do you know about headings? Why do you think headings are helpful tools for nonfiction writers?*

STEP 2: Cover the heading for the last paragraph. Have students compose a heading to fit.

Possible Think-Aloud: (Cover the last heading with sticky notes, and read the paragraph to the students.) *The heading is covered, so I am going to think really hard about a heading that would*

A Toothless President

Just Two

How Did He Eat?

No Smiles

Sample Modeled Writing

be good for this section. It is mostly about the fact that George Washington only had two teeth left when he was president. Isn't that sad? Listen as I think of headings for this section. My first heading is "A Toothless President." He wasn't really toothless. He had two teeth. Perhaps a better heading would be "Just Two." That might give a reader an idea about this section. I know that sometimes headings are questions. Another heading might be "How Did He Eat?" Are you noticing that the first letter in each word is a capital? Headings are like titles, and they need capital letters.

TURN &TALK *Think together about other headings that would be good for this passage.*

Analyze

STEP 3: Reread and reflect.

Possible Think-Aloud: *It is time to vote. I have listed several possible headings for this section, and we need to decide which one we think is best before we uncover the heading that the author wrote. Ready. Who wants to vote for . . . I can't wait to see how our headings compare with the one the author created.*

Sum It Up

Headings tell a reader what to expect from a section of writing. They can be a complete sentence, a phrase, or even a single word. As writers, we need to think about headings and include them in the pages we create. When we have a great heading, it is easy to remember the focus of our writing. Also, headings make our writing easier for others to read. Today as you begin writing, I am going to challenge you to insert headings. I know you can do it!

VARIATIONS

For Less Experienced Writers: During one-on-one conferences, guide writers in using sticky notes to add headings to existing pieces of writing.

For More Experienced Writers: Help more experienced writers to map out headings as they plan a piece of writing. This will help them to create cohesive, well-focused writing.

LINKS TO CD-ROM:
• Shared Reading:
  No Wooden Teeth

Questions Make Great Headings

WHEN TO USE IT: To add variety to headings students infuse into their nonfiction writing

FOCUS THE LEARNING

Questions make great headings that help young writers maintain and support a focused paragraph. There are many published books written in this format that would serve as powerful mentors to writers. To provide a visual for your students, you may want to make copies of the question and answer passage from the Resources CD ROM or use books like *How Do Flies Walk Upside Down?* by Melvin and Gilda Berger; *Why Don't Haircuts Hurt?* by Melvin and Gilda Berger; *Why? The Best Ever Question and Answer Book About Nature, Science, and the World Around You* by Catherine Ripley and Scot Ritchie.

Model

STEP 1: Read aloud from a passage written in a question and answer format such as those listed above. As you read, point out the question-answer structure for the headings.

Possible Think-Aloud: (Read a few pages.) *I am going to stop reading for a moment and look at the way the headings in this book are organized. I see that the author creates a heading that is a question and then answers the question. Once the question is answered, there is a new heading with a new question. Look closely at the pages as I turn them. Each section has the same format: a heading that is a question and then an answer.*

TURN &TALK *What do you think of this format? How might you use this in your writing?*

STEP 2: Post several sheets of paper, and model how to generate a heading that is a question on each page. Then draft an answer.

Possible Think-Aloud: *We have learned a lot about butterflies, so I am going to create some questions that could be great headings for some writing about butterflies. This will help my nonfiction writing because I will need to answer each question before I go on to the next heading. My first heading is "What Is the Difference Between a Butterfly and a Moth?"*

On page 2, my heading will be "Why Are Butterflies So Colorful?" Notice that I am just inserting questions. I will write my answers after I create some really great headings.

What Is the Difference Between a Butterfly and a Moth?

The biggest difference is that moths fly mostly at night and have a short, thick body. They have antennae that look like feathers.

Why Are Butterflies So Colorful?

The color absorbs heat and keeps the butterfly warm. It also provides camouflage to help the butterfly hide from enemies.

Sample Modeled Writing

TURN &TALK *Put your heads together. I am ready for a heading for page 3 and page 4. Identify some terrific butterfly questions that would make good headings for my writing. With your help, we will create some terrific headings and answers.*

Analyze

STEP 3: Reread and reflect.

Possible Think-Aloud: *Watch as I begin to write the answers to the questions in our headings. On page 1, the heading is about the difference between butterflies and moths so I will use the word* difference *in my answer. The biggest difference . . . Look at page 2 and think hard. What could we say that would answer the question in this heading?* (After reading.) *Get ready to analyze. Let's reread together to be sure that our headings, our questions, and the answers all match up.*

Sum It Up

When we organize writing around a series of questions, our writing is very clear and focused. Writers, as you begin writing today, I know that I can count on you to be thinking of questions that you could use as headings.

VARIATIONS

For Less Experienced Writers: In a small-group setting, model the construction of another piece of writing that mirrors the question and answer format of the class book but features a different topic. As students catch on to the structure of the writing, switch to interactive writing and have learners share the pen to create the headings and their corresponding answers.

For More Experienced Writers: Guide these writers in generating a series of questions as a prewriting strategy before they begin to research. Show them how to take notes and save key words under each question. Then, use their research in generating the answers.

LINKS TO CD-ROM:
• Shared Reading: The Earthworm

Add Captions to Illustrations

WHEN TO USE IT: To help writers learn to integrate captions into their nonfiction writing

FOCUS THE LEARNING

Captions are an essential tool for nonfiction writers, as they add clarity and information to visuals. Captions are often placed within text boxes and then set under or to the side of accompanying visuals.

Model

STEP 1: Show students a caption in an enlarged text or one provided on the Resources CD-ROM, highlighting the complete sentence and the surrounding text box.

Possible Think-Aloud: *A caption is a sentence or two that explain the content of a photograph, a drawing, or other visual. It is usually placed inside a text box. Watch as I create a caption for our chart about the water cycle. First, I draw a text box to the side. Then, I think of a sentence that tells about the picture: "Moisture comes down . . ." I am being careful to use a complete sentence. Labels can be a word or two, but a caption is a sentence.*

TURN &TALK *Talk about the difference between a label and a caption. What should you remember?*

STEP 2: Model the addition of a caption to a previously constructed piece of writing.

Possible Think-Aloud: *Remember this chart that we created about the water cycle? It has a great diagram and an explanation about the water cycle. But there isn't a caption. I know that a caption should explain or tell about a visual, and it needs to be at least one complete sentence. I also know that it needs to be in a text box. Watch as I draw a text box beside the diagram. Looking at the diagram helps me think of what to say. I will write, "Moisture comes down . . ." That is one sentence. But it isn't enough. That*

> Water falls to the earth in the form of rain, hail, sleet, or snow. The water then flows into rivers and streams and eventually into the ocean.
>
> During its journey, some water evaporates. Then, water vapor rises where it cools and forms clouds.

Sample Modeled Writing

Sample Modeled Writing

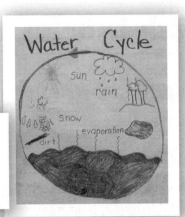

Moisture comes down as rain or snow. Then, evaporation carries moisture back into the clouds again.

only explains how moisture comes down. I need to tell how it gets back into the clouds. This caption is going to need two sentences. That is okay. Captions can have more than one sentence. They just can't be single words, because single words are labels.

TURN &TALK *Construct a sentence that I could use to finish this caption.*

Analyze

STEP 3: Reread and reflect.

Possible Think-Aloud: *Listen as I reread the poster and double-check my caption to be sure it is set up correctly. I see that it is in a text box. That is important. There are two complete sentences with capital letters and periods. That is important, too. I also notice that the caption tells about the visual. That is what good captions are supposed to do! Think together. What are you going to remember about creating captions?*

Sum It Up

Captions are important supports for photographs, illustrations, and diagrams. They explain the content of the visual and help a reader to understand the text. Captions are usually included in addition to the regular writing on the page. Sometimes they restate the same information. Sometimes they add a new fact or idea. I know you are ready to add captions to your writing!

VARIATIONS

For Less Experienced Writers: Provide a small-group experience with leveled nonfiction selections. Guide the students in using sticky notes to write captions and insert them into the pages of the book.

For More Experienced Writers: Have experienced writers review previously constructed pieces of writing and add captions to enhance their work.

LINKS TO CD-ROM:
• Visuals: Palomino Horses

Diagrams with Labels

WHEN TO USE IT: When students are ready to add nonfiction text features to their writing

FOCUS THE LEARNING

Diagrams are pictorial representations of information. Since emergent writers often convey meaning through pictures, we have a perfect opportunity to teach them how to include this text feature in their writing.

Model

STEP 1: Use a nonfiction big book or the diagram on the Resources CD-ROM to display a diagram with labels. Discuss how authors need to use factual information to create the diagram.

Possible Think-Aloud: *Today I want to show you how authors use diagrams to improve their writing. Writers create diagrams as a way to simplify the information they are writing about. Let's look at the diagram in this book. I notice that it is like a line drawing, not a picture. I also notice that there are lines or arrows linking parts of the diagram to labels. Watch as I trace my finger from the label to the portion of the diagram that the label matches. Labeled diagrams make ideas simpler and easier to understand.*

TURN &TALK *Partners, think together. How does a diagram help the reader of this book? Why do you think the author decided to include a diagram here?*

STEP 2: Display a short piece of writing. Demonstrate how you can create a diagram with labels from the information you have written.

Bees have two pairs of wings, two feelers, and six legs. Bees look like they have two eyes, but they actually have five! They have two main eyes and three tiny eyes on top of their heads.

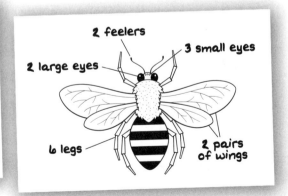

Sample Modeled Writing

Possible Think-Aloud: *I have written a paragraph about what bees look like, and I think that this might be a good place to insert a diagram. Watch me as I carefully draw a picture of a bee and then draw a line from the part of the bee to the word that tells what that part is. I'll draw lines from the wings and write the word "wings" there. Now I can do the same thing with the legs of my bee.* (Complete the diagram.)

TURN &TALK *What other information about the bee's body should be included in my diagram with labels?*

Analyze

STEP 3: Reread and reflect.

TURN &TALK *Let's reread this section and look at my diagram. Does the diagram help my reader understand more about bees? Is my diagram clear? I think my reader will really enjoy the diagram I made. And I think the paragraph and the diagram work together. Diagrams with labels and writing make good partners.*

Sum It Up

Today we learned that adding a diagram with labels can make your writing better. We saw how a published author used a diagram to teach the reader something new. As you begin work on your piece today, challenge yourself to create a diagram with labels. Who thinks they can try this today?

VARIATIONS

For Less Experienced Writers: Demonstrate how to start a section of writing with a diagram. Then, model how you can use the diagram to craft sentences.

For More Experienced Writers: Give each pair of students a different diagram. Challenge pairs to craft a paragraph based on the information in the diagram. Encourage them to share their paragraphs with the rest of the group.

LINKS TO CD-ROM:
- Diagram: Bee diagram
- Diagram: Grasshopper diagram

Bold Words

WHEN TO USE IT: When students have encountered bold words in text and are ready to try using them in their own writing

FOCUS THE LEARNING

When young writers learn how to choose important words and make them bold, it gives them a sense of power and helps them see that their writing can teach their reader.

Model

STEP 1: Select a nonfiction big book to examine how the author utilized words in bold print, or print the page from the Resources CD-ROM.

Possible Think-Aloud: *As we have been reading in our nonfiction books, we've noticed that some authors write a few words in bold. Bold words are a signal that the word is important and that we should pay close attention to it. Let's look at a section from this book. Which words did the author decide were important? Which words are in bold?*

TURN &TALK *Put your heads together and talk about why the author might have chosen these words to write in bold. Were there other words he could have chosen?*

STEP 2: Display a piece of writing. Demonstrate how you choose a few words to make into bold words.

Possible Think-Aloud: *I want to show you how to include bold words in your own writing. In this piece about rabbits, there are some words that I could make bold. The word "burrow" is an important word. I can go over the word with a black fine-tip marker, or I can go over it with my pencil to make it bold. Notice how the dark print makes the word stand out for a reader. I will make the word "herd" bold, too. My reader will know that it is an important word for sure.*

Most rabbits live in **burrows,** or holes in the ground. Hiding in a snug burrow keeps rabbits safe from most predators.

Rabbits are very social and live in groups. A group of rabbits is called a **herd.**

Sample Modeled Writing

TURN &TALK *Think about the bold words. What do the bold words help you to understand about rabbits?*

Analyze

STEP 3: Reread and reflect.

Possible Think-Aloud: *Let's look at my piece again. I am feeling really good about the bold words that I selected. These are words that are important to remember. I also notice that when I add some words in bold, my writing looks more and more like a polished, published piece of nonfiction. Think together. If you were going to teach someone about using bold words, what would you say? What would you want them to know?*

Sum It Up

Today we learned how to include words in bold in our writing. We learned that bold words alert the reader that the words are important, and we learned how to carefully choose the words that we want our reader to pay special attention to. As you begin writing today, challenge yourself to choose two or three words that are important and make those words bold. Let's get to work!

VARIATIONS

For Less Experienced Writers: Type out a short section from a published text, but do not denote which words were written in bold. Read the piece together, and challenge students to predict which word(s) the author chose to write in bold. Then, compare the predictions with the actual text.

For More Experienced Writers: Challenge writers to use the bold words they have included in their writing to create a glossary of terms for their book.

LINKS TO CD-ROM:
• Shared Text: How Does a Butterfly Begin?

Table of Contents

WHEN TO USE IT: When students have written several pages on a topic and the writing can easily be categorized into sections

FOCUS THE LEARNING

When we teach young writers to include a Table of Contents in their nonfiction texts, they learn the importance of this text feature both as a writer and as a reader.

Model

STEP 1: Display a nonfiction big book. Examine the Table of Contents, and discuss how it supports the reader.

Possible Think-Aloud: *Let's look at this big book. When I open up to the first page, I don't see a paragraph about the topic. The first thing I see is the Table of Contents. As I scroll down, I see all of the sections that the author has included in his book. Now I know that if I want to read about what bears eat, I can turn to page 8. Using the Table of Contents helps me locate information quickly.*

TURN &TALK *Think together. Have you seen a Table of Contents in other books you have read? Where have you seen them? How does the Table of Contents help you as a reader?*

STEP 2: Display a finished piece of nonfiction writing that has several pages, and demonstrate how to create a Table of Contents.

Possible Think-Aloud: *Watch me as I create a Table of Contents for my book about bats. In the first few pages, I have a section called "Bats: Hunters of the Night." That section begins on page 2, so I'll write the name of that section and then make lots of little dots that lead to the page number over here. My next few pages are all about where bats live. I'll add that section to my Table of Contents, too.* (Complete this Table of Contents.)

Table of Contents

Bats: Hunters of the Night 2

Where Bats Live 4

What Bats Eat 7

Protecting Bats 9

Sample Modeled Writing

TURN &TALK *What have you noticed about the Table of Contents so far? What are its features? What should you think about if you are going to create a Table of Contents for your writing?*

Analyze

STEP 3: Reread and reflect.

Possible Think-Aloud: *Let's look at my Table of Contents. It looks simple and organized, and I think it will help my reader find specific information in my book. Making the Table of Contents was fun. I used the headings for each section, a row of tiny dots, and page numbers.*

Sum It Up

When we are writing nonfiction texts, it's a good idea to add a Table of Contents. That way, our readers will be able to locate important information quickly. As you get to work on your nonfiction books today, challenge yourself to create your own Table of Contents.

VARIATIONS

For Less Experienced Writers: Provide partners with a copy of a nonfiction book with the Table of Contents covered. Challenge partners to create a Table of Contents based on the chapter or section headings. Uncover the actual Table of Contents and compare.

For More Experienced Writers: Build the expectation that a Table of Contents is a natural element of nonfiction writing that involves several pages. Expect writers to include a Table of Contents and a Glossary as well!

LINKS TO CD-ROM:
- Student Writing: Emergent Writing Sample
- Student Writing: Developing Writing Sample

Insert Page Numbers

WHEN TO USE IT: When students are writing multiple pages

FOCUS THE LEARNING

Once students begin crafting longer pieces, it's time to show them the text features that help readers to navigate informational text.

Model

STEP 1: Display a nonfiction big book. Draw attention to the page number on each page.

Possible Think-Aloud: *I've been noticing that many of you are writing several pages and that your books are getting longer and longer. That's fabulous! Today I want to show you one thing that writers do when they've written several pages. Take a look at this big book. The writer of this book wrote many pages, and when she was ready to publish the book, she put a page number on each page, right down here in the corner. Let's see the total number of pages that are in this book.*

TURN &TALK *Partners, why do you think this author put a page number on each page? How could that help the reader?*

STEP 2: In a pocket chart, display several pages of your own writing, placing each page on a separate piece of paper.

Have you ever seen a flying flashlight? Well, they may not be flying flashlights, but fireflies can light up the night sky the same way a flashlight can.

1

Fireflies can be found in warm environments. They love moisture and can live in humid sections of America and Asia.

2

Firefly eggs feed on worms and slugs, but adult fireflies eat nectar or pollen.

3

Sample Modeled Writing

Possible Think-Aloud: *Page numbers help a reader to locate information quickly. Today I want to show you how to add page numbers to your piece of writing. Here are several pages for my book on fireflies. This is the first page, so I'll write a little number 1 in the right-hand corner at the bottom, like this. On the next page, I'll write a number 2 in the bottom right-hand corner.* (Continue numbering pages.)

TURN &TALK *What are the benefits of putting numbers on the pages of your writing?*

Analyze

STEP 3: Reread and reflect.

Possible Think-Aloud: *Let's look at my book now. I've added a page number at the bottom of each page. My book is starting to look like the books in our book corner, isn't it? Once I have each page numbered, it helps me as I work on other parts of my book, like the Table of Contents.*

Sum It Up

Today we learned how to add page numbers to our writing. When we do that, we help our reader. And it is easy to do. As you work on your own books today, take some time to add page numbers. It will really improve the look of your nonfiction book. Let's get to work!

VARIATIONS

For Less Experienced Writers: Emergent writers feel a real sense of pride when they have a lot of writing. Support them as they organize for writing by planning each page of text before they begin writing.

For More Experienced Writers: Demonstrate how to create an index, with page numbers listed. Challenge them to create an index for their own books.

Chart/Table/Graph

WHEN TO USE IT: When writing includes information that can be represented using a chart, a table, or a graph

FOCUS THE LEARNING

There are times when words don't provide information as well as a well-placed graphic. As nonfiction authors, students need to learn how to include visually appealing and appropriate charts and tables in their writing.

Model

Before the lesson, create a chart such as the one on the Resources CD, and poll your students about their favorite pets.

STEP 1: Using a nonfiction big book or the charts on the Resources CD-ROM, demonstrate how the author used a chart or table.

Possible Think-Aloud: *I have created a graph on this chart paper and labeled it "Favorite Pets." This will give us a visual way to compare which pets are the favorites for our classroom. Notice I have written numbers going up the left side. Now watch as I write different kinds of pets across the bottom. I will write "Cats," "Dogs," "Fish," and "Birds." We learned that six people like cats best, so watch as I count up to six in the column above "Cats" and quickly color the column in. That is the first bar in our bar graph.*

TURN &TALK *I am getting ready to color in the column in the bar graph for dogs. Do you think this column will be shorter or taller than the column for cats? Why?*

STEP 2: Model adding columns to the graph.

Possible Think-Aloud: *Watch as I add the second column to my bar graph. We learned that nine people like dogs best, so count with me as I count up to nine on the left and then shade in the column for dogs. Notice that I am making the dogs column a different style because that helps me to compare. (Continue creating the bar graph.)*

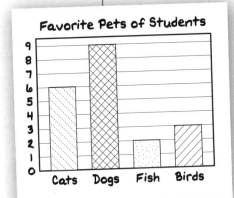

Favorite Pets of Students

Sample Modeled Writing

**TURN
&TALK** *Look at the bar graph we are creating, and summarize the information using words.*

Analyze

STEP 3: Reread and reflect.

Possible Think-Aloud: *Bar graphs such as this one make it easy to compare information. These are helpful tools to use in nonfiction writing. Watch as I create sentences to go with our bar graph. The students of Mrs. Hoyt's class have been polled, and it was discovered that nine people think that dogs are their favorite pet.*

Sum It Up

Today we learned how to add a bar graph to our writing. I think you'll have a lot of fun creating your own. Today, as you go back to your own piece of writing, think about how you can add a chart or a table to boost your writing. Let's begin!

VARIATIONS

For Less Experienced Writers: Provide additional examples of bar graphs by asking students to take off one shoe and then sorting the shoes using a variety of attributes (shoes that tie, shoes that use Velcro, tennis shoes, dress shoes, and so on). Once students have lined up the shoes, encourage them to record the information using a bar graph.

For More Experienced Writers: Demonstrate how to create a variety of graphs and charts, including pie graphs, Venn diagrams, and line graphs. Challenge writers to experiment with several different types.

LINKS TO CD-ROM:
• Student Writing: Animal Movement Chart

Bullets

WHEN TO USE IT: When writing includes lists

FOCUS THE LEARNING

Bullet points are helpful text features because they get the attention of the reader and they break up the text. Emergent writers love them because they are easy to read and easy to write.

Model

STEP 1: Demonstrate how to create a bulleted list.

Possible Think-Aloud: *Today I want to show you how to include bullets when making lists. I have started a piece about learning to ski. I'm going to tell my reader what equipment he or she will need. I could make one long sentence, but instead I'm going to use something called bullets. One thing you'll need is skis! I'll make a little mark that looks like a tiny meatball or a giant period. Then, I leave a space and write "skis." Notice that the bullet doesn't sit on the line; it is up a bit higher. The next item on my list is boots. I will insert a bullet and then the word boots.*

TURN &TALK *Partners, think together. What do you think of my bullets? Why do you think they make a list easier to read?*

STEP 2: Continue creating a bulleted list.

Possible Think-Aloud: *The next item on my list is bindings. Those are the clamps that hold your boots to the skis. Watch as I make my bullet, leave a space, and write the word "bindings." Think together: What else might we need if we are going to go skiing? I'll add those items next. Each time I add an item, I'll make a bullet and leave a space.*

Learning to ski is easier than you might think! But first, you'll need to gather the right equipment.

What you need:
- skis
- boots
- bindings
- poles
- warm clothes
- helmet
- patience!

Sample Modeled Writing

Analyze

STEP 3: Reread and reflect.

Possible Think-Aloud: *Let's read my writing so far. What do you think? Did I use a bullet with each item on the list? I like using bullets because it breaks up my writing, and it gets the attention of the reader. It's an easy way to include information in a list.*

Sum It Up

Today we learned how to include bullets in our writing. As you begin writing today, see if you can include some bullets in your piece. Remember to make the bullet mark, leave a space, and then write your word or words. Let's begin!

VARIATIONS

For Less Experienced Writers: Provide the group with several nonfiction texts. Encourage them to go on a "bullet scavenger hunt." Share examples with the group, and discuss what the author did when using bullets.

For More Experienced Writers: Demonstrate how to use bullets not only for items in a list but for broader ideas.

Word Choice

Seeking Precision and Excitement in Word Selection

Word choice is about the richness and precision that can be infused into communication. Word selection isn't a function of correctness but rather one of clarification and expansion of thinking. Carefully orchestrated word choice is the gateway to writing that features beautiful language and exquisite details.

LESSON	K	1	2	RELATED LESSONS
1 Use Descriptive Words and Phrases	●	●	●	*Revising:* Lesson 1, Revising to Add Details *Ideas:* Lesson 4, Infuse Interesting Details
2 Target Powerful Action Verbs	●	●	●	*Ideas:* Lesson 5, Add a Little Action
3 Select Words that Show Order or Sequence	●	●	●	
4 Use Words and Phrases to Focus on Location or Place	●	●	●	*Ideas:* Lesson 6, Make the Setting Stand Out
5 Beginning Sentences with *-ing* Words		●	●	
6 Add Action: Group *-ing* Words Together			●	
7 Use Onomatopoeia	●	●	●	*Sentence Fluency:* Lesson 2, Reading Aloud to Check Sentence Fluency
8 Compound Descriptors and Hyphens			●	
9 Have Fun with Alliteration	●	●	●	*Text Features:* Lesson 1, Choose a Title that Is Interesting
10 Transition Words to Add Information or Conclude			●	

Other Lessons to Create

You might also want to teach writers how to

- infuse figurative language into their writing,
- monitor their use of homophones and other tricky words, or
- use adverbs as sentence openers.

Use Descriptive Words and Phrases

WHEN TO USE IT: To improve descriptions in nonfiction writing

FOCUS THE LEARNING

Without rich descriptors, nonfiction writing can become flat, lifeless, and unappealing to a reader. It is important that young writers understand that their writing must bring a subject to life through descriptive words and phrases.

Model

STEP 1: Model describing a subject with rich details and precise word choice.

Possible Think-Aloud: *I am looking at this picture of a snake's tongue, and I want to describe it. I could say, "The snake has a long tongue." That is okay, but when I look at the picture, I realize that if I add words and phrases that describe the tongue, it would help my reader get a clear picture of the snake's tongue. Listen to this description of the tongue, and try to get a picture in your mind. The snake's tongue is shaped like a fork! It is longer than the snake's head and is shiny and wet.*

TURN &TALK *Consider my two descriptions: (1) The snake has a long tongue. (2) The snake's tongue is shaped like . . . Decide which description is better. Which one helps you get a clear picture in your mind? Why are great descriptions important in nonfiction writing?*

STEP 2: Model writing and emphasize clear descriptors.

The snake's tongue is shaped like a fork! It is longer than the snake's head and is shiny and wet. As it darts in and out of the snake's mouth, the tongue picks up smells and acts like a nose, helping the snake to know when food is near.

Sample Modeled Writing

Possible Think-Aloud: *I want to focus on the words and phrases I am selecting for my writing. Watch as I write the phrase "shaped like a fork!" That phrase really describes the end of the snake's tongue. I also want to add the phrase "shiny and wet." That tells me that the tongue isn't dry. Notice that a phrase is a group of words that describes. Now I need to choose a word that tells <u>how</u> the snake's tongue flicks in and out of his mouth, gathering smells for the snake. "Flicks" is a pretty good word. I also like "darts." If I write that the tongue "darts," my reader will know it is moving really fast.*

TURN &TALK *There are so many great words that would help us think about the snake's tongue and how it moves. I could say it zips, zooms, flashes, flicks, or darts. Move your tongue really fast like a snake, and think about words to describe the tongue. Think together, and identify the "best" describing word.*

Analyze

STEP 3: Reread and reflect.

Possible Think-Aloud: *Let's reread my writing and analyze this description. I need to be sure that the words and phrases I have selected give us a clear picture of the snake's tongue. As we reread, be thinking about my words and phrases. You may have an idea to help make this even better!*

Sum It Up

Nonfiction writers need to make careful choices so their words and phrases describe, giving a reader as much information as possible. One of the things we need to do is challenge ourselves to consider different words and then pick the ones that provide the best descriptions. As you begin writing today, reread a bit of what you have already written, and check your descriptions. Are you satisfied with the words and phrases you have chosen, or could you challenge yourself to do even better?

VARIATIONS

For Less Experienced Writers: Provide hands-on experience with real things, and have them practice generating describing words and phrases. You might consider using a classroom pet, real fruits and vegetables, or a real plant. As the students consider descriptive words and phrases, record their thinking on a chart so they have a rich cache of words and phrases to support their writing.

For More Experienced Writers: Have students read their writing to a partner without showing any photographs or illustrations. Then, have the partner create an illustration based ONLY on the writing—no additions from prior knowledge. Have the partners think together and evaluate the descriptive words and phrases to see if revisions might add strength.

LINKS TO CD-ROM:
• Visual: Snake's Tongue

Target Powerful Action Verbs

WHEN TO USE IT: To improve precision in description

FOCUS THE LEARNING

Young writers need to learn that verbs are the engines of sentences. Carefully chosen verbs make descriptions sparkle and enhance reader comprehension.

Model

STEP 1: Engage students in dramatizing various verbs, and then use each verb in a descriptive sentence.

Possible Think-Aloud: *Verbs are the engines of sentences. They bring action and help make descriptions come to life, so it is important to pick great verbs for our writing. I have written four great verbs on a chart. Let's start with "walk." Please walk to your desk. Now tiptoe back to the rug. Let's try "rocket." Alina, could you show us how to safely rocket to the sink?*

TURN & TALK *When you compare "tiptoe" and "rocket" to "walk," which ones are more precise? Which one gives us more specific information? Look at the other verbs on my chart, and identify the ones that you think are precise and helpful.*

STEP 2: Model writing as you think aloud about action verbs.

Possible Think-Aloud: *I am ready to put our thinking about verbs into action and write about a caterpillar. We know that caterpillars come out of their shells feeling really hungry. They start eating*

| walk | tiptoe | rocket | eat | munch | snack |
| scurry | scamper | leap | nibble | gobble | chomp |

The caterpillar begins to _____ the minute it hatches from its egg. It is ready to _____ on everything from leaves to sprouts or celery!

Sample Modeled Writing

and never stop. They don't even sleep. On the chart, I have a few words that describe how a caterpillar eats: eat, nibble, munch, gobble, snack, and chomp. Listen as I read the sentence and try each of these verbs in the blank. As I insert each verb, I need to keep visualizing the caterpillar and thinking about the verb that best describes.

TURN &TALK *It is time to vote! With your partner, dramatize these ways to eat, and get ready to vote on the best verb.*

Analyze

STEP 3: Reread and reflect.

Possible Think-Aloud: *You are cooking! I love the verb you selected, and I can really picture that caterpillar gobbling his way through the leaves. Let's try another sentence. Which verb would be the best choice for the sentence, "It is ready to . . ." Put your heads together, and choose a powerful action verb!*

Sum It Up

Remember that verbs are the engines of sentences. Nonfiction writers need to think of lots of options and include verbs that are powerful and show exactly the kind of action they want to describe. As you get ready to write today, think about verbs. Choose powerful action verbs that will make your writing sparkle.

VARIATIONS

For Less Experienced Writers: Assist writers in developing a classroom resource of terrific verbs that could be posted in the room to stimulate great verb choice. They could gather verbs from their own writing or from resources they are reading. Once the chart is posted, it can fuel powerful sentences for even your most emergent writers.

For More Experienced Writers: Teach more experienced writers to analyze their verb choices. Show them how to go back to their writing and check out the verbs. Help them identify passive verbs that show no action and replace them with powerful action-oriented selections.

LINKS TO CD-ROM:
• Teacher Tool: Powerful Verbs, Powerful Writing list

Select Words that Show Order or Sequence

WHEN TO USE IT: To emphasize sequence or order

FOCUS THE LEARNING

Transition words such as first, second, before, during, after, as soon as, while, and so on highlight sequence and set the stage for shifts in action. Conscious infusion of transition words into nonfiction writing produces smoother-sounding language and a clear sense of sequence for a reader.

Model

STEP 1: Create a chart with transition words that show order or sequence, and read it with the students. A sample chart can be found on the Resources CD. Use words from the chart to explain a familiar process such as lining up.

Possible Think-Aloud: *Transition words show the order in which things happen and alert a listener or a reader to a sequence of events. The chart I have posted lists sequence words that we use all the time when we talk. We need to challenge ourselves to use these helpful words in our writing, too.*

Think about getting ready for lunch. Picture the steps we follow for a moment. I am going to use words from the chart and point to them each time I use one. First, we wash our hands. Next, we gather our tickets and lunches. Then, we line up and go to the cafeteria. As soon as we get to our table, we get to sit down and eat!

TURN &TALK *Think together. If you were going to tell about getting ready to go home, what would you say? Use as many of our transition words as you can.*

STEP 2: Create a piece of modeled writing, and infuse it with transition words to show passage of time.

Making Soup

First, open the can, and pour the soup into a pan. Next, pour in water or milk and stir. Then, turn on the stove, and wait until the soup is hot. Finally, you get to eat!

Sample Modeled Writing

Possible Think-Aloud: *I am going to write about making soup. "First, open the can and pour the soup into a pan." Notice that I started with the word, "first." My next step will be adding milk or water. As I look at the transition words, I realize that I could use "second", "next", or even "then." I am going to use "next" because I like the way it sounds. I have used "first" and "next" so far. Those are helpful words to show order.*

TURN &TALK *I will be writing about heating the soup. I don't want to use the same transition words that I already used, so I need to select a new one for my next sentence. Look at the chart and think together. Select a word that I could use to start the sentence about heating the soup.*

Analyze

STEP 3: Reread and reflect.

Possible Think-Aloud: *We need to write one more sentence to tell that it is time to eat the soup. When I look at the transition words that show time-order, like now, soon, and once, I realize they are the right ones to choose from. I will use the word "finally" to begin my last sentence. "Finally, you get . . ." This makes it clear that this is the last step.*

Sum It Up

Writers use transition words to show order or sequence. These are important words that help a reader understand written directions, the life cycle of a butterfly, or a piece of writing about events during a school day. I will post this chart in a visible place, so you can find and use transition words that show order in your writing.

VARIATIONS

For Less Experienced Writers: Offer a chart with just ordinal numbers such as first, second, and third. Guide writers in using these words to retell more familiar events in school. Then, adjust the transition words to words of sequence such as first, then, next, and finally. Retell the same events with different transition words.

For More Experienced Writers: Stretch these writers by introducing them to a chart of words that establish time order. Model using time-order transition words so they can see how they add smoothness and flow to writing. An example: *At the first light of dawn, a hungry eagle circles overhead. Meanwhile, an unsuspecting mouse nudges the leaves from the top of his burrow and scuttles across a bare spot in the grass.*

LINKS TO CD-ROM:
- Chart: Words that Show Order or Sequence

Use Words and Phrases to Focus on Location or Place

WHEN TO USE IT: To help writers broaden the range of words they use to identify location of their subject

FOCUS THE LEARNING

Words that show location or place (above, across, against, below, by, high above, nearby, next to, to the right of, on top of, under, through, and so on) are helpful writing tools when developing specific descriptions. Young writers benefit from a clearly posted list of precise words for location so they can slip them into their writing, clarifying and adding specificity to their work.

Model

STEP 1: Orally describe the location of items in the classroom or in the school, placing emphasis on words that show place.

Possible Think-Aloud: *Today we are going to focus on words that show place or location.* (Display a chart of words that show location.) *For example, "Alicia could you please get the book that is sitting under the science display, next to the magnifying glasses?" Did you notice I used "under" and "next to"? These specific words helped Alicia to understand where to look for the book. My word choices helped to make my meaning clear. I am looking at the chart to select more words that show precise location. Listen carefully. "Miguel, could you please get the pencil that is beside my desk lamp and on top of the stack of papers?"* (Identify another object that a student can locate using your specific directions.)

TURN &TALK *You will each have a turn to ask your partner to go and get something, but you need to use specific location words that tell "where" the item is located. Look at the chart and think. What item are you going to request? Where is it located? Which transition words will you use? Partner B, you are first. Think for a minute, and then give your partner a thumbs up when you are ready to use specific words to describe a location.*

Nested safely <u>on</u> his father's feet, a tiny penguin peeks <u>through</u> his father's warm fur. The frozen ice field is just inches <u>below</u> the tiny chick, but the little bird stays warm and dry in his hiding place.

Sample Modeled Writing

STEP 2: Create a modeled writing example that utilizes transition words to show place or location.

Possible Think-Aloud: *Writers of nonfiction need to use specific words that show place. Specific words that tell location help a reader understand the information much more clearly. I really enjoyed reading about how father penguins care for their newly hatched chicks. I want to tell about the baby penguin being on his father's feet so it doesn't freeze on the ice. I am visualizing the baby penguin ON his father's feet and peeking out THROUGH his dad's warm coat. "On" and "through" are perfect choices for transition words. Watch as I include those in my first sentence.*

TURN &TALK *Are there any other words on my chart that would make it clear exactly where the baby penguin is standing?*

Analyze

STEP 3: Reread and reflect.

Possible Think-Aloud: *I think it would be helpful to explain that the baby is not on the ice. The ice is below his father's feet. The word "below" will be good to use in my next sentence. Watch as I write, "The frozen ice field is . . ."* (Read the passage out loud.) *Analyze the words I used to show the location of the baby penguin. Determine if I chose the best words from the chart or if there are other words that might help my writing.*

Sum It Up

Words that show location or place are important in nonfiction writing. Nonfiction writers need to work hard to ensure that their readers have a very clear picture in their mind of the location of the subject. We need to select words that are precise and very clear so our writing tells a reader exactly WHERE things are at.

VARIATIONS

For Less Experienced Writers: Use real objects that you can stack or line up. Then, have students generate sentences using location words from the chart. With real objects from the classroom, students might generate sentences, such as *The yellow marker is below the book. Ira's coat is to the left of Adam's backpack. The pocket chart hangs in front of the easel.*

For More Experienced Writers: Have writers take time to visualize and verbally describe the setting in which their subject is placed. Encourage them to use location words from the chart as sentence openers, such as *High above the treetops, the geese fly in perfect formation. Under the muddy surface, earthworms tunnel and continue their important work.*

Beginning Sentences with *-ing* Words

WHEN TO USE IT: To help writers understand that an *-ing* word can make a great sentence beginning

FOCUS THE LEARNING

Young writers write with more conviction when they start out with actions. The *-ing* words are perfect helpers to get them started. When we teach writers to turn verbs into *-ing* words, writing suddenly becomes rich in action and imagery.

Model

STEP 1: Create a list of verbs, and then turn them into *-ing* words.

Possible Think-Aloud: *I love earthworms.* (Write verbs on the left side of a T-chart as you name them.) *They can twist, turn, wiggle, chew, and so much more. They can stretch, dig, slither, hide, and even burrow. Look at all of the verbs I can write when I am describing an earthworm. Watch as I do something that is even more fun. On the right side of the chart, I am going to turn my verbs into* -ing *words. My first verb is twist. Watch as I write "twisting" in the second column. Let's look at the next words, turn and wiggle. Those can become "turning and wiggling."*

TURN &TALK *Think together about earthworms. What are some more things they can do? After you get your ideas ready, we will add your verbs to my chart, and then have fun turning them into* -ing *words.*

STEP 2: Utilize *-ing* words from the chart in sentences.

Possible Think-Aloud: *Today I am going to show you something new. I am going to begin my sentence with an* -ing *word. Watch as I write "Burrowing" and then a comma before I begin my sentence. Notice that this shifts the word "earthworm" to the middle of the sentence. Isn't that cool? When we start with an* -ing *word, we get to save the subject for the middle of the sentence. This is like eating an Oreo cookie. The best part is the middle!*

> Burrowing, the earthworm carves out tunnels that add air and help things grow. Chewing, he leaves castings that help things to grow.

Sample Modeled Writing

TURN & TALK *Analyze my sentence, and share your opinion about starting with an -ing word.*

Analyze

STEP 3: Reread and reflect.

Possible Think-Aloud: *Let's do another one. My next sentence is about the way that earthworms eat dead plants and then push castings out of their body to make the soil richer. I will use another* -ing *word, "chewing," to begin. Watch as I write "Chewing" and add a comma. Once I put in the comma, I am ready for the rest of the sentence. Now it's your turn. Think together and select another* -ing *word to begin sentence three.*

Sum It Up

Nonfiction writers can help their readers to focus on actions by starting sentences with *-ing* words. In this kind of sentence, we need to be ready to use a comma in the middle. Isn't this a great way to liven up our sentences and show readers that action is terrific in nonfiction writing?

VARIATIONS

For Less Experienced Writers: Prepare sentence strips with sentences such as: The worm digs tunnels. The worm comes to the surface to get air on a rainy day. Then, work with writers to experiment with adding an *-ing* word and a comma to the beginning of each sentence. The result may be something like: Twisting, the worm comes to the surface to get air on a rainy day. Wiggling, the worm digs tunnels.

For More Experienced Writers: Experiment with the effect of adding *-ing* words in the middle of sentences with structures such as: The worm, twisting and turning, plows his way through the soil. His bristles, grabbing and holding, anchor him to the ground when hungry birds think he is their dinner.

LINKS TO CD-ROM:
• Student Writing: Red-Eyed Tree Frog

Add Action: Group -*ing* Words Together

WHEN TO USE IT: To add sentence complexity and rich description

Seymour Simon, the highly esteemed author of more than 250 nonfiction books, says that -*ing* words and comparisons are the two top tools for nonfiction writing. When we teach young writers to cluster -*ing* words together, they can add action and rich sentence structures from the beginning.

Model

STEP 1: Model clustering -*ing* words together, inserting commas in the series.

Possible Think-Aloud: *In looking at this book on tornadoes, I am reminded of the amazing power of these storms. Watch as I make a list of* -ing *words that describe what a tornado can do. I want to include twisting, exploding, turning, howling, smashing, flattening, roaring, lifting, blasting, and destroying. These* -ing *words help me to visualize the action that occurs when a tornado comes roaring into life. Now watch as I write a sentence that clusters some of these words together. (Present sentences in a pocket chart so they can easily be manipulated.) "Twisting and howling, the tornado roared across the field." Notice that I used two* -ing *words to begin the sentence. Then, I placed a comma. I could have just said, "The tornado roared." But the* -ing *words show a lot more action. My sentence is in the pocket chart, but we are about to watch it change.*

TURN &TALK *Think together. Let's keep the base sentence, "The tornado roared across the field." You need to think of a new opening. Which* -ing *words would you select to begin this sentence? Pick two or three that help you visualize action. It will be fun to see how many combinations we can create!*

STEP 2: Add an additional sentence that clusters -*ing* words at the end of the sentence.

Possible Think-Aloud: *I am going to show you another great way that we can focus on action using* -ing *words. We can shift the* -ing *words to the end of the sentence. Our base sentence is "The tornado roared across the field." We added* -ing *words to the* beginning of the sentence to show action. Now let's shift the cluster of -ing words to the end of the sentence. "The tornado roared . . ." Isn't that great! What a terrific way to add interest and action to sentences.

> Twisting and howling, the tornado roared across the field.
>
> The tornado roared across the field, twisting and howling.
>
> The tornado, twisting and howling, roared across the field!

Sample Modeled Writing

TURN & TALK *It's your turn again. Select a cluster of -ing words to add action to the end of the sentence. Try some words that are different from mine, and think about the action.*

Analyze

STEP 3: Reread and reflect.

Possible Think-Aloud: *There is one more way that I can arrange this sentence to focus on action. Watch as I move the cluster of -ing words to the middle of the sentence. "The tornado, twisting and howling, roared across the field." Notice that I inserted the -ing words right after "tornado," the subject of the sentence. I used a comma before and after the cluster of -ing words. Put your heads together. Select some new -ing words to place in a cluster in the middle of my last sentence.*

Sum It Up

When we cluster *-ing* words together, it emphasizes action and helps our reader to visualize. These clusters can appear at the beginning, in the middle, or at the end of a sentence. It is important to notice that if you remove the cluster of *-ing* words, it is still a complete sentence.

VARIATIONS

For Less Experienced Writers: Revisit *Word Choice:* Lesson 6, and scaffold with more basic applications of *-ing* words.

For More Experienced Writers: Challenge writers to design sentences that use *-ing* words in clusters of three. (See examples on the Resources CD-ROM.)

LINKS TO CD-ROM:
• Student Writing: three examples

Use Onomatopoeia

WHEN TO USE IT: To add focused attention on sounds related to the subject and/or the setting

FOCUS THE LEARNING

When writers insert onomatopoeia, words that sound like the real sounds in life, writing sparkles with auditory images. Onomatopoeia is fun for young writers. Its use makes them feel like experts, and they love the lively language play that is always part of the auditory imaging.

Model

STEP 1: Direct attention to sounds in the environment, and show that you can put words together that sound like the real event.

Possible Think-Aloud: *Have you ever listened to a faucet drip? I can write those sounds. Watch . . . Drip, drop, drip, drop. That sounds just like a faucet dripping or even big fat raindrops. Think about the sound of a ball bouncing down a flight of stairs, "bump, bump, bump." I can write that, too. How about the sound of a big fly or a bumblebee? A doorbell makes noise, too. Ding-dong!*

TURN & TALK *Make the sound of a bee, and think about the letters you would need to write that word. How about the sound of a lamb or a baby chick? How would you write words that make those sounds?*

STEP 2: Model how to write using words that sound like what they mean.

Possible Think-Aloud: *Isn't this fun? We are writing words that are just like sounds in the real world. As a nonfiction writer, I can use this a lot. I want to use what I know about words that make sounds and write a poem about a big bulldozer. Bulldozers have big engines and they go rummm, rummm. They also creak and squeak. When the big arms move, they go crink, crink, crink. Watch as I write all these sounds. This will make a great poem!*

Drip, drop, drip, drop
Bump, bump, bump
Ding-dong
Buzzzz, buzzzz
Baa
Peep! Peep!

Sample Modeled Writing

TURN &TALK *What other sounds might I include in a poem about the sounds that a bulldozer can make?*

> Rummm, rummm
> Creak, squeak
> Crink, crink, crink
> Errr-eeek
> Scrape
> Thud

Sample Modeled Writing

Analyze

STEP 3: Reread and reflect.

Possible Think-Aloud: *Let's keep going. This bulldozer poem is going to be a lot of fun to read. I am thinking I want to add, "swoosh, scrape, thud." What do you think of those sound words? Do they sound like a bulldozer?*

Sum It Up

When nonfiction writers include words that sound like sounds in the real world, their writing captures the interest of their reader. Sound words tell a reader exactly what things sound like. In your writing, think of places where you could slip in a sound word or two and make your writing really exciting!

> Pop! Pop! Poppety! The popcorne is almoste rede.

Sample Modeled Writing

VARIATIONS

For Less Experienced Writers: Provide books on animals at a level that is easily accessible for these writers. Guide them in using sticky notes to insert onomatopoeia words on the photographs.

For More Experienced Writers: Show them how an onomatopoeia word slipped into a piece of narrative writing can add interest and sentence fluency. (An example appears at the bottom of the page.)

LINKS TO CD-ROM:
• Visuals: Frog Call!

Compound Descriptors and Hyphens

WHEN TO USE IT: To increase precision and add variety to descriptors

FOCUS THE LEARNING

When descriptors are linked by a hyphen and used to modify a noun, the result is richly textured internal punctuation and increased precision in descriptions. Compound descriptors might include structures such as: freckle-faced, fast-flying, wide-eyed, thin-skinned, and so on.

Model

STEP 1: Generate a list of compounds with hyphens to describe yourself.

Possible Think-Aloud: *I love hyphens. They are little dashes that I can place between words when I want to describe something in a way that is unique or very precise. Watch as I create some compounds to describe myself. I love to read, so I will create a compound that says "book-reading." Notice I use a hyphen, and the second word has an -ing ending—"read<u>ing</u>." When we create descriptive compounds, they need to end in -ing or -ed. I have brown hair, so I can write "brown-haired." Notice that I used a hyphen between the words again. That is important. See the -ed in brown-hair<u>ed</u>? Remember the second word must end in either -ing or -ed.*

TURN &TALK *I am ready for your help. Look at Michelle's eyes. They are blue, so I can say Michelle is "blue-eyed." Now look at my eyes. See if you can use two words to describe my eyes. Remember the second word needs to end with -ing or -ed. Compounds can help us be very precise in the way we describe things.*

Mrs. Hoyt is a
Book-reading
Brown-haired
Speckly-eyed
Teacher

Sharks are meat-eating,
fast-swimming, sharp-toothed
predators!

Sample Modeled Writing

STEP 2: Model how to insert a hyphen.

Possible Think-Aloud: *I loved the compound "speckly-eyed." That is so precise! My eyes are full of lots of different colors, and "speckly-eyed" really explains what they are like. Let's think about sharks. We can use compounds with a hyphen to show what we know about sharks. Watch as I write meat-eating. Notice the hyphen and the -ing ending on the second word. Meat-eating is a very precise descriptor for sharks, isn't it? We know they only eat meat.*

TURN &TALK *Think together. Use your whiteboards, and create another compound descriptor we could use to write about sharks.*

Analyze

STEP 3: Reread and reflect.

Possible Think-Aloud: *Watch as I use more compounds and hyphens to write some great descriptions of sharks. "Sharks are meat-eating, fast-swimming, sharp-toothed predators!" Wow! Compound descriptors provide precise information. That is important in nonfiction writing. Evaluate my compound descriptors. Think together and check each one to be sure that I included a hyphen. Then, check my endings. The second word needs to end in -ing or -ed.*

Sum It Up

As nonfiction writers, we need to describe our subjects very precisely. We need to give our reader information that is so clear that it is easy to form a mental picture. Compound descriptors with a hyphen are helpful tools that can make our nonfiction writing really terrific. Remember, to create a compound descriptor, we need to use two words that describe something, link them with a hyphen, and make sure the second word ends in *-ing* or *-ed*.

VARIATIONS

For Less Experienced Writers: Provide additional practice in a small-group setting. Build compound descriptors about familiar subjects. Students benefit from writing compound descriptor poems about each other following the first example in the modeled writing.

For More Experienced Writers: Stretch more experienced writers by challenging them to analyze previously completed pieces of their writing and insert compound descriptors.

LINKS TO CD-ROM:
• Teacher Tool:
  Compound Descriptors

Have Fun with Alliteration

WHEN TO USE IT: To jazz up titles or add lively language to descriptions

FOCUS THE LEARNING

Alliteration is a literary device often used in fiction, but it can have a presence in nonfiction writing as well. In alliteration, an author deliberately selects words that begin with the same sound. This calls attention to words and can give a lyrical sound to the language.

Model

STEP 1: Demonstrate alliteration.

Possible Think-Aloud: (Display a copy of *Some Smug Slug* by Pamela Duncan Edwards.)

TURN &TALK *I brought a book that uses a great writing technique called alliteration. That means that the author deliberately chose words that start with the same sounds and put them together in the title or in the writing inside the book. The title of this book is* Some Smug Slug. *Notice all of the /s/ sounds? Each word starts with the same letter. I am going to read a bit and look for more alliteration.* (After reading to page 7) *I am going to write down some of the great alliteration that I noticed. I saw slowly, slug, stringing, sparkling, silk. This author really likes the letter "s." Look at all of this alliteration.*

STEP 2: Model writing titles that use alliteration.

Possible Think-Aloud: *Alliteration can add a lot to titles, giving them a nice rhythm and flow. For example, if I were to create a title for a nonfiction writing selection on ants, I could write: "Awesome Ants." Both words start with "a," so this uses alliteration. What would you think of, "Adventurous Ants"? That uses alliteration, too. For writing on poisonous dart frogs, I could create a title like "Freaky Frogs." Watch as I write this, and notice the alliteration. I am thinking of more words to describe poisonous frogs, and I am wondering about "Frightening Frogs." What do you think of that?*

TURN &TALK *Put your heads together, and think about a title that uses alliteration for tornado. Select words you could put with tornado that would create alliteration.*

Analyze

STEP 3: Reread and reflect.

Possible Think-Aloud: *It is important to notice that alliteration doesn't require that every word start with the same letter. It is okay to include other words as long as the words that begin with the same letter are pretty close together. Watch as I write, "The Docile Dolphin," "Swimming with the Sharks," "Stumbling on a Stonefish," "Wild Winds of Winter." These titles all use alliteration, but they also have some words that do not begin with the same sound. Don't you love the way these titles sound?*

Awesome Ants
Adventurous Ants
Freaky Frogs
Frightening Frogs
Terrifying Tornadoes
Twirling Tornadoes
The Docile Dolphin
The Dance of the Dolphin
Dangers to Dolphins
Swimming with the Sharks
Stumbling on a Stonefish
Wild Winds of Winter

Sample Modeled Writing

Sum It Up

Alliteration occurs when a writer deliberately selects words that begin with the same letter of the alphabet and then uses those words closely together in a title or in a sentence. This is a literary device that can make your writing flow smoothly and seem very adult.

VARIATIONS

For Less Experienced Writers: Guide less experienced writers in writing phrases that use alliteration about familiar topics such as bouncing balls, perfect pizza, long lines, pointy pencils, and big brown bears, and so on. Once they catch on to these kinds of phrases, shift to conferencing, and assist them in adding alliteration to the body of their writing.

For More Experienced Writers: Encourage word play during drafting by having these students keep scratch paper next to their writing folder so they can play with alliterative phrases before committing them to their nonfiction writing selections.

Transition Words to Add Information or Conclude

WHEN TO USE IT: To add information, provide an example, or conclude a piece of writing

FOCUS THE LEARNING

When nonfiction writers learn to infuse transition words into their writing, the writing takes on a strong sense of internal organization and connectivity. Transition words signal readers that information is about to be added, an example is about to be showcased, or a conclusion or summary is the next step to expect in the writing. This lesson focuses on transition words to add information or provide a specific example. A more extensive listing of transition words used for other purposes can be found on the Resources CD-ROM.

Model

Post a chart of transition words and phrases from the Resources CD-ROM.

STEP 1: Model using transition words to add information.

Possible Think-Aloud: *I am writing about why nocturnal animals, those that see well at night, are able to do so. To make my writing sound smooth and connected, I am going to focus on inserting transition words that help my sentences link together. This chart of transition words is a helpful tool that I can use for ideas. I have already written the first sentence, "Nocturnal animals love . . ." Before I insert the next sentence, I want to select transition words that will link the next sentence together with the first one. Since I am going to talk about the size of their eyes, I could say, "for example." I could try the word "specifically." But I am going to choose "for instance." That will signal my reader that this is an example of why nocturnal animals see well at night.*

TURN &TALK *Try sentence two with "specifically" and "for example." Compare the transitions and select the one that you think sounds better.*

STEP 2: Demonstrate inserting additional transition words.

Possible Think-Aloud: *Transition words make my writing sound like the books in the library. I am ready to select one for sentence three. As I look at the chart, I am thinking that I could use "in addition" or "in fact." I like "in addition." Watch as I begin my sentence with that transition phrase and then write "nocturnal animals have . . ."*

Nocturnal animals love the dark because they can see very well. <u>For instance</u>, their eyes are especially large, and this extra size helps them to reflect even small amounts of light. <u>In addition</u>, nocturnal animals have a thick layer of material in their eyes that reflects light back into the eyes, making it easier to see. <u>Specifically</u>, this ability to reflect light is why you can often see the eyes of a cat or a deer in the dark.

Sample Modeled Writing

TURN &TALK *Sentence four is my conclusion—the end. I need transition words that signal that an example is coming next. Look at the chart. Which transitions might be the best choice for a sentence that gives an example of why they see so well at night?*

Analyze

STEP 3: Reread and reflect.

Possible Think-Aloud: *Time to reread and think about the transitions. I used three transitions in four sentences. That might be too much, or it might be perfect. As we reread, analyze my choices. I want this writing to have transitions that really make the sentences feel connected.*

Sum It Up

To improve your nonfiction writing, you need to be sure that your ideas stick together and that sentences flow nicely into one another. Transition words and phrases are helpful tools that make your writing feel connected and very adult. As you write today, consider opportunities to insert transitions into your work. I will hang this chart in a visible place so you can use it to support your thinking about transitions for your sentences.

VARIATIONS

For Less Experienced Writers: Provide a short list of simple transitions such as in addition, because, also, and finally. Support writers as they insert these transitions into sentences within an existing piece of writing.

For More Experienced Writers: Consider requiring the use of transition words before an ending or concluding statement. As writers gain experience, it is important that their nonfiction writing have a clear and satisfying conclusion that signals the reader to prepare for the end.

LINKS TO CD-ROM:
- Teacher Tool: Transition Words and Phrases list

Sentence Fluency

Creating Sentences that Flow Smoothly

Sentence fluency is best tested with the ear. Pieces that have sentence fluency are easy to read aloud, with a rhythm and flow that draw us along. To achieve sentence fluency, writers must weave a tapestry of sentences that are of varying lengths and styles while offering variety in sentence beginnings. Interesting sentence structures can significantly enhance sentence fluency.

LESSON	K	1	2	RELATED LESSONS
1 Sentences Are of Varying Lengths	●	●	●	*Sentence Structure:* Lesson 1, Two-Word Sentences *Word Choice:* Lesson 5, Beginning Sentences with *-ing* Words
2 Reading Aloud to Check Sentence Fluency	●	●	●	*Word Choice:* Lesson 7, Use Onomatopoeia
3 Varied Sentence Beginnings		●	●	*Revising:* Lesson 6, Revising to Add Variety to Sentence Beginnings
4 Varying Sentence Beginnings with Prepositional Phrases		●	●	*Word Choice:* Lesson 5, Beginning Sentences with *-ing* Words *Revising:* Lesson 6, Revising to Add Variety to Sentence Beginnings
5 Varying Sentence Beginnings with Phrases Focused on Time		●	●	*Word Choice:* Lesson 4, Use Words and Phrases to Focus on Location or Place
6 The Rule of Three		●	●	*Revising:* Lesson 4, Sentence Combining *Punctuation:* Lesson 4, Comma in a Series

Other Lessons to Create

You might also want to teach writers how to

- vary their sentence structures (statements, questions, exclamations),
- listen for pleasing sentences in books read aloud (check "sentence fluency" online for recommended titles), or
- become aware of rhythmic sentences by clapping to read-alouds of rhyming texts.

247

Sentences Are of Varying Lengths

WHEN TO USE IT: When students are writing several sentences, but the sentences are either short and choppy or long and rambling

FOCUS THE LEARNING

Once students build up writing stamina and can write more than one sentence, it's time to show them how to fine-tune their sentences so that the writing sounds natural and one sentence flows effortlessly into the next.

Model

STEP 1: Display a short section of writing, and think aloud about the variety of sentence lengths using the Varying Sentence Length Checklist from the Resources CD-ROM.

Possible Think-Aloud: *When I am writing, I want to make sure that my sentences differ in length so they are easy to read aloud. If all of my sentences were short, it would make my writing sound choppy. I don't want the sentences to go on forever, either. I need to be sure that some sentences are short, some are long, and some are medium length. Watch as I use this Varying Sentence Length Checklist. I will count the number of words in each sentence to be sure that some are long and some are short. Sentence one, "Snap!" is just one word. Sentence two has 11 words! I used sentence fluency—a short sentence followed by a long sentence.*

Snap! Crocodiles have powerful jaws that they use to crush their prey. They eat fish, turtles, crabs, and lobsters. Look out! They have also been known to hurt people!

Sample Modeled Writing

Count the number of words in each of your sentences.

Sentence #	Number of words
1	I
2	II
3	

TURN &TALK *Count the words in the third sentence and think together. Is this a short sentence, a long sentence, or a medium-length sentence?*

STEP 2: Finish completing the Sentence Fluency Checklist.

Possible Think-Aloud: *I am feeling really good about my sentence fluency. I have one short, one long, and one medium-length sentence so far. I am going to put the word counts for the last two sentences into the chart and then read my writing out loud. One of the best ways to check for sentence fluency is to read your writing out loud and see how it sounds. Our writing should sound smooth and natural when we read it out loud, just like talking.*

TURN &TALK *What did you notice about the fluency of my writing? Did it sound smooth when it was read aloud? Were the sentences of different lengths?*

Analyze

STEP 3: Reread and reflect.

Possible Think-Aloud: *Let's look at my checklist. Notice that I used both short and long sentences. I have some medium-sized sentences, too. So far, I think I'm on track! I have a variety of sentence lengths that will help my writing sound natural when it is read aloud. Let's all read it aloud one more time.*

Sum It Up

Today we learned one way to do a check on our writing to see if it has sentence fluency. When we count the number of words in each sentence, we may find that all of our sentences are short or that all of our sentences are long. That would lead us to revise. Who thinks they are ready to try this checklist with their own piece of writing?

VARIATIONS

For Less Experienced Writers: Emergent writers may need support in defining what makes a *word* and what makes a *sentence*. Gather a small group of students, and provide modeling and guided practice in finding a *word* and a *sentence*.

For More Experienced Writers: Challenge partners to take a short and choppy piece of writing and revise it. Demonstrate how to combine sentences to add flavor and variety while keeping the content intact.

LINKS TO CD-ROM:
- Checklist: Varying Sentence Length Checklist
- Checklist: Sentence Fluency Checklist

Reading Aloud to Check Sentence Fluency

WHEN TO USE IT: To move writers beyond short, choppy sentences

FOCUS THE LEARNING

Good sentence fluency stands out when a piece of writing is read aloud. When we help students develop an expectation that they need to reread for sentence fluency, their writing develops smoothness and flow.

Model

STEP 1: Display a piece of writing, and think aloud as you listen for fluency in the sentences.

Possible Think-Aloud: *Writers, when I think I am finished with a piece of writing, one of my important jobs is to focus on how my writing might sound to my reader. It should sound natural and be pleasant to read aloud. It is also important that the sentences are of different lengths and that each sentence begins with a different word.* (Read the writing.) *Uh-oh. I have a nice long sentence to begin, but sentences two, three, and four sound really choppy when I read them out loud. My middle sentences are too short, and two of them start with the same word.*

TURN &TALK *Partners, analyze my writing. What can I do to help these sentences have more fluency?*

First draft:

A ladybug can beat its wings 85 times a second. The wings are thin. You can see through them. Ladybugs can fly a long way. Ladybugs won't fly if the temperature is less than 55 degrees.

Revised draft:

A ladybug can beat its wings 85 times a second. **Bzzzz!** The wings are **so thin that** you can see through them. Ladybugs **can fly a long way if the temperature is more than 55 degrees.**

Sample Modeled Writing

STEP 2: Model how to improve sentence fluency.

Possible Think-Aloud: *I am going to add sentence fluency in two ways. First, I am going to add a bit of onomatopoeia, words that sound like a noise. I will slip in "Bzzzz!" after sentence one. A ladybug's wings beat so fast you can hear them, but they are hard to see. Next, I am going to combine sentences two and three into "The wings are so thin that you can see right through them."*

TURN &TALK *Writers, is this helping? Read this out loud and determine if my sentence fluency is getting better.*

Analyze

STEP 3: Reread and reflect.

Possible Think-Aloud: *We are getting it. Each time we reread, it helps us think of more ways to improve the fluency of the sentences. Let's look at the last two sentences. Do they have sentence fluency, or do we need to revise them?*

Sum It Up

Today we learned that the best way to see if a piece of writing is fluent is to read it out loud and pay close attention to how it sounds to our ears. Fluent writing needs to have sentences that vary in length and sentence beginnings that use different words. I'm going to give each one of you a "whisper phone" that will help you read your piece aloud without distracting other writers. As you get out your writing folders today, I know I can count on you to use your whisper phones and check your sentence fluency. (See Resources CD-ROM for directions for whisper phones.)

VARIATIONS

For Less Experienced Writers: Collect or write several short pieces of writing that are strong and weak in sentence fluency. Read the pieces, and discuss how to tell which piece is fluent and which piece is not.

For More Experienced Writers: Challenge writers to work with a partner to revise their writing to enhance sentence fluency. Coach them in how to combine and rearrange sentences for improved fluency.

LINKS TO CD-ROM: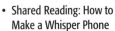
- Shared Reading: How to Make a Whisper Phone

Varied Sentence Beginnings

WHEN TO USE IT: When students are crafting several sentences, but sentence beginnings are lacking variety

FOCUS THE LEARNING

Many emergent writers have difficulty utilizing variety in sentence beginnings. We want to draw attention to this challenge and offer a range of options that will help them broaden their range of openings.

Model

STEP 1: Think aloud as you craft a piece of writing and consider how to keep your sentence beginnings varied.

Possible Think-Aloud: *Writers, one challenge we have in crafting any piece of writing is making sure that our sentences don't all start the same way. I'm working on a piece about koalas, and I want to show you what I'm thinking as I begin each sentence. (Read piece.) I want to add, "Koalas eat eucalyptus leaves and bark," but then I stop and think. I just used the word "koalas" to start the last sentence. I need to choose another way to begin!*

TURN &TALK *Partners, put your heads together and see if you have some ideas for me. How could I start my next sentence?*

STEP 2: Continue writing and thinking about sentence beginnings.

Possible Think-Aloud: *I heard some fantastic ideas. Some of you suggested that I use the word "they" to begin the next sentence. That would work! Watch me as I write the next sentence. I'll write, "They eat eucalyptus leaves and bark." Next, I want to add, "They also eat mistletoe and box leaves." Whoa! If I start with the word "they," it will be just like my last sentence. I think I'll start with an action word instead. "Chewing" would make a good opener, so I will write, "Chewing mistletoe and box leaves is one of their favorite things to do."*

What are you learning about varying

> Have you ever seen a koala bear? If you have, you are one of the lucky ones. There are fewer than 100,000 koalas on earth! Koalas live in Australia, in eucalyptus forests. **They eat eucalyptus leaves and bark. Chewing mistletoe and box leaves is one of their favorite things to do.**

Sample Modeled Writing

**TURN
&TALK** *sentence beginnings? Help each other remember what
we should think about when looking at the beginnings of
sentences.*

Analyze

STEP 3: Reread and reflect.

Possible Think-Aloud: *Let's reread my piece and see how it sounds.
It is important to check the sentence beginnings and be sure that
they start in a variety of ways. I like the way my sentences sound,
and I think my reader will, too!*

Sum It Up

Today I showed you how I think about each sentence before I write
it. I think about what word I've used for the last few sentences, and
I take the time to consider other words I can use to spice it up. As
you continue to write your own pieces today, challenge yourself to
think about each sentence beginning. You may even want to use
the Sentence Beginnings Checklist to help you think about your
work. Let's write!

VARIATIONS

**For Less Experienced
Writers:** Provide
additional opportunities
to craft a common text,
pausing to think before
beginning each new
sentence. Coach them
in using a variety of
words.

**For More Experienced
Writers:** Give partners
a short piece of writing
in which each sentence
begins with the same
word. Challenge them
to revise the piece
for varied sentence
beginnings. Encourage
them to share the
"before" and "after"
piece with the rest of
the group.

LINKS TO CD-ROM:
• Checklist: Sentence
Beginnings Checklist

Varying Sentence Beginnings with Prepositional Phrases

WHEN TO USE IT: When students are ready to experiment with phrases to begin sentences

FOCUS THE LEARNING

It's never too early to teach students the parts of speech. The goal of this lesson is to teach writers how using prepositional phrases to start sentences adds richness and variety to their writing.

Model

STEP 1: Work with students to create a description chart such as the one below (see Link to Resources CD-ROM).

Possible Think-Aloud: *We've been collecting information about whales on our description chart. And we've been learning the parts of speech as we add them. Today I want to show you how this chart can help you start your sentences in a fun and interesting way. I am writing a section about why whales sing. I want to tell that "some whales sing." I see in my chart that we listed "deep in the ocean." That might be a great sentence beginning.*

Personal Sentence Planning Chart

Author _____ Date _____

Topic **Whales** _____

Prepositional Phrases (where)	Adjectives (describing words)	Verbs (action words)
beyond the reef		
at the aquarium		
deep in the ocean		
in the North Atlantic		
in warm water		
in the North Pacific		

TURN &TALK *What do you think of our chart? Does it help you to visualize?*

STEP 2: Model a sentence beginning with a prepositional phrase.

Possible Think-Aloud: *I really like the phrase "deep in the ocean." Watch me as I write, "Deep in the ocean, some whales sing." That sounds great! Now I can go on to tell my reader what I know about why whales sing.*

> **Deep in the ocean,** some whales sing. Scientists aren't sure why some whales break into song, but some believe that the whales use the song to communicate with other whales.

Sample Modeled Writing

TURN &TALK *Examine the chart and create a sentence that begins with a prepositional phrase. Give me a thumbs up when you and your partner are ready to share.*

Analyze

STEP 3: Reread and reflect.

Possible Think-Aloud: *Let's reread the piece so far. What do you think? I think we added a lot of richness, detail, and variety by using a prepositional phrase to begin one of the sentences.*

Sum It Up

Writers, today I showed you how to begin a sentence in a fresh and exciting way. You've been working on your own topic chart. Challenge yourself today to use the chart to craft a sentence or two that start with a prepositional phrase. Be ready to share your sentence or sentences with your partner.

VARIATIONS

For Less Experienced Writers: Have some fun with the topic chart. Invite students to choose three adjectives, one verb, and one prepositional phrase. Ask them to write the sentence they have created. For example, "Slow, enormous, mysterious whales sing in the ocean."

For More Experienced Writers: Challenge writers to be on the look out for prepositional phrases in their reading selections. Ask them to record the prepositional phrases in their reading log and bring the collection to the next writer's workshop minilesson to share.

LINKS TO CD-ROM: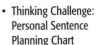
• Thinking Challenge: Personal Sentence Planning Chart

Varying Sentence Beginnings with Phrases Focused on Time

WHEN TO USE IT: When students are able to craft several sentences and are ready to experiment with another way to begin sentences

FOCUS THE LEARNING

Some young writers begin each sentence the same way, and their piece becomes choppy and lackluster. We want to expose them to a variety of ways in which writers begin a sentence.

Model

In advance of the lesson, prepare a chart with phrases that focus on time as per the Resources CD-ROM.

STEP 1: Show students how to begin a sentence by focusing on time.

Possible Think-Aloud: *Writers, I made a chart to help us start thinking about phrases that tell about* **when** *something happened. Today I want to show you how I can use a focus on time to help me begin a sentence in a new way. I'm writing about bats. I could write, "Bats begin their day at night." That would be fine, but I think I can do better. As I look at the phrases on the chart, I really like "When the sun sets." That is a great match for thinking about bats because sunset is when bats wake up. Watch as I use this phrase to begin my first sentence.*

TURN &TALK *Think together. Analyze my sentence. What are the benefits of opening a sentence in this way? Do you see any other phrases on the chart that we could use as we continue writing about bats?*

STEP 2: Continue thinking aloud about time as a focus for sentence beginnings.

Possible Think-Aloud: *I heard some fabulous phrases that I could use to begin my next sentence. "As the night creeps in" tells me that the time is changing. It is getting darker. This phrase signals time as well. Watch as I write, "As the night creeps in." I need to place a comma here to*

When the sun sets, bats begin their day. As the night creeps in, these winged mammals burst from their hiding places in search of a meal.

Sample Modeled Writing

separate my phrase from the rest of the sentence. This will tell my reader to take a breath here.

TURN &TALK *Read my writing about bats. Be sure to take a breath when you come to the comma after the opening phrase. Think together about the opening phrase and the comma. What do you need to remember if you are going to use fabulous phrases to begin your sentences?*

Analyze

STEP 3: Reread and reflect.

Possible Think-Aloud: *This chart of phrases that show time is filled with great sentence beginnings that can help us be really fluent when we write. I used two in my writing today, and I think that is enough for this piece about bats. If I started every sentence this way, my writing wouldn't be fluent anymore, because all of the sentences would sound the same and be the same length. I want to choose carefully and have just one or two sentences open with a focus on time.*

Sum It Up

Today I showed you how to use phrases that tell about time to begin your sentences. Deciding on a phrase was easy when we looked at the chart, but I'm sure that there are more phrases we could come up with. As you find great phrases about time in your reading or create them in your writing, be sure to add them to our chart. We want this helpful tool to grow and grow. As you work on your piece of writing today, try using a phrase that shows time to start one or more of your sentences.

VARIATIONS

For Less Experienced Writers: Use pictures on the chart to help support emergent and developing readers. Confer one-on-one with students as they work to craft their sentences.

For More Experienced Writers: Provide partners with several cards on which are written sentence fragments that are meant to go together. Challenge them to find the fragments that fit together. For example, one card might read, "In the morning" and another card might read, "dew settles on the flowers."

LINKS TO CD-ROM:
- Teacher Tool: Phrases that Focus on Time

The Rule of Three

WHEN TO USE IT: When writing is choppy and loaded with short sentences

FOCUS THE LEARNING

Writers can improve sentence fluency and descriptions by following the "rule of three," or organizing descriptions in sets of three. We know students often write something like "I went to the parade. I saw a band. There was a float." Or: "Turtles have shells. They have four legs. They pull their head and legs into the shell." If we teach writers to create complex sentences that combine three descriptions, the writing becomes richer and nonfiction communication is enhanced.

Model

STEP 1: Display a pocket chart with three short sentences, and use drama to focus on the actions.

Possible Think-Aloud: *I have placed three sentences in my pocket chart. Watch as I use the "rule of three" and turn these three short sentences into one longer sentence. First, I need to focus on the verbs. These sentences have verbs that tell what happened at the beach: What I saw, heard, and felt.*

TURN &TALK *Let's imagine we are at the ocean. Dramatize these important actions. We see people. We hear the waves crash. We feel the warm sand on our toes. Partners, act it out!*

STEP 2: Use scissors and additional sentence strips to create one sentence that uses the rule of three.

Possible Think-Aloud: *For the "rule of three," you need three actions. We have saw, heard, and felt. The trick is to put them all in one sentence! Watch as I use my scissors and snip the word "I" from sentence two and sentence three. Now I am going to turn the period at the end of sentences one and two into commas.*

Draft 1:

I saw people along the beach.

I heard the waves crash and boom.

I felt the warm sand on my bare toes.

Sample Modeled Writing

Draft 2:

I saw people along the beach, heard the waves crash and boom, and felt the warm sand on my bare toes.

Sample Modeled Writing

TURN &TALK *Analyze my new "rule of three" sentence. What is your opinion of this new sentence? Why is the "rule of three" a great rule for nonfiction writers to consider using?*

Analyze

STEP 3: Reread and reflect.

Possible Think-Aloud: *Listen as I reread my new "rule of three" sentence. (After reading.) Rereading helped me notice something important. I think I need to slip the word "and" into the sentence after the last comma. Adding "and" after the last comma makes the sentence sound much smoother when I read it aloud.*

Sum It Up

The "rule of three" helped me create a great sentence with three actions. By writing one sentence with three actions, I have an <u>interesting</u> sentence that sounds great when I read it aloud. I wouldn't want to do this to all sentences; that would be boring. The "rule of three" is a great tool for nonfiction writers.

VARIATIONS

For Less Experienced Writers: In a small-group setting, provide additional practice using a pocket chart and combining sentences using the rule of three. With English language learners, scaffold their understanding by focusing on events in their lives such as three actions at recess, three actions in the cafeteria, or three things they do when reading a book.

For More Experienced Writers: Broaden their range of thinking to include the "rule of three" for topics outside of their own experience. An example: *The turtle quickly flattened himself to the ground, pulled his legs and head into the safety of his shell, and then waited for the hungry possum to pass.* Help writers to notice the use of a transition word after the last comma.

Voice and Audience

Bringing Personality to the Page— Thinking About Our Readers

Nonfiction writing can represent a range of voices from quiet and objective to energetic and enthusiastic. When a nonfiction writer integrates voice into his or her work, there is a sense that a real person with feelings and emotions is speaking to you. It is clear that the author cares about the message and has consciously thought about you—the reader.

LESSON	K	1	2	RELATED LESSONS
1 Developing an Awareness of Voice	●	●	●	
2 Speak Directly to Your Reader		●	●	*Voice and Audience:* Lesson 12, Shifting Point of View
3 Consider: Capture the Interest of Your Reader		●	●	*Research:* Lesson 1, Identify Facts in a Visual
4 Pick a Topic You Find Interesting	●	●	●	*Text Features:* Lesson 1, Choose a Title that Is Interesting
5 Pick an Enticing Title	●	●	●	*Word Choice:* Lesson 9, Have Fun with Alliteration *Text Features:* Lesson 1, Choose a Title that Is Interesting
6 Make Your Writing Sound	●	●	●	*Planning:* Lesson 2, Talk Before Your Write
7 At the End, Reveal Your Thoughts, Feelings, and Opinions		●	●	*Ideas:* Lesson 8, Separating Fact and Opinion *Organization:* Lesson 7, Craft a Satisfying Ending
8 Show Excitement in Writing		●	●	*Punctuation:* Lesson 5, Comma: After Introductory Element or Clause
9 Include Humor or Surprise	●	●	●	
10 Voice Shifts with Your Audience		●		
11 Draw Your Reader into the Setting		●	●	*Organization:* Lesson 6, Create an Inviting Lead *Word Choice:* Lesson 4, Use Words or Phrases to Focus on Location or Place
12 Shifting Point of View	●	●	●	

Other Lessons to Create

You might also want to teach writers how to

- become aware of voice (for example, by comparing a dictionary entry with an imaginative alphabet book),
- compare the different feelings voice creates in two nonfiction picture books, or
- discuss voice in books with a strong voice (for example, *So You Want to Be President?* by Judith St. George).

Developing an Awareness of Voice

WHEN TO USE IT: When students are comfortable writing several sentences and are ready to focus on the qualities of strong writing

FOCUS THE LEARNING

Students are often confused by the vague nature of voice. Our goal in this lesson is to introduce them to this powerful trait and foster an awareness of its importance.

Model

STEP 1: Read two nonfiction passages aloud. One should include voice and one should not. (See Sample Modeled Writing for examples.)

Possible Think-Aloud: *Writing is more interesting and fun to read when it has what is called voice. When there is voice, readers understand the feelings and attitudes of the author. They sense the author's passion for a topic. This makes readers want to read more. I'm going to read two passages about chocolate. (After reading.) Wow! What a difference! The first passage sounded like a real person talking, and I could tell that this person really likes chocolate! The author's voice is so strong, I felt like the author was right here.*

TURN &TALK *Partners, analyze the passages. Share your thinking about the writing, and discuss why one makes us feel more connected to the author than the other.*

Strong voice:

I can smell the chocolate candy before I take that first luscious bite. It smells as if all the cacao trees in heaven have come down to earth in the form of small edible morsels. I try to eat it slowly, but I can't help myself. I gobble the whole thing in two bites!

Weak voice:

I like chocolate. I like the way it smells. I like the way it tastes. If I could eat chocolate all day, I'd be happy. Chocolate comes from the cacao tree.

Sample Modeled Writing

STEP 2: Discuss which piece of writing was stronger and why.

Possible Think-Aloud: *I heard several of you say that the first piece of writing had a lot more voice. I agree! When I read it, I can tell that the writer has written from his or her heart and really cares about the topic. The second example sounds just okay. There isn't much emotion or excitement in it, so there isn't much voice. The writing makes it sound like the author doesn't care a lot about chocolate. If a writer isn't excited about the topic, it is hard for voice to come through in the writing.*

TURN &TALK *Talk with your partner. What are you learning about voice? What are you going to try to do in your own writing?*

Analyze

STEP 3: Reread and reflect.

Possible Think-Aloud: *When I think about including voice in my writing, it helps me to imagine that I am talking to my reader. I want to choose words and use phrases that show how I feel. I want to help my reader understand that my writing is really "me" doing the talking! To have voice, writing needs to be lively and show emotion, so I am going to read the first passage again and think about how I can get more voice in my own writing.*

Sum It Up

Today we talked about voice. Voice is what makes a piece of writing fun or interesting to read. As you work on your own piece of writing today, take some time to read your writing and see if yours has voice. If not, make it sound like you are talking to a friend. That will bring voice to your writing.

VARIATIONS

For Less Experienced Writers: Play "Guess Who?" Gather students in a small group with their eyes closed. Tap one student and have him or her say something to the group. Challenge the group to guess who was speaking. Explain how we can listen for someone's distinct voice when they are speaking *and* when they are writing.

For More Experienced Writers: Collect excerpts from books by several authors with whom the students are familiar (examples: Dr. Seuss, Tedd Arnold, Mo Willems). As you read the excerpts aloud, challenge students to identify the author. Consider: How did you identify the author? Could you hear the author's voice come through?

LINKS TO CD-ROM:
• Teacher Tool: How to Tell If Your Writing Has Voice

Speak Directly to Your Reader

WHEN TO USE IT: To add voice and connection between the author and reader

FOCUS THE LEARNING

When writers speak directly to their readers and invite them to "imagine themselves in the action," writing becomes much more personal, and readers find it easier to consider the content.

Model

STEP 1: Model talking directly to a reader.

Possible Think-Aloud: *When I create writing in which I talk directly to a reader, I don't just describe the subject. I try to make the reader feel like he or she is right there in the action. When I start writing, I need to change my sentences and say things like "Reach out and touch his tough, wrinkled skin." Notice that I am telling the reader to touch the skin. This kind of writing sounds a little bit bossy because you are telling your reader to do something. But that is part of the fun when you are speaking directly to a reader.*

TURN &TALK *Listen as I read my first four sentences, and try to think like you are my reader. (Read the first four sentences.) Describe the mental picture you are getting. How does it make you feel when I talk directly to you and tell you to touch the skin? In your mind, do you see yourself next to the elephant?*

STEP 2: Continue writing and speaking directly to a reader.

Possible Think-Aloud: *I am ready to speak to my reader again. This time, I want to focus on the elephant's eye. I don't want to say reach out and touch; that might hurt an elephant in real life. I will write, "Look into its eye . . ."*

Imagine that you are next to an elephant. Reach out and touch his tough, wrinkled skin. It's rough to the touch, and filled with bumps and ridges. Notice that near his ears, the skin is as thin as paper and feels like an eraser to the touch. Look into its eye. It's as big as a dinner plate and the color of dark honey.

Sample Modeled Writing

Analyze the part about the eye. How did I do at talking to the reader? Is there anything else I could do to make it clear that I am not talking to the world but just to the person who is reading my writing?

Analyze

STEP 3: Reread and reflect.

Possible Think-Aloud: *In talking to my reader, I invited my reader into the action. I got to be a little bit bossy by saying things like "touch" and "look." Think together. My goal was to speak directly to my reader. Do I deserve a thumbs up or a thumbs down on this writing?*

Sum It Up

Writers can add voice to writing by talking directly to a reader and inviting the reader into the action on the page. In this kind of writing, you get to be a bit bossy and say things like "Look at me. I'm a red-winged blackbird. Or, You dive into the frigid waters of the Antarctic with your penguin brothers all around. Or, Run! The bald eagle is diving right at us." These statements all speak directly to a reader and are one more kind of writing you can use to create variety and add voice to your work.

VARIATIONS

For Less Experienced Writers: Guide these writers through Lesson 12 in this section on shifting point of view to give them additional experience in talking directly to a reader.

For More Experienced Writers: Stretch more experienced writers by having them create a chart of questions and statements that speak directly to the reader. Questions and stems you might consider include: "Did you know… Are you aware? I have a surprise for you … A tiger's nose is huge, bigger than your fist. If you were close enough, you could _____."

Consider: Capture the Interest of Your Reader

WHEN TO USE IT: When writing is stilted, is dull, or lacks voice

FOCUS THE LEARNING

Voice separates writing that is read from writing that is not read. Many readers have abandoned a text because it's simply not interesting. We need to model how to write with a reader in mind.

Model

STEP 1: Challenge students to think about what makes a strong piece of writing.

Possible Think-Aloud: *Writers, have you ever read a book that wasn't very exciting? When I read a book like that, I usually don't finish it. I know that one of my jobs as a writer is to stop and ask, "Would my reader think this is interesting?" "Have I added some things that might surprise him or her?" I want the words I write to come to life for my readers and keep them interested and engaged.*

TURN &TALK *Think together. What is the last book you read that was interesting or surprising? What did the author do to keep you engaged?*

STEP 2: In advance of the lesson, create a chart with facts about your topic. Think aloud as you craft a short piece of writing, and consider what fact or facts would interest and/or surprise the reader.

Possible Think-Aloud: *I'm working on a piece about penguins. As I begin to write, I'm thinking about my readers. What would be interesting or surprising to them? I've collected several facts on this chart. As I read them, I'm thinking I could write a bit about how penguins have wings like birds but cannot fly. That might be surprising. I think I'll write, "Did you know that even though penguins are birds and have wings, they can't fly?" Capturing the interest of a reader is a great way to add voice.*

TURN &TALK *Identify other facts that might capture the interest of a reader or offer an element of surprise!*

PENGUIN FACTS

· Eat fish, krill, squid, and silverfish
· Swim to get away from predators
· Penguins are birds
· Have wings but cannot fly

Did you know that even though penguins are birds and have wings, they can't fly? Instead, they swim quickly through the icy waters to escape hungry predators.

Sample Modeled Writing

Analyze

STEP 3: Reread and reflect.

Possible Think-Aloud: *Let's read my piece so far. I think I've done a good job using the facts that I've collected to create a couple of sentences that would be interesting and might even surprise my reader. It helped to have my reader in mind as I was writing.*

Sum It Up

We all want our writing to be read! When you take time to think about your reader, it helps you to create a piece of writing that is interesting and fun to read. One way you can check to see if your piece is working is to read it to a friend. Ask your friend, "Does my writing need to be spiced up a bit?" Who is ready to begin writing?

VARIATIONS

For Less Experienced Writers: Remind emergent readers how to gather facts from photographs, diagrams, and illustrations. Support each student as he or she collects interesting facts about a topic.

For More Experienced Writers: Demonstrate how to take notes on interesting or surprising facts when researching. Introduce a Note Taker Graphic Organizer, and challenge students to try it out with their next piece of writing. (See Resources CD-ROM.)

LINKS TO CD-ROM:
• Graphic Organizer: Note Taker Graphic Organizer

Pick a Topic You Find Interesting

WHEN TO USE IT: When writing sounds like the author has no interest or passion for the topic

FOCUS THE LEARNING

When we show students how to pick a topic that interests them and how to showcase that interest, voice shines through. Careful topic selection and a conscious effort to let personal interest in the topic shine through the writing develop strong voice.

Model

STEP 1: Write a list of animals that interest you and about which you would like to write.

Possible Think-Aloud: *Writers, when you write about things you know about and things you care about, you usually have a lot to say. Picking the right topic is important! Once you have a topic you love, it is easier to show that interest through your writing. You want your reader to know you are excited and interested in your subject. I'm going to make a list of animals that interest me. I would love to know more about sharks, grizzly bears, and sea turtles.*

TURN &TALK *What are some topics that interest you? Tell your partner about some of the animals that make you curious. What would you enjoy learning about?*

STEP 2: Choose a topic and begin crafting a short piece.

Possible Think-Aloud: *Today I'll begin writing about sea turtles. I know that they have been around for millions of years but that there are six kinds of turtles that might become extinct. I think I'll start my writing with a question. That is a great way to add voice and show that I am very interested in my topic. I also want to react to*

Did you know that sea turtles have been swimming in the earth's oceans and seas for millions of years? That's a long time! That means they were in the ocean when the dinosaurs roamed the earth. Sadly, there are now six kinds of sea turtles that are in danger of becoming extinct. What can we do to protect them?

Sample Modeled Writing

the question and show interest, so I will write, "That's a . . ." Notice that I use an exclamation point. That is another way to show that I am passionate about my topic.

TURN &TALK *Think about voice. What do you need to remember when you are trying to infuse voice into your work?*

Analyze

STEP 3: Reread and reflect.

Possible Think-Aloud: *Let's reread my piece and see what we think. Did I show an interest in my topic, or does my writing sound bland? Will my reader know that I really care about sea turtles? When I pick a topic that interests me, I'm off to a good start in developing voice!*

Sum It Up

Writers, today we learned how to choose a topic that we know and care about. We also learned that it's important to choose a topic that we are curious about. As you prepare to write today, ask yourself if you've chosen a topic that interests you. Once you begin writing, pause to ask yourself if that interest is coming through in your writing. Let's get to work!

VARIATIONS

For Less Experienced Writers: Show writers two writing samples on a similar topic. One sample should be dull and lack interest. The other should be full of voice. Read both pieces, and discuss which piece is better and why.

For More Experienced Writers: Challenge partners to revise a weak piece of writing so that it contains more voice and shows more interest in the topic. Encourage partners to share their revisions with the group.

Pick an Enticing Title

WHEN TO USE IT: When students are omitting a title, or when the titles they choose are lackluster

FOCUS THE LEARNING

It has been said that you never get a second chance to make a first impression. The title is the author's chance to set the tone and entice a reader to read the piece. The best titles are often selected after writing is complete, so help your writers learn a bit of patience by crafting their titles after drafting.

Model

STEP 1: Display a short piece of writing. Explain the importance of choosing a good title.

Possible Think-Aloud: *I have been working hard on my piece about kangaroos, and I think I'm finished. Now all that is left is the title. I want to write a title that is clear, concise, and interesting. I'm going to think of a few titles and then choose the one that I think will work the best. One title could be "All About Kangaroos." But my piece isn't really **all** about kangaroos. My piece is mostly about how kangaroos can swim and hop. I could try something like, "Kicking Kangaroos." What do you think of that?*

TURN &TALK *Partners, put your heads together and think. If you were the author of this piece, what title would you write? What title would tell my readers what my piece is about while making them curious to know more?*

STEP 2: Think aloud as you choose a title for the piece.

You may know that kangaroos are amazing hoppers. But did you know that they are also strong swimmers? In Australia's southern areas, kangaroos have been known to swim to land from small islands. Their powerful hind legs help them propel through the water.

Sample Modeled Writing

Possible Think-Aloud: *I heard some great ideas for a title for my piece! I know that I want my title to be short, snappy, interesting, and clear. My piece is mostly about how kangaroos use their mighty hind legs to swim. I want to include something in my title about that. I have decided that my title will be "Mighty Marsupials." I know that kangaroos are marsupials and that they are mighty because they can both hop and swim. I am so glad I didn't try to create a title until the writing was finished. I never would have thought of this title before I did my research and writing.*

TURN &TALK *Are there any other titles that I should consider?*

Analyze

STEP 3: Reread and reflect.

Possible Think-Aloud: *Let's reread my title and my piece of writing. Do they go together? Is it short and snappy? I think my title will work to draw my reader in and make him or her want to read more.*

Sum It Up

Today we talked about the importance of choosing an enticing title. We know that readers often decide whether they want to read something after reading the title, so we want to choose our title carefully. As you work on your own writing today, take some time to come up with a few titles that might work. Then, choose one that you think will interest your reader the most. Let's begin!

VARIATIONS

For Less Experienced Writers: Collect a few short nonfiction books with strong titles. Read the books, and have partners brainstorm some possible titles. Then, reveal the author's choice of title.

For More Experienced Writers: Challenge writers to be collecting strong titles from books they are reading during independent reading time. Encourage them to bring their lists to writer's workshop and share with the group. Collect strong titles on a chart, and discuss what makes the titles work.

LINKS TO CD-ROM:
• Chart: An Enticing Title

Make Your Writing Sound Like <u>You</u>

WHEN TO USE IT: When writing is dry and lacks personality

FOCUS THE LEARNING

Young writers are often so focused on writing each word that they forget that sentences should sound natural. When we teach them to say each sentence aloud before they write, they can utilize their own personal voice.

Did you know that dragonflies are meat-eaters? They eat ants, mosquitoes, termites, bees, and even butterflies! Some dragonflies will eat tadpoles and tiny fish, too. Who knew that dragonflies were such mighty hunters?

Sample Modeled Writing

Model

STEP 1: Think aloud as you write a short piece, pausing to say each sentence out loud before writing it.

Possible Think-Aloud: *Today I want to show you one smart thing that writers do to make sure each sentence sounds like them. Before I write a sentence on paper, I say it out loud. That way, I can check to see if it sounds like me talking. Listen as I say my first sentence about dragonflies.* Did you know that dragonflies are meat-eaters? *I say, "Did you know" all the time. If I write that sentence on my paper, it will sound like my voice. That is just what I wanted!*

TURN &TALK *Think together. Why do you think it helps me to say the sentence out loud before I write it? When I listen to the sentence, what I am trying to notice?*

STEP 2: Continue writing, pausing to say each sentence aloud.

Possible Think-Aloud: *Listen as I say another sentence. "Some dragonflies will eat tadpoles and tiny fish, too." Does that sound like something I would say? I like the way it sounds, and I think my reader will, too. I'll add that sentence for sure. Now I want to use a sentence that shows my surprise. I will start, "Who knew . . ."*

TURN &TALK   _Does that sound like me? Is there another sentence that would show my voice a little better and keep my reader interested?_

Analyze

STEP 3: Reread and reflect.

Possible Think-Aloud: _Let's read my piece so far and see what we think. Did I use my own words? Does my writing sound like me? Did I say each sentence out loud before I wrote it down? Saying the sentences out loud before I wrote them helped me to write sentences that had voice._

Sum It Up

Today we learned how to say a sentence out loud before we write it. When we do that, we can hear what our sentence sounds like and make sure that we are using our own words. As you begin to write today, try saying each sentence out loud before you write it. I'll be anxious to hear how it helps you as a writer.

VARIATIONS

For Less Experienced Writers: Gather writers in a small group, and have them write a short piece together, pausing to say each sentence out loud. Reread often to check for voice.

For More Experienced Writers: Explain that, eventually, writers start to hear each sentence in their head before they write them rather than saying each sentence out loud. Challenge them to try this and report back on how it helped them as a writer.

At the End, Reveal Your Thoughts, Feelings, and Opinions

WHEN TO USE IT: To showcase feelings and opinions of the author

FOCUS THE LEARNING

Although most nonfiction writing tasks require us to be unbiased providers of information, there are times when a well-placed opinion or personal thought can add power to a piece of writing.

Model

STEP 1: Display a short piece of unfinished writing. Think aloud about how to include your thoughts, feelings, or opinions.

Possible Think-Aloud: *We've been talking about how to add voice to our writing. One way to do that is to share your thoughts, feelings, or opinions at the end of your piece. These give your writing voice. I've written a short piece about sea turtles. I'm ready to add some of my own thoughts and opinions at the end. Let's read my piece so far and think about what I could add.*

TURN &TALK *Think together. What could I add next that would reveal my thoughts or feelings about protecting sea turtles?*

STEP 2: Think aloud as you end the section of writing with your own thoughts, feelings, and opinions.

Possible Think-Aloud: *As I listened to your conversations, I heard some great ideas. I want to let my reader know that, in my opinion, we should protect the sea turtles. I think I'll say, "We*

> Sea turtles have lived since dinosaurs roamed the earth. But, today some are in danger. People are building near nesting grounds, and baby sea turtles become confused by the bright lights. We need to work to protect these beautiful creatures so they will be around for years to come.

Sample Modeled Writing

need to protect these creatures so they will be around for years to come." I also want to tell them that I think sea turtles are beautiful, so I could add the word "beautiful" before the word "creatures." To say a turtle is beautiful is an opinion. That word shows what I think.

TURN &TALK *Would you describe a turtle as beautiful? If not, what words would express your thoughts and opinions about sea turtles?*

Analyze

STEP 3: Reread and reflect.

Possible Think-Aloud: *Let's read my whole piece together. Did I add some thoughts, feelings, or opinions at the end? Do you think it improved my writing? I think that by adding that last sentence, I boosted the voice in my piece.*

Sum It Up

Today we learned how to add some spice to our writing by ending with our thoughts, feelings, and opinions. If you've chosen a topic that you really care about, you'll have a lot of thoughts and opinions. The end of your piece is a great place to make those thoughts clear to your reader. When you go back to your writing today, challenge yourself to add some of your feelings at the end.

VARIATIONS

For Less Experienced Writers: Emergent writers may need more explicit instruction on the difference between **fact** and **opinion**. Provide guided practice by giving partners several facts and several opinions written on strips. Challenge them to sort the sentences.

For More Experienced Writers: Challenge students to support their opinions with specific details and reasons. Explain that if you really believe in something, you need to prove to your reader that you are right. Model how to do this with a common text.

Show Excitement in Writing

WHEN TO USE IT: When students are ready to show excitement and enthusiasm on the page

FOCUS THE LEARNING

Young children are naturally filled with excitement and voice in oral language. Showing them how to convey excitement on paper can infuse additional voice.

Model

STEP 1: Display a copy of *Don't Let the Pigeon Drive the Bus* by Mo Willems or *Surprising Sharks* by Nicola Davies. Guide a conversation about showing excitement in writing.

Possible Think-Aloud: *I love* Don't Let the Pigeon Drive the Bus. *Mo Willems, the author, talks directly to the reader, and it is so much fun to see the excitement building for the bus driver and the pigeon. As I read it, pay attention to the ways in which the author tells us that there is excitement.* (After reading.) *Wow! I noticed lots of ways to show excitement. I noticed exclamation points. I also noticed that some of the words were in capital letters. Capitals in the middle of a sentence tell a reader that someone is shouting. I also notice that there are sound words on some of the pages.*

TURN &TALK *Think together. Do sound words like vroom-vroom, vroomy make the writing sound exciting?*

STEP 2: Continue writing, considering other ways to infuse excitement.

Possible Think-Aloud: *So far we know that we can make writing more exciting by using exclamation points, capitalize words in the middle of a sentence, and add sound words. I am writing about bees. Watch as I write, Eeek, watch out! Notice the exclamation point? I can't use an exclamation point for every sentence, just this one. Now I am going to write a bit in all capital letters to act like I am talking really loud on paper. Watch as I write, BE CAREFUL.*

TURN &TALK *Analyze my writing. Is it showing excitement yet?*

It's summer and bees are buzzing all around searching for nectar. That's okay until they come too close. Eeek, watch out! BE CAREFUL. Bzzzzz. Bzzzz. Beware.

Sample Modeled Writing

Analyze

STEP 3: Reread and reflect.

Possible Think-Aloud: *Now I am ready for a sound word. Get your lips ready and make the sound of a bee for me. I want to include that next. Let's reread my writing. How does it sound? I think adding that exclamation point added some excitement and voice. I think it also added excitement when I wrote BE CAREFUL in capital letters. That is how we would say it if a bee really did come too close.*

Sum It Up

Writing can sound exciting. We just need to think about how to make excitement show on paper. Today we learned three ways to do it. An exclamation point, some sound words, and a word or two in capital letters like someone is yelling. That will add excitement to the page.

VARIATIONS

For Less Experienced Writers: Challenge students to talk about a topic and show their excitement in conversation. Then, show them how to infuse exclamation points, capital letters, and sound words for emphasis as their own words are written down. Assist writers in placing a limited number of exclamation points into their own writing.

For More Experienced Writers: Work together to create a chart of ways in which to show excitement on paper. Guide writers in reviewing nonfiction titles with excitement and adding strategies to the list. Some examples: *Dogteam* by Gary Paulson, Picture Yearling, 1991 (repetition); *Surprising Sharks* by Nicola Davies, Candlewick Press, 2003; *Emperor's Egg* by Martin Jenkins, Candlewick Press, 1999 (pages 25–29); *Earthquakes* by Seymour Simon, Smithsonian, 2006 (notice hyphens on page 1).

Include Humor or a Surprise

WHEN TO USE IT: To add variety and enhance voice

FOCUS THE LEARNING

Children are natural humorists, and they love surprises. The trick is to help them add the element of surprise or humor to a piece of nonfiction writing. Once they catch on, they realize that their writing sparkles with voice, and readers will love to read their work.

Model

STEP 1: Think aloud as you utilize surprise and humor.

Possible Think-Aloud: *Today I want to show you how you can spice up your writing by adding a sentence or two that are suspenseful or funny. As I've been researching about giraffes, I've discovered something surprising. Giraffes can use their tongues to clean their ears! I know that I surely can't reach my ears with my tongue. That is both surprising and funny. Watch as I write, "We all know that . . ." I want to write a bit on the topic before I launch my big surprise! I could put the surprise almost anywhere, but today I will put the surprise in the middle of my writing.*

TURN &TALK *Why do you think it is a good idea to use humor or surprise in nonfiction writing?*

STEP 2: Add to your piece of writing as you think aloud.

We all know that giraffes have long necks, but did you know that they also have extremely long tongues? The long tongues help them reach leaves on trees. Get ready for a surprise . . . a giraffe can use its tongue to clean its ears! Can you imagine cleaning your ears with your tongue?

Possible Think-Aloud: *I am going to tell my reader that a surprise is coming. If I write, "Get ready for a surprise," my reader will have a bit of suspense, a reason to guess what is coming. Here is the surprise: "a giraffe can . . ." This line definitely needs an exclamation point. I want this surprising fact to be noticed!*

Sample Modeled Writing

Analyze

STEP 3: Reread and reflect.

Possible Think-Aloud: *Let's reread my piece and see if adding some surprise and humor helped to boost the voice in my writing. Surprise and humor are both helpful tools for creating voice. I'm glad I took the time to give my writing some voice with suspense and humor!*

Sum It Up

Today, we talked about how to add voice by including some surprises and funny facts. When you are researching, be on the look out for facts that might be funny or surprising to your reader. Challenge yourself to add those to your piece. Off you go!

VARIATIONS

For Less Experienced Writers: Provide more guided practice by leading students in a shared writing experience on a familiar topic. Encourage them to utilize humor and surprise.

For More Experienced Writers: As students are reading independently, challenge them to look for the author's use of humor or surprise. Gather students in a small group, and encourage them to share what they have discovered.

Voice Shifts with Your Audience

WHEN TO USE IT: When the writing doesn't match the audience

FOCUS THE LEARNING

Audience and purpose determine the type of voice and tone each piece of writing should have. Young writers need to learn how to shift and adjust the voice so that it is appropriate for the intended audience.

Model

STEP 1: Think aloud as you write a short letter to a friend.

Possible Think-Aloud: *Writers, we've been talking about the importance of voice in your writing. Today I want to show you how your voice can change based on the person or persons you hope will read your piece. I'm going to write two letters. The first one is to my friend, Kerry. Sometimes we start a letter with "Dear" and then the person's name. But Kerry is a good friend. I think I'll start with something more casual, like "Hey Kerry,"* (Continue writing letter.)

TURN &TALK *Think about the way you talk to your friends. Is this the same way you would talk to the principal or a police officer? How does your talk change when you speak to different people in your life?*

STEP 2: Write the second letter.

Possible Think-Aloud:
The second letter that I'm writing is to our principal, asking him to allow the first graders to play dodge ball. It wouldn't be okay to start this letter with "Hey!" I need to show respect, so I want my voice and my words to sound more formal. For this letter, I think

First letter:

Hey Kerry,

I was thinking it would be a blast to have you over for dinner next week. Are you free? I'll make my special pizza that we both adore. Let me know if you want to hang out!

Hugs,

Kelly

Sample Modeled Writing

Second letter:

Dear Mr. Hess,

I am writing to ask you to please consider allowing the first graders to play dodge ball during morning recess. They are learning to play this game in PE and have shown themselves to be safe and responsible when they play. Please let me know what you think of this suggestion.

Sincerely,

Mrs. Boswell

Sample Modeled Writing

I'll start with "Dear Mr. Hess." I'm going to try and use more formal words for this letter.

TURN &TALK *Compare and contrast the two letters. What differences do you see? What are you noticing about the voice in each?*

Analyze

STEP 3: Reread and reflect.

Possible Think-Aloud: *Let's read both letters again. I want to double-check the voice in each. I need to be sure that my letter to the principal sounds respectful and polite. With my friend, I just want to have a little fun, so I can use a voice that is relaxed.*

Sum It Up

Today we learned how our voice shifts based on the person or persons we hope will read our piece. It's important to think about the kind of voice that is appropriate for each kind of writing. As you begin writing today, take some time to think about your potential audience, and then consider the kind of voice that would be best for your piece.

Draw Your Reader into the Setting

WHEN TO USE IT: When leads are flat and written from a third person, outsider view

FOCUS THE LEARNING

When nonfiction writers begin by describing the setting, they invite their reader in for a closer look. While all nonfiction writing does not need to start with setting, writers should know how to create a nonfiction lead that utilizes setting, as it supports visualization for a reader and enhances voice.

Model

STEP 1: Create a list of words and phrases that describe the setting or habitat of an animal.

Possible Think-Aloud: *I learned in one of our books that toads are nocturnal. That means they are awake at night. During the day, they rest in nests of leaves or pine needles. To get ready to write, I am making a list of phrases that tell about the setting where I am likely to find a toad. "Almost night, hiding place, nest of leaves or pine needles" are phrases I could use to help my reader understand the time of day and where the toad is hiding. Writing out these phrases that describe the setting will help me draw my reader into the setting and give him or her a better understanding of the life of a toad.*

TURN & TALK *Visualize a time when it is almost dark. The toad is stirring around in his nest of pine needles, trying to wake up. He has a small, flat head that starts to poke up out of the nest. He is sleepy, so his eyes blink. Partners, dramatize a toad waking up in his nest. Then think about the words and phrases I have listed. Are there any other words I should add to describe the setting?*

STEP 2: Write a lead that includes the words and phrases you listed in Step 1.

Possible Think-Aloud: *When you open your writing with a focus on setting, it helps your reader visualize and want to read more. I am going to use the phrases we listed and write, "It is almost evening . . ." I am trying*

Toad

It is almost evening, and from deep within a pile of mud and leaves, a small flat head pokes up. Toad's sleepy eyes blink as he stretches and stares into the mist.

Sample Modeled Writing

to write a lead that will help my reader to visualize the toad just as you did when you were dramatizing the way the toad wakes up! I want to get in the part about his sleepy eyes, so I will begin sentence two, "Toad's sleepy eyes blink as he . . ."

TURN &TALK *Get ready to visualize as I read my writing out loud. Analyze my lead. Does it paint a picture of the setting? Can you get a mental picture of the toad in his nest of mud and leaves? What else could I say that would draw my reader right into this setting?*

Analyze

STEP 3: Reread and reflect.

Possible Think-Aloud: *Have you noticed that I keep returning to my visualization? I want to be sure that the words I write expose the details I see in my mind. When we visualized the last time, I thought of another detail to include. I want to add something about the mud. When you open with the setting, it helps to have a really great picture in your mind so your reader understands what you are thinking. Let's reread one more time and wonder together. Is there anything else we can do to make this setting come alive and give a reader a strong visual image of the setting?*

Sum It Up

Nonfiction writing does not need to be boring. We can capture the interest of our readers by inviting them into the setting. If we use words and phrases that describe the picture we are getting in our own minds, we can help a reader to see and understand what we are saying. This kind of writing takes a bit more time, but it is worth it. Let's get started inviting our readers into the setting within our writing!

VARIATIONS

For Less Experienced Writers: Use a terrarium with a live animal or a series of high-quality photos to help your writers come up with phrases that describe the setting. Once they have a rich list of phrases, support them as they recast their phrases into sentences.

For More Experienced Writers: During one-on-one conferences, guide these writers in examining the leads in their writing to consider enriching the setting in a way that invites the reader in. Assist them in writing from a view within the setting rather than a third person view.

LINKS TO CD-ROM:
• Visual: Red-Eyed Tree Frog

Shifting Point of View

WHEN TO USE IT: To help writers understand that shifting point of view can offer an artistic and highly personal tone to nonfiction writing

FOCUS THE LEARNING

Visualization is a well-known support to deep comprehension. When students visualize themselves as taking on the persona of an animal, a bird, a river, or a slowly shifting glacier, they must engage in sensory imaging. They must also consider more deeply the essence of the topic, describing from within rather than outside a subject.

Model

STEP 1: Think aloud and demonstrate how you create a mental image, shift point of view, and write from within the topic.

Possible Think-Aloud: *If I were snow, I would have lots of little crystals in beautiful patterns. I would sparkle in the sunshine and float on the wind. When I finally touch the earth, I would cling tightly to the branch of a tree or settle softly on top of a tall, fluffy drift. Did you notice that my point of view was as though I was the snow? That is really different than if I write,* Snow is white. It drifts. It has little crystals.

TURN &TALK *Use the stem, "If I were snow . . ." Tell your partner what you would do if you were snow. Dramatize falling snow and the way that it whirls and floats. Make your body move like the snow.*

STEP 2: Demonstrate writing using the stem, "I am . . ."

Possible Think-Aloud: *When we shift our point of view and visualize ourselves as being the snow, it helps us to write great descriptions. Because I am writing as though I were the snow, I want to start*

> I am the snow. I twirl and float as I fall softly toward the earth. My tiny flakes are filled with beautiful icy patterns. I begin as mist in the clouds, but then cold air causes the mist to freeze, and I begin my swirling journey to the earth. I am the snow.

Sample Modeled Writing

with, "I am the snow." As I watched you dramatize being the snow, I noticed that you twirled and floated, so I will write, "I fall softly . . ." Notice that I am selecting words that make it sound like the snow is doing the writing.

TURN &TALK *What else can snow do? What else do we know about the way snow is formed? Use "I am" and think of more that we could write about the snow.*

Analyze

STEP 3: Reread and reflect.

Possible Think-Aloud: *As I reread this piece of writing, close your eyes and visualize. Make a movie in your head, and "see" the snow as it falls.* (After reading) *That visualization helped me to realize that I left out important information about how snow crystals are formed. I need to add that, so I will write, "I begin as mist." Wonder together: Are we helping our reader understand what it would be like to be the snow? Have we included enough facts and descriptions of the snow?*

Sum It Up

Nonfiction writers can write about their subjects as though they are observing from far away. Or they can think about what it would be like to BE the subject and write in a much more personal way. Writers need to be able to do both kinds of writing, so as we confer this week, let's plan to talk about shifting point of view and writing, "I am . . ."

VARIATIONS

For Less Experienced Writers: It is especially helpful to select topics for which these writers have personal experience. A few topics to consider: I am the rain. I am a river. I am a caterpillar wriggling from my egg. I am the snake slithering through the grass. I am the red-winged blackbird.

For More Experienced Writers: Begin by creating a list of facts and understandings that would be good to include in the writing. Then, guide writers in shifting to the "I am" format using mentor books by Diane Siebert, such as *Heartland* and *Sierra*.

LINKS TO CD-ROM:

- Student Writing: I Am a Tornado
- Student Writing: I Am a Raindrop

Punctuation

Controlling the Pace and Flow of Messages

Well-designed punctuation controls the flow of a message, helps the reader understand nuances of meaning, and makes the texts we construct more interesting. Interesting phrasing and complex sentences depend on internal punctuation to control pace and meaning. End-of-sentence punctuation is more often a function of correctness. A key feature for writers to understand is that punctuation should be considered during drafting to add interest and support meaning. Waiting until editing to work on punctuation is not likely to lift sentence quality or improve sentence fluency.

LESSON	K	1	2	RELATED LESSONS
1 End Punctuation (statement)	●	●		*Sentence Structure:* Lesson 2, Simple Sentences
2 End Punctuation (question)	●	●	●	*Organization:* Lesson 11, Create a Question and Answer Book
3 End Punctuation (exclamation point)	●	●	●	*Voice and Audience:* Lesson 8, Show Excitement in Writing
4 Comma in a Series		●	●	*Word Choice:* Lesson 6, Add Action: Group *-ing* Words Together
5 Comma: After Introductory			●	*Word Choice:* Lesson 4, Use Words and Phrases to Focus on Location or Place *Word Choice:* Lesson 5, Beginning Sentences with *-ing* Words
6 Use a Variety of Punctuation Elements	●	●	●	*Word Choice:* Lesson 7, Use Onomatopoeia

Other Lessons to Create

You might also want to teach writers how to use

- apostrophes in contractions,
- apostrophes with possessives, or
- quotation marks around direct quotes from research sources.

End Punctuation (statement)

WHEN TO USE IT: When writers are ready to identify complete sentences

FOCUS THE LEARNING

Punctuation exists to support the reader's understanding of the text. Our goal is to support our emergent writers in their understanding of effective use of punctuation.

Model

STEP 1: Display a chart that asks these questions: *Who or what did something? What did they do?*

Possible Think-Aloud: *When we craft a complete sentence, we tell who or what did something, and we tell about what they did. When we do that, we've created a complete sentence, and we're ready to add a period. A period is a kind of stop sign for our readers. It tells them to stop briefly and get ready for another complete sentence.*

TURN &TALK *Talk with your partner. How do you know when to use a period?*

STEP 2: Craft a piece of writing, pausing to think aloud about when to add a period.

Possible Think-Aloud: *I'll start by writing, "My cat." Let's check to see if I can add a period yet. Did I tell "who"? Yes. Did I tell what my cat did? No. I can't use a period yet. "My cat likes to end her day by . . ." Am I ready for a period now? Did I tell what she does yet? I'll keep writing. "My cat likes to end her day by sitting next to the fire." Can I add a period now? I can! This is a complete sentence. (Model the second sentence with the writers.)*

My cat likes to end her day by sitting next to the fire. She heads for her favorite spot and settles down for her evening nap.

Sample Modeled Writing

TURN &TALK *How do you know when you have written a complete sentence? Remind each other of the two important questions you have to ask yourself before you get to use a period.*

Analyze

STEP 3: Reread and reflect.

Possible Think-Aloud: *Let's reread my sentences. Do they answer both of the questions on our chart? Did I use a period to give the signal to my reader that he or she should stop and then get ready for the next sentence? When I thought about the two questions on our chart, it helped me know where to place a period in my writing. Nonfiction writers need periods, and they need to know when to use them.*

Sum It Up

Today I showed you how writers use a period to end a sentence that tells us something. As you are writing today, remember to use a period at the end of your sentences.

VARIATIONS

For Less Experienced Writers: Give students a section of text photocopied from a familiar leveled reading selection. Challenge them to cut the words apart, mix them up, and put them back together. Discuss where the periods should be placed and why.

For More Experienced Writers: Display a familiar piece of writing, but do not include the periods. Encourage partners to decide where the periods should be placed and why.

LINKS TO CD-ROM: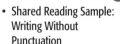
- Shared Reading Sample: Writing Without Punctuation

End Punctuation (question)

WHEN TO USE IT: When writers are ready to insert questions into their writing

FOCUS THE LEARNING

When we teach young children a new convention, we give them the opportunity to improve their writing and support the reader.

Model

STEP 1: Display the first three sentences of the modeled writing. Explain why you placed a question mark at the end of the first sentence.

Possible Think-Aloud: *Let's read the first few sentences of my piece on grasshoppers. Do you see the mark I used at the end of my first sentence? I used a question mark because I was asking my reader a question. We know that we use a period at the end of a "telling sentence." When we write questions, we use a different kind of mark. We use a question mark. A question mark tells the reader that they need to respond or that an answer is about to be provided in the writing.*

TURN &TALK *Practice together. Ask your partner a question about things they like to eat or things they like to do. Listen carefully and see what you learn.*

STEP 2: Continue writing, thinking aloud as you add another question to your piece.

Did you know that grasshoppers have no ears? They hear by using an organ called the tympanum. The tympanum is found on the grasshopper's abdomen. Can you imagine having an ear on **your** belly?

Sample Modeled Writing

Possible Think-Aloud: *I think I'll add another question at the end of this section. I'll write, "Can you imagine having an ear on your belly—" I am not going to put any punctuation on this. I will leave a blank and give you a minute to think together.*

TURN &TALK *Should I use a period or a question mark? How do you know?*

Analyze

STEP 3: Reread and reflect.

Possible Think-Aloud: *You are so smart! I'll place a question mark at the end of that sentence. Now I have some telling sentences <u>and</u> some questions in my piece. Let's reread my piece and think together. Did I use some questions in my writing? Did I remember to put a question mark at the end of my questions? I think these questions will boost my writing!*

Sum It Up

Today we learned how to put a question mark at the end of a question. That's an important thing to remember. When you start working today, look back over what you have written so far, and see if you can weave in some questions so you can use a question mark in your writing. I can't wait to admire your questions!

VARIATIONS

For Less Experienced Writers: Give each student an index card with a question mark written on one side and a period on the other. Read a variety of sentences and questions orally, and ask students to decide which kind of end punctuation would be necessary for that sentence.

For More Experienced Writers: Model the use of questions as headings for a nonfiction piece of writing.

End Punctuation (exclamation point)

WHEN TO USE IT: When writers are ready to convey excitement on the page

Model

STEP 1: Craft a short piece of writing, pausing to think aloud about adding an exclamation point.

Possible Think-Aloud: *I've been working on a piece about bees. I want to add a bit about being careful not to bother bees. I want my sentence to say, "Look out," and I want my reader to read that sentence in an excited way. One way that writers show excitement in their writing is to add a special mark called an exclamation point. Watch me as I add an exclamation point after the word "out."*

TURN &TALK *Partners, have you seen this kind of mark before? Where have you seen it?*

STEP 2: Continue writing, adding another exclamation point.

Possible Think-Aloud: *I'm going to keep working on my piece. I'll add a sentence about how the bee might sting you. I think I'll end this paragraph with the sentence, "Ouch!" I could use another exclamation point there. Watch me as I write an exclamation point after the word "ouch."*

> When you see a bee sipping nectar, be careful not to bother him. If you don't bother a bee, he usually won't bother you. Sometimes you can accidentally annoy a bee. Look out! He might just sting you. Ouch!

Sample Modeled Writing

TURN &TALK *How do you know when to use an exclamation point? Why can't you use it with every sentence you write?*

Analyze

STEP 3: Reread and reflect.

Possible Think-Aloud: *Let's reread my writing. How does it sound? I think adding those exclamation points added some excitement and voice. I like the way my writing sounds, and I think my reader will, too. As you're writing today, challenge yourself to try using an exclamation point to liven up your piece. Let's write!*

Sum It Up

Remember that we have a way to add excitement or emphasis to our writing by using an exclamation point. Just remember not to use it too often.

VARIATIONS

For Less Experienced Writers: Challenge students to locate exclamation points around the room on charts, in poems, and in big books. Discuss why the author chose to utilize the exclamation point in each example.

For More Experienced Writers: Photocopy a page from a nonfiction text that includes a variety of punctuation. Lead students on a "punctuation scavenger hunt," asking students to find a period, a question mark, and an exclamation point. Lead a discussion about **why** the author chose to use each mark.

Comma in a Series

WHEN TO USE IT: When student writing shows more complexity, and when students are ready to include several things in one sentence

Model

STEP 1: Display a chart with facts about your topic. Demonstrate how you think about combining facts.

Possible Think-Aloud: *I've been collecting interesting facts about eagles on this chart, and I'm ready to write. I want to write about what eagles eat. I could write, "Eagles eat fish. Eagles eat small rodents. Eagles eat birds." However, I think that might make my writing sound choppy. It might sound more natural to say, "Eagles eat fish, small rodents, and birds."*

TURN &TALK *Partners, what do you think? Does it sound smoother when you link ideas together in the same sentence?*

STEP 2: Continue writing and model how to insert commas in a series.

Eagles eat small fish, small rodents, and birds.

Sample Modeled Writing

Possible Think-Aloud: *When writers write about several things in one sentence, they use a comma to separate those things. A comma tells the reader to take a little pause. Watch me as I write the sentence, "Eagles eat fish, small rodents, and birds." I add the comma on the line right after each thing the eagle eats. Notice that before I write my very last item, I use the word "and" to show that this is the end of my list.*

TURN &TALK *Explain where to put the comma. Think together about exactly where it goes.*

Analyze

STEP 3: Reread and reflect.

Possible Think-Aloud: *Let's reread my sentence. I am pleased that I remembered to include a comma to separate the names of the animals that eagles eat. I also notice that I remembered to put the comma on the line, not up in the air. My sentence sounds natural, and I think the commas will remind my reader to take a little pause.*

Sum It Up

Today we learned that when writers tell about one thing after another in the same sentence, they use a comma to separate each thing. As you begin writing today, think about what we learned, and try it out with your piece. Be ready to share a sentence in which you used commas. Let's begin!

VARIATIONS

For Less Experienced Writers: Craft several more sentences together, modeling when and how to use commas in a series.

For More Experienced Writers: Lead readers and writers on a "scavenger hunt" for commas in a series. Collect sentences and display them on sentence strips for others to enjoy.

LINKS TO CD-ROM:
• Student Writing

Comma: After Introductory Element or Clause

WHEN TO USE IT: When students are ready to experiment with complex sentences

FOCUS THE LEARNING

Introductory clauses make writing more interesting while supporting sentence fluency. They add richness and texture to the writing and stimulate sensory imaging.

Model

Post a list of helper words that can initiate a clause. A few examples include with, above, below, at, as, across, against, by, and just.

STEP 1: Think aloud about how to craft a sentence with an introductory element.

Possible Think-Aloud: *I want to create a picture in the reader's mind of what an eagle looks like when it hunts for food. Watch as I use a helper word from my list and create a sentence that has two parts. Notice that I use a comma after the word "treetops." This isn't a sentence yet. This is just a beginning. Now I need to use the word eagle and tell what it did. Watch as I write the rest of the sentence. The last three words, "an eagle soars," are actually a sentence all by themselves, but when I start with a helper word and begin my sentence with a clause—wow! This sounds really great.*

TURN &TALK *Analyze my sentence. What do you notice?*

STEP 2: Think aloud as you craft the sentence using a comma after the introductory element.

Possible Think-Aloud: *Let's try another one. When an eagle soars, its wings are spread wide. Watch as I write, "With wings spread wide, the eagle plunges toward its prey." Notice that I started with the helper word "with." I found that word right here on the chart. Watch as I use a comma to separate the opening element from the main sentence. Notice that this kind of sentence has*

Just above the treetops, an eagle soars. With wings spread wide, the eagle plunges toward its prey.

Sample Modeled Writing

two distinct parts—an opening element followed by a comma and then the main sentence.

TURN &TALK *If you were going to write a sentence like this, what are the steps that you would need to follow?*

Analyze

STEP 3: Reread and reflect.

Possible Think-Aloud: *Let's reread from the beginning. How does my piece sound so far? I really like the sound of these sentences with an opening element and a comma before the main sentence. These sentences make my writing sound really adult!*

Sum It Up

Today we learned how to add a comma after an introductory element in a sentence. Adding an introductory phrase is a great way to spice up your sentences! Once you get the hang of it, it's really fun to do! Use this chart to get started, but let's keep thinking of helper words that can help us write great introductory elements for our sentences.

VARIATIONS

For Less Experienced Writers: Give students more opportunities to see you model using a comma after an introductory element. You may even want to consider writing the introductory element in one color and the main sentence in another. Think aloud about the two essential parts of this style of sentence as you model.

For More Experienced Writers: During independent reading, challenge students to be on the lookout for introductory clauses in sentences. When they find one, encourage them to write the sentence down in their Writer's Notebook to share with the class. Keep a chart displaying the sentences.

Use a Variety of Punctuation Elements

WHEN TO USE IT: When students have learned how to use a variety of punctuation marks and are ready to experiment with using them to improve their writing

FOCUS THE LEARNING

Once students have learned the different kinds of punctuation, they are ready to learn how they can all fit together to add some spice to a nonfiction piece.

Model

STEP 1: Briefly review the kinds of punctuation marks you have taught so far.

Possible Think-Aloud: *We've been learning about a lot of different kinds of punctuation marks. We've learned how writers use a period to end a sentence that tells us something and an exclamation point to end a sentence that shows excitement. We have learned that when we write questions, we use a question mark. Finally, we've learned how to add a comma when we are writing about several things in one sentence or after an introductory clause. All of these punctuation marks exist to support our reader.*

TURN &TALK *Talk with your partner. Which punctuation marks have you tried in your own writing? Are you using one more often than the others?*

STEP 2: Craft a short piece of writing, thinking aloud about the punctuation marks you can use.

Possible Think-Aloud: *Today I want to show you how you can use a variety of punctuation marks to spice up your writing! I'm writing a piece on popcorn. I'd like to start with something exciting like "Pop! Pop! Pop!" I can use some exclamation points there. Next, I'll add a telling sentence. I'll write, "The kernels of popcorn explode as they heat." I'll need a period there. I think I'll use an introductory element to begin my next sentence. That means I need a helper word and a comma.*

TURN &TALK *With your partner, discuss the purpose of the punctuation marks we've used so far, and tell why they are needed.*

Pop! Pop! Pop! The kernels of popcorn explode as they heat. With eager anticipation, I pour the popcorn in a bowl. I add salt, butter, and a little cheese. Will I be able to eat it all?

Sample Modeled Writing

Analyze

STEP 3: Reread and reflect.

Possible Think-Aloud: *Let's reread my piece so far. What do you think? Have I used a variety of punctuation? Is my piece interesting? I like the way it looks and sounds so far, and I think my reader will, too! I'll keep writing now and see if I can maybe add a question or use a comma in a series. When I use a variety of punctuation, it really boosts my writing!*

Sum It Up

Today we remembered all of the different punctuation marks we have learned and how we can put them all together to make our writing look and sound more interesting. Remember that punctuation marks are there to act as road signs for your reader. They tell your reader how to read your piece. Today, as you begin writing, think about the punctuation marks you can use to add some variety. Let's write!

VARIATIONS

For Less Experienced Writers: Provide additional opportunities for modeled writing and guided practice as you craft another piece of writing in which you utilize a variety of punctuation.

For More Experienced Writers: Examine text from published authors, and discuss the variety of punctuation that the author employs. Offer opportunities to peer edit with an eye for a variety of punctuation marks.

Grammar

Structures and Patterns that Support Messages

The rich conversations we have with children all day long are essential building blocks of grammar development. Within the context of the language we hear in our lives and the works of our favorite authors, our ears become tuned to what "sounds right." When focusing on grammar, take cues from your students. Listen to their oral language patterns, and look closely at the grammar within their writing. With careful attention to the patterns that are already in place, you can open their eyes to structures and forms within a read-aloud or a favored nonfiction selection—helping young writers to apply the more formal registers of English that are seen in published books and expected of proficient writers.

LESSON	K	1	2	RELATED LESSONS
1 Singular and Plural Nouns	●	●	●	
2 Subject and Verb Agreement		●	●	
3 Verb Tense		●	●	
4 Pronoun Order	●	●	●	
5 Single vs Double Subject	●	●	●	
6 Open with an Adverb	●	●	●	*Sentence Fluency:* Lesson 4, Varying Sentence Beginnings with Prepositional Phrases
7 Use Stellar Adjectives	●	●	●	*Word Choice:* Lesson 1, Use Descriptive Words and Phrases *Word Choice:* Lesson 8, Compound Descriptors and Hyphens

Other Lessons to Create

You might also want to teach writers how to

- use irregular verb forms (run and ran),
- form comparative and superlative adjectives (big, bigger, biggest), or
- check for uniform verb tense throughout a piece of writing.

Singular and Plural Nouns

WHEN TO USE IT: When written language doesn't reflect correct usage

FOCUS THE LEARNING

Singular and plural nouns are part of everyday language. For writers who are learning English as an additional language or for those whose oral language systems are still developing, an explicit focus on singular and plural forms can enrich both oral and written communication.

Model

STEP 1: Think aloud as you create a chart of singular and plural nouns.

Possible Think-Aloud: *I have a chart that says "Singular Noun . . . Plural Noun" at the top. I have one book. Watch as I write "book" in the singular column. If there are two books or a bookcase full of books, then we add an "s" to the end of the word and make it plural. One book is singular. I don't need an "s" at the end. If I have more than one book, then I need to add the letter "s" to the end to show that it is a plural.*

TURN &TALK *I am about to write "books" on the plural side of my chart. What do I have to write at the end of the word "book" to show that there are lots of books?*

STEP 2: Identify additional items in the classroom, and add them to the chart showing the singular and plural forms.

Possible Think-Aloud: *I love nonfiction books. Watch as I write, "Who can read . . ." Notice that when I write "book" there is no "s."*

Singular Noun	Plural Noun
book	books
shoe	shoes
finger	fingers
coat	coats

Who can read just one nonfiction book? No one! Nonfiction books are filled with wonderful facts and information. There is nothing better than a terrific nonfiction book.

Sample Modeled Writing

That is because I am writing about one book. Next, I will write, "Nonfiction books . . ." Since I am talking about lots of books, I am going to be sure that I add an "s." The letter "s" at the end tells my reader that I mean more than one. Let's try this with some more items in our room. Look at my left shoe. We are looking at one shoe, so we don't need an "s" at the end of the word. Now look at both of my shoes. Do you hear the "s" in shoes? That says there are more than one.

TURN &TALK *Look at your hands. Hold up your pointer finger. That is one finger. Talk together. Do you need to add an "s" to write about one finger? If I said fingers, what is the difference? What does the "s" at the end tell you?*

Analyze

STEP 3: Reread and reflect.

Possible Think-Aloud: *Let's reread my chart of singular and plural words. If we look around our classroom, there are lots of things we could add to these lists. We can add pencil and pencils. How about coat and coats? It's your turn. Think together of items in our classroom that we could put on our chart for singular and plural.*

Sum It Up

Nonfiction writers need to be careful to think about how many items they are describing when they write. It makes a big difference if you are writing about one snake, or many snakes. To be the best writers we can be, we need to pay attention and think about when to add the letter "s" and turn words into plurals.

VARIATIONS

For Less Experienced Writers: Provide more practice with real items, identifying singular and plural and then creating personal lists similar to the class chart. Guide these writers in reviewing their writing to identify places where they used singular and plural forms.

For More Experienced Writers: Introduce the concept of plural being formed with "es" instead of "s." Examples: branch, branches; box, boxes. Or create plurals from words that end in the letter "y." Examples: puppy, puppies; party, parties.

Subject and Verb Agreement

WHEN TO USE IT: When writers have not yet acquired subject-verb agreement

FOCUS THE LEARNING

Subject-verb agreement is a tricky concept for some students, especially if they are learning English as an additional language or speak non-standard English at home. Support this important concept with lots of modeling and positive coaching.

Model

STEP 1: Post a T-chart labeled "Singular Subject" and "Plural Subjects." Model how to shift verbs to match singular and plural forms.

Possible Think-Aloud: *As I write today, I want to focus on making the subjects of my sentences match my verbs. Watch as I write, "Tony runs." Tony is just one person, so I add an "s" at the end of run. When I write "All the boys," I need to decide if I should say run or runs. "All the boys runs" doesn't sound right. Saying the sentence aloud is a good way to check. Let's try another one. The rabbit hops.*

TURN &TALK *Watch as I write, "Lots of rabbits . . ." Think together. Should it be "Lots of rabbits hop" or "Lots of rabbits hops"? How do you know which one is correct?*

STEP 2: Continue thinking aloud and modeling adjustment of the verb "climb" to create subject-verb agreement.

Possible Think-Aloud: *You are getting it! Let's try it another way. Sometimes we create subject and verb agreement by changing a word completely. We do this when we have an irregular verb, like "is." Watch as I write, "A bear is . . ." Now I will change it to "The bears _____." I need to be careful. I can't add an "s" to "is." That wouldn't sound*

Level I

Singular Subject

Tony runs.

The rabbit hops.

A bear climbs fast.

Plural Subjects

All the boys run.

Lots of rabbits hop.

All bears climb fast.

Sample Modeled Writing

Level II

Singular Subject

A bear is swimming.
A worm is crawling.

She is writing.

The baby is crying.

Plural Subjects

The bears are swimming
The worms are crawling.

They are writing.

The babies are crying.

Sample Modeled Writing

right at all. I need to say "The bears ARE swimming." Because I have a plural subject, "bears," I need a whole new word! Get ready. Here is another one. "She is writing." "They _____ writing."

TURN &TALK *Think together. What word should I put in the blank to make the plural subject ("They") have a good partner in the sentence? What would sound right?*

Analyze

STEP 3: Reread and reflect.

Possible Think-Aloud: *When we write sentences, it is important to think about singular and plural subjects and then make sure that the verbs match. Let's reread my sentences and think about what we have learned. (After rereading and pointing out verb changes.) Think together. If you were going to tell someone how to make subjects and verbs be good partners, what would you say to him or her? What would you want that person to know?*

Sum It Up

When we use singular subjects and write about just one thing, the verbs should be singular. When we use plural subjects and write about lots of things, those verbs need to be plural. If the verb is irregular, you might need to use a new word. The best test is to read a sentence out loud and listen to how it sounds. As you begin writing today, I know I will hear you reading your sentences aloud and checking to be sure that nouns and verbs agree.

VARIATIONS

For Less Experienced Writers: Work with a pocket chart, inserting a variety of sentences such as those in the modeled writing of this lesson. Omit the verbs, and have writers consider which verbs will best match the singular or plural subject.

For More Experienced Writers: Read *Animals Nobody Loves* by Seymour Simon, and help students notice that the subjects of some sections are singular and others are plural. Begin a chart of the verbs that Seymour Simon matches to his subjects, and post it in a visible place so that writers can use it as a reference.

Verb Tense

WHEN TO USE IT: To bring the selection of past versus present tense verbs to a conscious level

FOCUS THE LEARNING

Verb tense has a big impact on voice and reader involvement in nonfiction writing. As we coach young writers, it is important to help them become conscious of tense. They need to deliberately select a tense for each piece of writing, realizing that the tense will affect the reader. Once tense is selected, writers need to be consistent throughout the selection.

Model

STEP 1: Think aloud about selecting present or past tense verbs as you tell about a bird hatching. Create a chart of present and past tense verbs so writers can see the differences in structure.

Possible Think-Aloud: *I am going to write about a robin's egg hatching. I have to decide if I should sound like the egg already hatched or invite the reader to watch the egg hatching right now. Listen as I practice. First, I will sound like the egg already hatched.* A mother robin **watched** over her eggs. Inside one of the eggs, a baby bird **peeped**. Then, the shell **cracked,** and the beak **popped** through. *Did you notice that all the verbs, "watched, peeped, cracked, and popped," were past tense? The -ed endings tell us that they are past tense verbs, so the action happened in the past. Watch as I write the verbs in present tense and then past tense.*

TURN &TALK *Read these words together. Think about the difference in present tense and past tense verbs. Which of these verbs tell that something already happened? Which ones say something is happening right now? How do you know?*

STEP 2: Use the verbs highlighted in Step 1 to create a present and past tense version of the writing.

Possible Think-Aloud: *Now I will try again, as though my reader and I are right beside the nest watching. I will use present tense verbs to make it clear this is happening now. "A mother robin watches . . ." Notice the difference in the verbs! The endings are present tense endings.*

Present	Past
watches	watched
peeps	peeped
cracks	cracked
pops	popped

Sample Modeled Writing

Past Tense: A mother robin **watched** over her eggs. Inside one of the eggs, a baby bird **peeped**. Then, the shell **cracked** and a tiny beak **popped** through.

Present Tense: A mother robin **watches** over her eggs. Inside one of the eggs, a baby bird **peeps**. Suddenly, the shell **cracks** and a tiny beak **pops** through.

TURN & TALK *What differences do you notice in the two types of writing? Which version do you like better? What are you learning about present tense and past tense verbs?*

Analyze

STEP 3: Reread and reflect.

Possible Think-Aloud: *I am ready to reread these pieces of writing. Once I select a tense for my writing—either present tense or past tense, I need to be sure that I stick to it and that I am consistent. Nonfiction writers need to be very careful not to use some present tense and some past tense verbs in the same piece of writing. I will start with the past tense writing.* (Pause in the middle of reading the passage.) *The first two verbs are both past tense. That is good. Now I am ready to think about "cracked." Think together. Is "cracked" present tense or past tense? Is this the right tense to use in this writing about something that already happened?*

Sum It Up

Writers have an important decision to make in every piece of writing. They need to decide if they are going to make their reader feel like the action is happening right now or if they want to describe it as though it has already happened. As you begin writing today, take a moment to look back through your writing and identify pieces that are written in past tense—like they already happened. Notice if you have written any in present tense, inviting your reader into the moment. I can hardly wait to see what you notice!

VARIATIONS

For Less Experienced Writers: Model additional think-alouds and writing in which you involve students in deciding which verb tense to use, as well as assisting in selecting verbs within the writing. It is often helpful to focus past tense writing on shared experiences and to base present tense writing on drama.

For More Experienced Writers: During one-on-one conferences, guide writers in evaluating their own work by having them identify the verbs and decide if they are present or past tense. They should also check entire selections to see if they were consistent in the tenses used.

LINKS TO CD-ROM:
• Teacher Tool: Regular and Irregular Verbs chart

Pronoun Order

WHEN TO USE IT: When crafting nonfiction narratives in which the author is part of the story line

Applying rules about pronoun order can be challenging when explaining the concept but suddenly become quite clear when the distinction is modeled in a piece of meaningful writing. In addition to modeling this important grammatical concept in writing, try practicing it in daily conversation with your writers. For example: Garett and I need to chat for a moment. Wylie and I will be collecting your paintbrushes. Please get your math manipulatives ready. Serena and I will be passing out your thinking challenge for today.

Model

STEP 1: Model appropriate pronoun order in oral speech and in writing.

Possible Think-Aloud: *When I share an experience that includes someone else as well as myself, I need to be polite and use the other person's name before mine. For example, I could say, "Mrs. Fisher and I walked down the hall together." Did you notice that I used Mrs. Fisher's name first and then said "I"? It is polite to name the other person before yourself. Today I am writing about the pancakes that my sister, Nancy, and I used to make with our grandmother. My sister and I were both there, so I need to be careful and use her name first. Watch as I write my first sentence, "When I was young, Nancy and I . . ." In sentence two, I want to say that Grandma and I were the ones who made the pancakes because my sister was too little.*

TURN &TALK *I will be writing about my grandma and myself. How should I write that? What will I write first?*

STEP 2: Continue thinking aloud and modeling.

Possible Think-Aloud: *Okay. I am ready to tell how my sister and I got to eat those wonderful pancake designs. I want to be polite, so watch the way I write "my sister and I" in the sentence. This is just like having a party. When I have people over to my house, I try to be polite and serve them first, before myself. It is the same way in talking and writing. The other person first and then "I."*

The Best Pancakes

When I was young, Nancy and I loved to visit our grandparents and eat pancakes made into different shapes. Grandma and I would stand at the stove and create fish, bear, and even cartoon character shapes out of pancake batter. Then, my sister and I would get to eat all of our wonderful "art."

Sample Modeled Writing

TURN & TALK *We need to create a chart to remind everyone about the rule we are going to use in talking and writing. Think together. What should we write on our chart that would remind us all to say or write the other person's name first and then say "I"?*

Analyze

STEP 3: Reread and reflect.

Possible Think-Aloud: *It is time to reread my work and recheck the way I wrote about my grandmother, my sister, and me. As I reread, watch how I touch the words and check very carefully to make sure that this is correct. I don't want to write in a way that makes me look rude. I really want to be sure I name the other person first and then say "I."*

Sum It Up

Writers, we have a great chart that will help us remember to say or write another person's name and then say "I." Being polite is important, and it will be great to work on it both in the way we talk and in the way we write. If you have an idea for an illustration for our chart, please let me know. It will look even better with a bit of color.

VARIATIONS

For Less Experienced Writers: Practice using the oral format of saying the other person's name and then "I" while retelling events on the playground, in the cafeteria, on the school bus, and so on.

For More Experienced Writers: Use the tool on the Resources CD-ROM, and project sentences on an overhead projector, document camera, or smart board for writers to analyze. The goal is not to have students rewrite the sentences but rather to analyze and discuss them.

LINKS TO CD-ROM:
• Student Writing: Fire blizzard text
• Teacher Tool: Invitations for Analysis

Single vs Double Subject

WHEN TO USE IT: To adjust double subject use in oral and written language

FOCUS THE LEARNING

The use of double subjects, such as "My mom, she" or "The penguin, he," is a very common error in oral and written language. To help young writers attend to a conventional pattern of use, provide oral models in daily interactions and several rounds of modeled writing on this topic.

Model

STEP 1: Think aloud about identifying a subject only once in each sentence.

Possible Think-Aloud: *My dog is kind of silly. He loves to chase his tail. Watch as I write about this really funny way he entertains himself. "My dog he . . ." Oops! That's not right. Did you see what I did? I wrote "my dog" and then I also said "he." I only need to tell you once that I am talking about my dog. I will cross out "he." Listen as I reread my sentence the correct way. "My dog loves to chase his tail." That sounds ever so much better, doesn't it? My next sentence is, "When he gets going, my dog he . . ." Ooops! I did it again.* (Point to the two "he"s in the sentence.) *I don't need this twice.*

TURN & TALK *Think together. I need to get rid of one of the "he"s in this sentence. Which one should I cross out? Let's fix this sentence.*

STEP 2: Continue writing and thinking aloud about single and double subjects.

Possible Think-Aloud: *Now I want to tell about my sister. I need to decide. Should I say "My sister she laughs" or "My sister laughs . . ." I definitely don't want to tell you twice who is laughing, so I won't use "she." I will say, "My sister laughs . . ." That is better.*

> My dog ~~he~~ loves to chase his tail. When he gets going, my dog he goes round and round and round. My sister ~~she~~ laughs so hard that she almost falls out of her chair.

Sample Modeled Writing

TURN &TALK *Analyze the writing that I just did. Why is it important to name the subject of your sentence just once? Why shouldn't I say, "My sister she" or "The penguin he"?*

Analyze

STEP 3: Reread and reflect.

Possible Think-Aloud: *Listen as I reread my sentences. I want to be sure that I have crossed out all of the times when I named the subject of my sentence twice. This rule is a little tricky, but rereading will help me get it right. Read: My dog loves to chase his tail. I am so glad I crossed out "he." "My dog loves to . . ." sounds much better. Read the next sentence with your partner and talk about what I did to be sure that I named the subject just once.*

Sum It Up

Naming the subject of a sentence just once is important. We need to remember this when we talk and when we write. You can't name the subject and still say he or she. That is like saying, "Angela, Angela, please shut the window." I wouldn't say her name twice, would I? That would sound very strange. As you begin writing today, take a minute to check your narratives for places you might have named a subject twice. This is a good time to snip out the extra words!

VARIATIONS

For Less Experienced Writers: Provide a sentence frame in a pocket chart, such as: My mother _____. My father _____. My friend _____. Have writers work together to think of various ways in which these frames could be completed, being careful to name the subject of the sentence only once.

For More Experienced Writers: Have writers analyze any of their nonfiction passages in which the subjects have been doubled. Guide a conversation about words that should be removed to improve the writing quality. See the Resources CD-ROM for examples.

LINKS TO CD-ROM:
• Practice passages (4)

Open with an Adverb

WHEN TO USE IT: To introduce another format for creating interesting sentence structures

FOCUS THE LEARNING

Adverbs make terrific sentence openers. To assist young writers in using these helpful parts of speech to liven up their work, post a chart of interesting adverbs so they can refer to the list while drafting. Adverbs are great stimulants to vocabulary development as well.

Model

STEP 1: Collaborate with students to generate a list of adverbs to post on a chart. (A sample list is on the Resources CD-ROM.)

Possible Think-Aloud: *Adverbs are great words that can be used to help us create interesting sentences. They often have "ly" at the end of the word. It helps to think about ways we can move and use adverbs to describe our actions. I know we can move slowly, cautiously, quickly, painfully, or tiredly.*

TURN &TALK *Get ready to dramatize. Let's act out these adverbs. Please move very slowly. Now move cautiously, as if you are walking on a wire high above the ground. Get ready, the next adverb is quickly. How would you move quickly to your chair? Put your heads together. How else can you move? Try to think of words that end in "ly." I will write your ideas on my chart.*

STEP 2: Model crafting sentences that begin with an adverb followed by a comma.

Possible Think-Aloud: *I am thinking about a book I read about tree frogs and the danger they face from snakes. I visualize a little frog sleeping while the snake creeps toward him. I am going to select "quietly" as my adverb for the snake. Watch as I write "Quietly" and then follow it with a comma. One of the tricks to this kind of sentence is to use an adverb followed by a comma and then write the rest of the sentence. The main action in my sentence*

> Quietly, the snake slithers toward the sleeping frog. Suddenly, the little frog's eyes pop open. Abruptly, the snake is alone. The little frog has disappeared.

Sample Modeled Writing

is the snake slithering. Now that I have my adverb and comma in place, I am ready to write, "the snake . . ."

TURN &TALK *Think together. What did you just see me do with the adverb and the comma? What is your analysis of this kind of sentence? Do you like it? Why?*

Analyze

STEP 3: Reread and reflect.

Possible Think-Aloud: *I am looking at the chart to find a word for when the little frog wakes up. I want to show that it happened fast. Watch as I write "Suddenly" and place my comma. Now I am ready for the rest of the sentence, "the little frog's . . ." Isn't this a good way to create interesting sentences! I love the way the adverbs show HOW something is happening. Quickly, suddenly, abruptly, slowly—these are all great adverbs that we can use every day.*

Sum It Up

We have started a chart with some great adverbs. Now I am going to challenge you to do two important things. First, keep thinking of adverbs that tell how things move. It would be great if they ended in *-ly*. Next, use the adverbs on our chart with a comma to launch some really fabulous sentences. I can't wait to see what you write.

VARIATIONS

For Less Experienced Writers: Gather less experienced writers around a pocket chart containing a very basic sentence or two, such as Anna walked to the office. The bear caught a fish. The bird pulled on a worm. Then, work as a team to try adding different adverbs and a comma to each sentence, identifying the sentences the team thinks are the best.

For More Experienced Writers: Show these writers how to insert an adverb into the center of a sentence to increase precision in communication. Examples: The waves rushed quickly over the rocks. The geese flew rapidly away from the approaching eagle.

LINKS TO CD-ROM:
- Teacher Tool: Adverbs Primary Students Can Use to Open Sentences list

Use Stellar Adjectives

WHEN TO USE IT: To heighten awareness of adjectives as tools for description

FOCUS THE LEARNING

While we wouldn't want writers to think that piling on adjectives will ever take the place of precise nouns and powerful verbs, adjectives are important. They fine-tune understanding and add details. They give rhythm and flow to the cadence of language as well. An important understanding is that adjectives are not all created equal. Some are stellar!

Model

STEP 1: Post a chart labeled "Stellar Descriptions." Read aloud from *Bat Loves the Night* by Nicola Davies, or from another book with stellar adjectives, such as *Amos and Boris* by William Steig.

Possible Think-Aloud: (After reading.) *Do you know what the word "stellar" means? It means "outstanding." Some descriptions are better than good; they are outstanding, or stellar. I need to stop for a minute and focus on some of the stellar descriptions I am reading. I like these so much I am going to use them to start a chart for us, focused on Stellar Descriptions. Nicola Davies said that the bat has beady eyes, pixie ears, and thistledown fur. Those descriptions are so good. I can make a picture in my mind. For beady eyes, I see tiny round eyes that look like dark beads on a necklace. Nicola Davies could have said small eyes. But instead she chose "beady eyes"! That is a stellar description for sure.*

TURN &TALK *Think together about pixie ears. What mental picture do you get from that stellar description?*

STEP 2: Read pages 22–24 in *Bat Loves the Night,* and add more words to the chart.

Possible Think-Aloud: *Wow! Let's focus for a minute on the way Nicola Davies describes feet. She said the bats have "oversized feet." Then, she said they have "coat-hanger feet." Look at these descriptions as I write them on the chart. Both of these tell about feet, but they tell us different things. The adjective, the word that describes the feet, makes a big difference. Watch as I underline the adjectives "oversized" and "coat-hanger." These adjectives work* with "feet" to explain and tell us more. The adjectives really help to make these descriptions stellar!

TURN &TALK *What do you think "coat-hanger" or "oversized feet" look like? Think together.*

Analyze

STEP 3: Reread and reflect.

Possible Think-Aloud: *I am going to reread the rest of the stellar descriptions that we collected from this book. As I read each one, I will underline the adjective. That is the word that describes and tells more about something. For example, in "beady eyes," "beady" tells us what the eyes are like. That is the adjective in this description. Think together. What other adjectives could we put with eyes? Small eyes, big eyes, bulging eyes . . . keep going! Use adjectives to describe all kinds of eyes.*

Sum It Up

As we continue to grow as writers, one of the most important things we can do is to take descriptions seriously. We need to visualize our subject and then choose words that help a reader get a really clear mental picture. Adjectives, like these words that are underlined on our chart, help a lot. It will be fun to capture stellar descriptions from your writing and from the books we read. Then, we can add them to our chart. Let's make our list of stellar descriptions grow into a terrific resource.

Stellar Descriptions

Beady eyes

Pixie Ears

Thistledown Fur

Tangled Hedge

Hungry Batlings

Oversized Feet

Coat-hanger feet

Sample Modeled Writing

VARIATIONS

For Less Experienced Writers: Working in a small-group setting, display a picture of an animal such as a rabbit, a dog, or another animal that your writers enjoy. Provide them with sentence strips, and assist them in creating stellar descriptions with precise language such as "slender toes," "bulging eyes," and "sleek fur."

For More Experienced Writers: Provide an opportunity for these writers to re-evaluate a piece of work they have already completed and consider points where descriptions could be improved with precise adjectives.

Sentence Structure

A Tapestry of Pattern and Possibility

As with all expressions of language, sentences come in many forms and formats. When learning about sentence structure, it is helpful to teach young writers the basic sentence elements and patterns so they can vary sentences in terms of both length and style of internal organization.

The basic sentence structures include:

- Simple sentence
- Compound sentence
- Complex sentence
- Introductory element followed by a comma
- Appositive, an interrupter, in the middle of the sentence
- Closing element at the end of the sentence set off by a comma

LESSON	K	1	2	RELATED LESSONS
1 Two-Word Sentences	●	●	●	*Sentence Fluency:* Lesson 1, Sentences Are of Varying Lengths *Word Choice:* Lesson 2, Target Powerful Action Verbs
2 Simple Sentences	●	●	●	*Editing:* Lesson 5, Using Spelling Consciousness While Editing
3 Compound Sentences		●	●	*Revising:* Lesson 4, Sentence Combining
4 Introductory Phrases or Clauses		●	●	*Sentence Fluency:* Lesson 3, Varied Sentence Beginnings *Sentence Fluency:* Lesson 4, Varying Sentence Beginnings with Prepositional Phrases
5 Appositive: An Interrupter that Clarifies or Explains			●	

Other Lessons to Create

You might also want to teach writers how to use

- sentence fragments for dramatic effect in dialog ("Oh, no!"),
- the correct article with nouns in sentences (a dog or the dog), or
- adverbs to make more specific sentences (quickly, slowly).

Two-Word Sentences

WHEN TO USE IT: To strip sentences down to core components

FOCUS THE LEARNING

Two-word sentences are fun and lively ways to show writers that sentences can be of almost any length. When writers create two-word sentences, all they can work with is a noun and verb—subject and predicate. This helps them see that every sentence has an internal structure that, like the skeletal system of our body, helps everything else stand tall.

Model

STEP 1: Engage in language play, creating two-word sentences and writing them down on a chart.

Possible Think-Aloud: *Did you know that you can make sentences with only two words? Two-word sentences are really fun, and they remind us that, as writers, we need to use sentences of many different lengths. Watch as I write some two-word sentences. "Babies cry." This is short, but it is a sentence. It tells who or what did something: Babies. Then, it tells what they did: cry. It has all the components of a sentence, so I need to give it a period. Isn't that cool? Watch as I do another one. "Children run." Remember the two key questions: Who or what did something? (Children) What did they do? (run) This is a sentence, too. I need to place a period at the end, because I know that it is a real sentence. Get ready. It's your turn.*

TURN &TALK *Horses . . . What can horses do? Think together and identify one word that would finish this sentence! Create a two-word sentence about horses.*

STEP 2: Create a poem about school filled with two-word sentences.

Possible Think-Aloud: *We're on a roll. Let's switch gears and do two-word sentences about school. I will write them in a list format so we can read them like a poem.*

Babies cry.
Children run.
Horses gallop.
Worms wiggle.
We laugh.

School
Children read.
Teachers teach.
Buses rumble.
Everyone learns.
School

Sample Modeled Writing

My first sentence is "Children read." This is an important part of school, isn't it? Now I need to check my sentence with our two questions: Who or what did something? What did they do? Who did something? Children. What did they do? Read. This passes the test. "Children read" is a sentence. My next sentence is, "Teachers teach."

TURN &TALK *Think together and use the two questions that tell if this is a sentence. Who or what did something? What did they do? Assess my sentence.*

Analyze

STEP 3: Reread and reflect.

Possible Think-Aloud: *We have all noticed how noisy the school buses can be. They have those big engines that rumble. Rumble is a perfect verb for my next sentence. "Buses rumble" is a great two-word sentence because it helps me to visualize. It's your turn. Put your heads together, and create a two-word sentence about school!*

Sum It Up

One of the things nonfiction writers need to do is be sure that writing has a mixture of sentences, some short, some long, and some medium. Now that you know how to make two-word sentences, I suspect that they will appear in all kinds of wonderful writing. Remember also that two-word sentence poems are terrific ways to share our learning. You could do two-word sentence poems about koala bears, owls, the weather—almost anything.

VARIATIONS

For Less Experienced Writers: Place a two-word sentence in a pocket chart, and work with these writers to expand the sentence. For example: "Children read" could be turned into "Curious children read exciting nonfiction resources." "Clouds gather" could become "Storm clouds gather, bringing heavy rains and gray skies."

For More Experienced Writers: Examine *Sylvester and the Magic Pebble* by William Steig, and search for the two-word sentence, "It ceased." Engage writers in a conversation about why the author used a two-word sentence, and then have them look for places where a two-word sentence might be infused into their own writing.

LINKS TO CD-ROM:
- Shared Reading: Weather
- Shared Reading: Koala

Simple Sentences

WHEN TO USE IT: To heighten awareness of complete sentences versus fragments

FOCUS THE LEARNING

Emergent writers are often wrestling with concepts focused on word and word boundaries. As they gain experience, they are ready to examine sentences. It is very helpful to create a poster featuring the two key questions writers can use to determine if a sentence is complete: *Who or what did something? What did they do?*

Model

Display a poster with the two key sentences: *Who or what did something? What did they do?*

STEP 1: Model how to analyze sentences and determine if they are complete.

Possible Think-Aloud: *I am writing about a lion at a time when he is really hungry. My first sentence is, "The mighty lion . . ." Watch as I do two important things. First, I will write the sentence; then I will check it with the two key questions on my poster.* (After writing.) *Okay, let's check this sentence. Who or what did something? The lion. What did he do? He roared. This is a sentence! Watch as I write the next line, "He thrashes . . ." Let's check it. Who did something? Hmmm. It says "He." I need to think about that. I know that "He" means the lion because the first sentence is about the lion. So the first question is okay. "He" means the lion, and that tells me who did something. The next question is: What did he do? He thrashed. That means he tossed his head and shook it.*

TURN &TALK *Think together. Is this a sentence? Test it yourselves with our two key questions.*

The mighty lion roars and paces. He thrashes his head and roars again. The king of the jungle.

STEP 2: Continue modeling an analysis to determine if sentences are complete.

Possible Think-Aloud: *I have often heard lions called the kings of the jungle, so I will write that next. "The king of the jungle."*

Sample Modeled Writing

TURN &TALK *You know what to do. Test this last line with our two questions: Who or what did something? What did they do?*

(After partners discuss.) You are right! I didn't write a sentence. I told who, but my sentence didn't tell what the lion did. Put your heads together, and think of a way to make this into a real sentence.

Analyze

STEP 3: Reread and reflect.

Possible Think-Aloud: *As we reread this piece about the lion, it will be important to recheck and be sure that all of the sentences are really sentences. I need to use my two key questions and check every line.*

Sum It Up

Nonfiction writers need to check their writing, using our two key sentences. It is important to know if a sentence is a sentence so we know where to place a period. When a sentence isn't complete, like "The king of the jungle," it doesn't make sense to a reader. So, writers, be sure to use our two key questions and check your writing. Make sure that you are writing sentences by asking yourself: Who or what did something? What did they do?

VARIATIONS

For Less Experienced Writers: During one-to-one conferences, guide less experienced writers as they evaluate their own work. Help them use the key questions to reflect on and identify simple sentences in their writing.

For More Experienced Writers: For more experienced writers, have them analyze sentences in books using the two questions. They will quickly notice that many of the verbs are passive and don't necessarily suggest "action."

Compound Sentences

WHEN TO USE IT: To help writers link short sentences with conjunctions

FOCUS THE LEARNING

Compound sentences are formed when two simple sentences are linked together with a conjunction such as *and, for, but, yet, or,* or *so.* In creating compound sentences, it is important to note that both of the linked sentences must be complete and capable of standing on their own.

Model

STEP 1: Display the first two sentences from the first draft (below) in a pocket chart, and model the insertion of a conjunction and a comma to create a compound sentence. Post a list of conjunctions: and, for, but, yet, or, so.

Possible Think-Aloud: *As nonfiction writers, we need to be able to create many different kinds of sentences. Compound sentences occur when two short sentences are connected by a linking word and a comma. Watch as I use my scissors and work on the first two sentences in the chart. First, I snip out the period after "eyes" and turn it into a comma. Now I need to add a linking word. I could choose and, for, but, yet, or, or so. I am going to choose "and." Watch as I write "and" on a sentence strip and slip it into the chart after the comma. My last step is to fix "It." This is now in the middle of a sentence, so it doesn't need a capital letter. Watch as I cut off the "I" and replace it with a lowercase "i." Let's read my compound sentence!*

First draft:

A spider can have big eyes. It can have little eyes as well. Most species have eight eyes in all! All spiders have eight legs. They have only two body parts. Some spiders are hairy. Some spiders have smooth skin.

Draft with compound words:

A spider can have big eyes, _and_ it can have little eyes as well. Most species have eight eyes in all! All spiders have eight legs, _but_ they have only two body parts.

Sample Modeled Writing

TURN &TALK *Consider what you just saw me do. What steps did I take to turn two short sentences into a terrific compound sentence? Think together.*

STEP 2: Model merging two more sentences.

Possible Think-Aloud: *The next sentence says, "Most species . . ." This sentence sounds pretty good. It isn't too short, and it is interesting. I will move to the next two sentences and see if they would be good to use in creating a compound sentence. (Read the last two sentences.) These two sentences will make a great compound. First, I turn the period after "legs" into a comma. Next, I need to select a linking word. This time I will choose "but." All spiders have eight legs, but they have only two body parts. I like the way that sounds. Now I need to change the capital letter on "They," which is in the middle of the sentence, to a lowercase "t."*

TURN &TALK *See if I followed all of the steps in creating a compound sentence. Evaluate my linking word. Do you think "but" is a good choice? Would another one be better?*

Analyze

STEP 3: Reread and reflect.

Possible Think-Aloud: *I am ready to analyze the last two sentences and see if they should be left alone or turned into a compound. It is important not to have every sentence be a long one. We need some long, short, and medium sentences. Think together about the last two sentences. Should we turn them into a compound sentence? If so, how?*

Sum It Up

To turn short sentences into longer, more interesting ones, you can create compound sentences. You need to change the period to a comma and insert a linking word, such as and, for, but, yet, or, or so. The last step is to change the capital letter of the second sentence into a lowercase letter. Compound sentences make your sentences look really adult. I know you will try this in your writing today!

VARIATIONS

For Less Experienced Writers: Meet with less experienced writers individually, and assist them in identifying places in their own writing where they could create a compound sentence. Teach them to celebrate the fun of reading longer sentences aloud and appreciating the smooth flow they create in the writing.

For More Experienced Writers: Expect more experienced writers to produce sentences in a variety of lengths. To assist them in integrating compound sentences into their writing, you might want to have these writers create a poster or bulletin board showcasing compound sentences. As part of this display, they could show the steps in creating compound sentences and give examples from favorite books.

LINKS TO CD-ROM:
• Thinking Challenge: Orcas

Introductory Phrases or Clauses

WHEN TO USE IT: To lift complexity and interest in sentence construction

FOCUS THE LEARNING

Introductory phrases and clauses lift sentence structure and create a lyrical flow to language. Introductory phrases are not difficult to learn, and young writers have fun playing with language and considering different ways to say the same thing.

Model

STEP 1: Post starter words: when, as, before, with, if, after, until. Show writers how to play with sentences orally, as you consider different ways to say the same thing.

Possible Think-Aloud: *I love pizza, and I know you do, too. As I get ready to write about pizza today, I want to experiment a bit and think of different sentences that I could create when I write. The starter words on this chart can help. I am going to use these words to begin some sentences and then decide which one I like the best. Listen as I try one with the starter word "when." "When I eat pizza, I . . ." That was okay. Now I am going to try to start with the word "as." "As I lift that first slice of pizza and . . ." Wow! I like that even better. It makes me think of that wonderful moment when I am lifting the pizza to my lips for the first bite! I am going to write both of these down so I don't forget what I said.*

TURN &TALK *Evaluate my sentences. What did you notice about the difference in my writing when I started with " when" and then with "as"? Which sentence do you like better and why?*

When I eat pizza, I want it loaded up . . .

As I lift that first slice of pizza and watch the cheese drip, . . .

With a grin of delight, I carry the pizza to the table.

Before the pizza arrives, the smell of melting cheese and warm crust . . .

Sample Modeled Writing

STEP 2: Use two more starter words to create sentences, and add them to the chart.

Possible Think-Aloud: *It is amazing that a different starter word changes the way my sentence turns out. These are so much more interesting than reading "I like pizza."*

It is important to notice that these sentences need a little break in the middle so the reader knows where to take a breath. Let's read the top two sentences again and make a real point to take a breath at the comma.

TURN &TALK *It is your turn to take the challenge. Your starter word is "before." Think together and create a sentence about pizza that begins with the word "before."*

Analyze

STEP 3: Reread and reflect.

Possible Think-Aloud: *To use a starter word and an introductory phrase, I need to look at the starter words and try out more than one. Then, I need to select the best sentence and starter word for my writing. My last step is to think about a little breath. I want to be sure these sentences get a comma in the middle so my reader knows where to take a breath.*

Sum It Up

Starter words really do affect the way sentences sound. We also need to remember that if we take away the starter and all the words up to the comma, we still have a sentence that answers our two key questions: Who or what did something? What did they do? Watch as I cover up the introductory part of this sentence up to the comma and read the rest. Notice that this is still a sentence. The starter word and the part up to the comma are like icing on the cake! As you begin writing today, use starter words and be ready to see some exciting sentences in your writing.

VARIATIONS

For Less Experienced Writers: Provide 3 x 5 cards with starter words for each writer. Then, have each of them hold up a starter word and tell about a shared experience, beginning with the special word they are holding.

For More Experienced Writers: Assist more experienced writers in learning to use the correct labels for this sentence structure. They should be able to talk about using an introductory element with a comma or an introductory phrase. Labeling their actions with explicit language will assist them in analyzing their writing and working on sentence fluency.

Appositives: An Interrupter that Clarifies or Explains

WHEN TO USE IT: To promote varied sentence structures and increase precision in descriptions

FOCUS THE LEARNING

An appositive, or an interrupter, is a noun or a noun phrase that renames or clarifies. This is a structure very commonly seen in nonfiction resources and is quite attainable for primary students when they are given explicit modeling and practice.

Model

STEP 1: Display a sentence in a pocket chart, and show how you can add an interrupter—an appositive.

Possible Think-Aloud: *I placed a sentence in the pocket chart, "Mrs. Hoyt loves to read." Watch as I add something really exciting. It is called an interrupter, and it slips right into the middle of the sentence. First, I will cut the strip after Mrs. Hoyt and make room for more words. An interrupter breaks the sentence to give more information, so I will write "a teacher" on a new strip and slip it into the sentence. My sentence now reads, "Mrs. Hoyt a teacher . . ." The interrupter needs to have a comma just before and just after it appears, so I will now slip in two commas. Isn't this great? The interrupter, "a teacher" tells more about Mrs. Hoyt.*

TURN &TALK *Think together. What did you just see me do? What did you learn about creating a sentence with an interrupter?*

STEP 2: Model another sentence.

Possible Think-Aloud: *Oakley is my dog. She loves to play catch with sticks, balls, and anything she can find. My sentence says, "Oakley loves to play catch." Here comes the interrupter. I will snip right after "Oakley" and make some space.*

Mrs. Hoyt, a teacher, loves to read.

Oakley, my dog, loves to play catch.

Mr. Williams, our principal, eats lunch with us every week.

The orca, a killer whale, eats ocean mammals and fish.

Sample Modeled Writing

TURN &TALK *Consider options for this interrupter. What could I insert to tell who or what Oakley is?*

Analyze

STEP 3: Reread and reflect.

Possible Think-Aloud: *We have got it. "My dog" is a good interrupter. Let's try it with the orca, a black and white killer whale that you often see on TV. I want to remember the steps. An interrupter renames or gives more information. It has to have a comma before it and after it. When I think of an orca, I remember that it is also called a killer whale. That would make a good interrupter. Think together. Can you think of another interrupter that we might use for this sentence about an orca?*

Sum It Up

Interrupters are fun to add to nonfiction writing. They add information and look very adult in our writing. When we create an interrupter, we rename the subject of the sentence—giving more information. We also surround the interrupter with commas—one before and one after. As you begin writing today, look at your sentences and identify some places where you could insert an interrupter and commas.

VARIATIONS

For Less Experienced Writers: Use writers' names in sentences in a pocket chart, and have them insert interrupters about themselves. An example: Emilio, a soccer player, loves to read about sharks.

For More Experienced Writers: Demonstrate more complex interrupters in which adjectives are added. For example: The teacher's desk, a terrible mess of papers and books, needs to be moved. Oakley, the 12-year-old shoe-chewing Chesapeake, loves to play catch.

Capitalization

Saving Capital Letters for Special Purposes

Young writers often have a merry mix of lowercase letters and capitals. The challenge comes in helping them understand that they need to write mostly in lowercase formats and save capital letters for special purposes. Capital letters transmit a message of "Take notice: this word has special significance." This is important in helping emergent writers to use capital letters sparingly.

LESSON	K	1	2	RELATED LESSONS
1 Capitalize Beginning of Sentences	●	●		*Drafting:* Lesson 5, Use Mostly Lowercase Letters
2 Proper Nouns: Names and Places	●	●		
3 Capitalize Important Words in a Title	●	●	●	*Text Features:* Lesson 1, Choose a Title that Is Interesting *Text Features:* Lesson 2, Headings Help Your Reader
4 Capitalize for Emphasis	●	●	●	

Other Lessons to Create

You might also want to teach writers how to capitalize

- a title before a name (Mrs. Jones),
- names of cities and states, or
- days of the week.

Capitalize Beginning of Sentences

WHEN TO USE IT: When writers can produce a line or two of text

FOCUS THE LEARNING

Capitalization of the first word in a sentence is an understanding that writers can develop quickly. As soon as they can differentiate capital letters from lowercase letters, they are ready to go.

Model

STEP 1: Model beginning a sentence with a capital letter.

Possible Think-Aloud: *Did you know that writers always capitalize the first word of a sentence, no matter what kind of sentence they are writing? As I write today, watch how I use a capital letter to begin every sentence. I am writing about my cat, Samantha. The first word in my sentence is "My." Watch as I make a capital M to begin this sentence. I will use lots of lowercase letters as I write the rest of the sentence, but the first letter is always a capital. Let's move on to sentence two. "Her fur is soft . . ."*

TURN &TALK *The first word is "Her." Remind yourselves of the correct way to write a capital H. Use your finger, and draw a capital H on your leg. Visualize it.*

STEP 2: Continue modeling.

Possible Think-Aloud: *My next sentence begins with "Everyone . . ." Hold your finger in the air, and make a capital E in the air. Now watch as I place a capital E on my paper. Does it look like the one you just made in the air? Writers use capital letters at the beginning of every sentence.*

My cat's name is Samantha. Her fur is soft and silky. Everyone in my family likes to hold Samantha, because she purrs and curls up in a round little ball.

Sample Modeled Writing

TURN &TALK *Remind each other. What is the rule for the first word in every sentence? What do you capitalize?*

Analyze

STEP 3: Reread and reflect.

Possible Think-Aloud: *I have three sentences, so I should have at least three capital letters in my writing. Let's reread and check.* (After rereading) *We have three sentences, but I have five capital letters! Help me analyze this.*

TURN &TALK *Why do I have extra capital letters? You are so smart! You noticed that Samantha, the name of my cat, is capitalized. We also use capital letters for names.*

Sum It Up

Writers always begin sentences with a capital letter—always. We can use capital letters for other reasons, too. But we always begin a sentence with a capital letter.

VARIATIONS

For Less Experienced Writers: Provide personal sentence strips that less experienced writers can lay in front of them as they work. Offer support as each new sentence is started in correct formation with the capital letter.

For More Experienced Writers: Begin a chart of reasons why nonfiction writers use capital letters, and have these writers analyze their own writing to explain why they have used capital letters.

Proper Nouns: Names and Places

WHEN TO USE IT: When writers begin integrating the names of people and places into their work

FOCUS THE LEARNING

Young children love to learn to write their names and the names of their family members and friends. As they begin to understand that these special words are capitalized, you can help them realize that the names of their pets, their school, and their town all deserve capital letters, too.

Model

STEP 1: Demonstrate identifying and capitalizing property names.

Possible Think-Aloud: *Today I am going to write about our school and some of the people who make it special. My goal is to focus on using a capital letter when I write the name of a person or a place. Nonfiction writers need to be very careful with capital letters. My first sentence is, "I love McKinley School." Notice that I used a capital letter for McKinley and another one for School. McKinley School is the name of a place, so it needs to be capitalized. My second sentence begins, "Mr. Hawkins . . ." The term "Mr." is part of Mr. Hawkins' name. Watch as I write a capital M and a lowercase r, followed by a period. The second part of his name, Hawkins, is next.*

TURN &TALK *Think together. Which letter in Hawkins do I need to capitalize as I add "Mr. Hawkins" to my writing?*

STEP 2: Continue modeling.

I love McKinley School. Mr. Hawkins, our principal, and Mrs. Evans, our secretary, are always nice when I visit the office.

Possible Think-Aloud: *I am ready to add "Mrs. Evans" to my writing. We know that Mrs. is part of her name, so I will write a capital M. In Evans, watch as I write a capital E. Capitalizing for names and places is fun!*

Sample Modeled Writing

TURN &TALK *If you were going to tell someone the rule for capitalizing the names of people and places, what would you tell them? What do they need to know?*

Analyze

STEP 3: Reread and reflect.

Possible Think-Aloud: *Let's reread and recheck. I want to be sure that I used a capital letter for the names of people and places. First, I will draw a line under the names like McKinley School and Mr. Hawkins. That is one way that I can check to be sure that I have all the capital letters I need.*

Sum It Up

Names of people and places are special. They need to be capitalized every time we include them in our writing. Let's think about middle names. Would I need to capitalize those, too?

VARIATIONS

For Less Experienced Writers: Provide an opportunity for these writers to take a survey such as the one on the Resources CD-ROM. As they interview their classmates, have them write names in the appropriate columns. Make sure they use a capital letter at the beginning of each name.

For More Experienced Writers: Broaden the range of proper nouns to include days of the week, titles on books, cities, and states.

LINKS TO CD-ROM
- Teacher Tool: "Do You Have a Dog?" survey

Capitalize Important Words in a Title

WHEN TO USE IT: To support correct format in published work

FOCUS THE LEARNING

Writers love to create titles for their written messages. As they do so, this is a perfect time to focus on correct capitalization so their titles are presented to others in conventional form.

Model

Display an array of nonfiction books with titles that are large enough for students to clearly see them.

STEP 1: Model writing.

Possible Think-Aloud: *Let's look at the titles of these books and notice the way the authors have used capital letters. My first book,* Snowflake Bentley *by Jacqueline Briggs Martin, has just two words in the title. Both words, "Snowflake" and "Bentley," are capitalized. The rest of the title is lowercase. The next book,* What Do You Do with a Tail Like This?, *by Steve Jenkins and Robin Page, has a lot more words in the title.*

TURN & TALK *As I touch the words in the title, count them with me. Wow! Nine words is a long title. Now let's count the capital letters in the title and see how many we find. Ready? 1 . . . 2 . . . (After counting.) I bet you notice what I noticed. Every important word starts with a capital because a title is a name! It is the name of a book, so we need to use capital letters.*

STEP 2: Model writing a list of book titles.

Possible Think-Aloud: *I am going to make a list of the nonfiction books that I plan to read aloud this week. As always, I want to include books from the library as well as books written by students. We know that titles*

Books to Read Aloud This Week

Actual Size by Steve Jenkins
Animals Nobody Loves by Seymour Simon
Frogs by Mrs. Allen's class
Spots On My Face by Javier

Sample Modeled Writing

are names for books, so we will be using some capital letters. Watch as I write the first title, Actual Size. *There are two words, so I will be sure to make each of them start with a capital letter.*

TURN &TALK *My next book is* Animals Nobody Loves *by Seymour Simon. Count the words in the title, and decide how many capital letters I will need to write.*

Analyze

STEP 3: Reread and reflect.

Possible Think-Aloud: *Javier has volunteered to let us read his book this week. It is called "Spots On My Face." There are four words. Watch as I write the title on our read-aloud list, placing a capital letter at the beginning of each word.*

Sum It Up

Capital letters are special. We don't use them very much, just at the beginning of sentences and in names. We use capitals for names of people, places, and titles of books!

VARIATIONS

For Less Experienced Writers: Guide less experienced writers in analyzing titles for books used in small-group instruction as well as in the classroom library. Assist them as they identify and name the capital letters they find.

For More Experienced Writers: Introduce these writers to the next level of capitalization with titles by showing them titles such as "Frog and Toad," "Blueberries for Sal," and "If You Give a Mouse a Cookie." Assist them in noticing that small words like and, a, and the are capitalized only if they are the first word in the title.

Capitalize for Emphasis

WHEN TO USE IT: To highlight a word as especially important

FOCUS THE LEARNING

When capitalization is used for emphasis, a reader realizes that a word in all capitals is stated very loudly or is read with significant expression.

Model

STEP 1: Demonstrate how to capitalize for emphasis.

Possible Think-Aloud: *I hate bee stings, but I love the sound that bees make. Bzzzz. Isn't that a great sound? I love to write it, too. As I write about bees today, I am going to use bzzzz in two different ways. Watch as I write "bzzzz." All lowercase letters suggest that I make the sound in a normal voice. Watch this time: "BZZZZ." When we use all capital letters in a word, you say it in a big voice and give it extra emphasis.*

TURN &TALK *Turn to your partner, and read my two versions of "bzzzz," changing your voice to make one normal and one in a big voice.*

STEP 2: Insert an emphasized word into writing.

Bzzzz. BZZZZ.

Bees flit and float gathering pollen for their hive. LOOK OUT! Don't let one land on you.

Sample Modeled Writing

Possible Think-Aloud: *Notice in my first sentence that I only capitalized the first word. But I want to put in two words and give them big emphasis. I want to say "look out" like I am warning my reader. Watch as I write "LOOK OUT!" all in capital letters. We don't want to do this very often, but once in a while, it is an interesting way to use capital letters for emphasis.*

TURN &TALK *Read my writing so far, and practice reading my capitalized words to show emphasis. What do you think of having one word or maybe two that are capitalized so a reader knows to read them in a different way? When would you want to do this in your writing?*

Analyze

STEP 3: Reread and reflect.

Possible Think-Aloud: *Capital letters are tools that we can use in our writing. But we need to be careful and use them very cautiously. Too many capital letters just wouldn't look right. Reread my writing and analyze. What do you think of the way I used capital letters today? Did I use too many, too few, or just the right number?*

Sum It Up

Capital letters are special and should only be used for a specific reason. We know we use them at the beginning of a sentence and in a name. Now we know that they are also helpful to show emphasis in our writing. The trick is to be careful and not do this very often.

VARIATIONS

For Less Experienced Writers: Provide sticky notes, and have writers add sound and other statements of emphasis to familiar books such as *Rosie's Walk*. Help them understand that they want to use a limited number of capital letters, saving them for important purposes.

For More Experienced Writers: Engage more experienced writers in creating safety posters warning readers of dangers in the school building. Guide them in making wise selections about the use of capital letters for emphasis.

Spelling Consciousness

Thinking Strategically—Making My Message Accessible to Others

When writers approach spelling tasks strategically, they have a sense of when to rely upon themselves and their knowledge of letters and sounds or when to turn to other resources for support. Strategic spellers pay attention to the way words look, and they search for patterns in words. These spellers have a distinct sense of spelling consciousness that guides them as they write.

LESSON	K	1	2	RELATED LESSONS
1 Spelling Consciousness: Notice When Words Are Not Spelled Correctly	●	●	●	*Editing:* Lesson 5, Using Spelling Consciousness While Editing
2 Stretching Words . . . Writing Sounds You Know	●	●		
3 Strategic Spellers Pay Attention to Syllables	●	●	●	
4 Strategic Spellers Use a Variety of Resources		●	●	*Editing:* Lesson 8, Using Familiar Resources to Help You Edit
5 Navigating Homophones			●	

Other Lessons to Create

You might also want to teach writers how to

- reread to add more letters to words,
- use a word wall, or
- try different spellings to see which looks most right.

Spelling Consciousness: Notice When Words Are Not Spelled Correctly

WHEN TO USE IT: To help writers develop a system of noticing misspelled words and preparing to deal with them

FOCUS THE LEARNING

With our youngest writers, the most important goal is to extend and expand communication. However, when they are ready to present their work to others, they need to focus on specific words and their spellings, noticing when words don't look quite right.

Model

STEP 1: Model how to edit and underline words that don't look quite right.

Possible Think-Aloud: *As I edit this writing today, I am going to focus on my spelling. I want to be sure that I am paying attention to the letters in each word and noticing if a word doesn't look right. In my writing about the grizzly bear, I have some great facts. Now it is time to look at my spelling. I will begin by reading very slowly and touching each word to look at the letters. In the first sentence, I think that "grizle" doesn't look quite right, so I will draw a line under that word. I also think that I should check on "liks," so I will draw a line under that as well.*

TURN &TALK *Look at my writing. Are there any other words that you think I should underline and check for spelling?*

STEP 2: Model how to use resources such as word walls and resource books to check spellings.

A grizle bear liks to eat salmon. When these bears can't find salmon, they eet honey and buggs.

Sample Modeled Writing

Possible Think-Aloud: *Great! You have identified two more words that we need to check, "eet" and "buggs." For "grizle," I can look in this great book about bears and see how grizzly is spelled. The word "likes" is on our word wall. Alina, can you go check the word wall so we know how to spell "likes"?*

TURN &TALK *Think together. How can we check the other two words that we have decided need a bit of attention to spelling? What can writers do when they aren't sure of how to spell a word?*

Analyze

STEP 3: Reread and reflect.

Possible Think-Aloud: *Let's reread this one more time. We underlined four words and checked them for spelling. Let's reread and see how we did. We know that the most important thing is to have great facts, but spelling counts, too!*

Sum It Up

When we write, we always think first about our message. But if our spelling isn't pretty good, then no one can read our writing, and they don't know what we said! Before we present our writing to others, it is a good idea to reread and underline words that don't look quite right. Then, we can use resources like the word wall and books to check on the words.

VARIATIONS

For Less Experienced Writers: Have writers underline words they think they need help with, and then have them select only one or two high-frequency words to actually investigate. Limiting the number of spellings they investigate actually increases the likelihood that they will remember the correct spellings.

For More Experienced Writers: Broaden the scope of resources writers use by providing Portable Word Walls and lists of homophones such as those in the Resources CD-ROM for this lesson.

LINKS TO CD-ROM:
- Checklist: Spelling Consciousness Checklist
- Checklist: Spelling Consciousness: Self Reflection

Stretching Words . . . Writing Sounds You Know

WHEN TO USE IT: To help writers use the sounds they know and keep writing

FOCUS THE LEARNING

Writers who develop spelling consciousness learn to trust themselves and build words using sounds they already know.

Model

STEP 1: Stretch each word out very slowly, emphasizing individual phonemes. Then, write the sounds that are easily heard, explaining to the students that you are writing the sounds you know and will work later at adding more letters.

Possible Think-Aloud: *Writers, we are going to practice stretching out words and using sounds we know as I write about plants. My first sentence is, "Plants need water and light." Watch how I say each word very slowly. That helps me to hear the sounds in the word and think about spelling. My first word is "plants." (Say it very slowly: "/p/ . . . /l/ . . . /a/ . . . /n/ . . . /t/ . . . /s/.") I know that /p/ is spelled with the letter "p." I hear a /t/ sound toward the end. That is the letter "t." Watch as I draw a line and then place a "t." I know there are more letters in the middle, but I won't work on those right now. I need to write quickly and get my idea down before I forget!*

TURN &TALK *What did you notice about the way I stretched out the word "plant"? Did I get most of the sounds? My next word is "need." Say it together, and think about the sounds you can hear. What letters would you write for "need"?*

STEP 2: Continue drafting— saying each word slowly and showing students how you listen for the sounds. Draw lines for missing letters to demonstrate that you can quickly write the sounds you know and keep going.

Pl___ts eed w___r and li___t to sta uliv.

(Plants need water and light to stay alive.)

Sample Modeled Writing

Possible Think-Aloud: *I had a great idea for spelling "need." Reed is a student in our classroom, so we can use his name to help us spell "need." Watch as I use a whiteboard and write Reed. All I have to do is change the R to n, and I have "need." Spellers have lots of tools! My next word is water. I hear /w/ at the beginning of the word, and I hear /r/ at the end, so I am going to draw a line for the middle of the word to remind myself to check on the spelling after I am finished writing. Remember, we stretch words out and think of letters we know. We also use words we already know to help us remember spelling patterns.*

TURN &TALK *Listen to my sentence again: Plants need water and light to stay alive. Think together. What should we do to help ourselves spell the rest of these words? What strategies can we use?*

Analyze

STEP 3: Reread and reflect.

Possible Think-Aloud: *Let's reread. Good spellers start with the letters they know so they don't forget their ideas.Then, they go back and add more letters and word parts. Think together. What will you remember about stretching out words and using the sounds you can hear? Why is it important to keep adding letters as you reread your work? How can you remind yourself to use words you already know, like Reed's name, to spell other words?*

Sum It Up

When we are drafting, it is important to get our ideas down quickly so we don't forget what we have to say. You don't want to wait for the teacher to come and help you spell words, because you have strategies that help you to keep going. But good spellers don't stop there! Each time they reread, they think about additional letters they can add. They can also go to the word wall and use familiar books to keep improving the spelling in their writing so their spelling just keeps getting better and better.

VARIATIONS

For Less Experienced Writers: Coach less experienced writers in stretching words so they have a better chance to hear the internal sounds. Show them how they can say the entire sentence first so it is clear to them.

For More Experienced Writers: Help these writers clap out the syllables in words and write the sounds they hear in each syllable. This will help them to make better approximations of spelling and increase writing fluency.

Strategic Spellers Pay Attention to Syllables

WHEN TO USE IT: When writers have learned to clap out syllables

FOCUS THE LEARNING

Strategic spellers need to learn that each syllable should have a vowel. This understanding reminds writers to integrate a vowel into each syllable as they draft and edit.

Model

STEP 1: Model counting syllables and checking to be sure the word you wrote has as many syllables as you heard. (Writers will need whiteboards or paper for this lesson.)

Possible Think-Aloud: *There are two important rules about syllables that help us to be strategic spellers. The first is: Notice syllables. To spell well, we need to notice the syllables in the words we are trying to write. If we count the syllables out and then check to be sure we wrote as many syllables as we heard, our spelling will be better! I am going to write a poem today about fishing. My first line is "Darting and flashing." Watch as I clap the syllables in the first word. /Dart/ . . . /ing/. I heard two syllables. Watch as I write: The first syllable is "dart." The second syllable is "ing." "dart-ing." I heard two syllables, and I wrote two as well.*

TURN &TALK *Think about the spelling strategy I just used. Identify the steps I used to help myself be a better speller.*

STEP 2: Model checking for a vowel in each syllable.

Possible Think-Aloud: *We have identified that darting has two syllables. We counted two syllables, and I wrote two on my paper. There is one more thing we need to check. Each syllable needs to have a vowel. We remember that the vowels are a,e,i,o,u and sometimes y or w. I will use my hands and frame each of the syllables in darting. (Check for a vowel in each syllable.) We followed both important steps. We counted the syllables and made sure we wrote the same number of syllables. Then, we checked each syllable to be sure it had a vowel.*

Darting and flashing

Quivering and alert

Water Sparkles

Fishing!

Sample Modeled Writing

TURN & TALK *It's your turn. Be strategic spellers with the word "flashing." I will be watching as you clap it out and count the syllables. Then, use your whiteboards to write the same number of syllables you heard. Finally, check for vowels. Each syllable needs to have one. Writers, put your heads together!*

Analyze

STEP 3: Reread and reflect.

Possible Think-Aloud: *You've got it. The next line is "Quivering and alert." Grab your whiteboards and think together. You have three words. How many syllables and how many vowels will you need? Go, writers!*

Sum It Up

Strategic spellers use syllables to assist them as they spell. First, they count the number of syllables they hear in a word. Then, they make sure they write as many syllables as they hear. Finally, it is time to check for vowels and be sure that there is a vowel in every syllable. These steps are things you can do during drafting as well as editing. If you remember that syllables are your friends, you will be a better speller!

VARIATIONS

For Less Experienced Writers: Provide additional coaching on counting syllables in words. It is important that writers learn to clap out the syllables if they are to reach maximum potential as strategic spellers.

For More Experienced Writers: Have these students make a poster of how to use syllables to be better spellers, and then have them meet with a partner from another classroom and teach that partner this important rule.

Strategic Spellers Use a Variety of Resources

WHEN TO USE IT: To help spellers use resources while spelling

FOCUS THE LEARNING

Modeled writing, familiar charts of songs and poems, big books, word walls, and nonfiction selections are all tools that assist writers as they draft and edit. A key to strategic spelling is to help writers realize that they can utilize a variety of resources as they verify spelling.

Model

STEP 1: Model how to use familiar texts and tools to check spelling.

Possible Think-Aloud: *I am working on a draft of an invitation for our author tea. Watch how I use some of the resources in our room to check the spelling. "Come" is a word we use a lot. AJ, could you go stand at the word wall and help us check the spelling on "come"? As you spell it, I will match it against my draft. The word tea is very important in this invitation. But how could I check that word? It isn't on the word wall. It isn't in this picture dictionary. I know! We could check the song chart for I'm a Little Teacup! Who would like to get the song chart so we can check on the spelling of this word?*

TURN &TALK *Think together. What are some of the resources that I have just used to check my spelling? Write together and list them.*

STEP 2: Model using additional resources to check punctuation.

Possible Think-Aloud: *We are getting really good at using a variety of resources as we check spelling. Let's try another one. The word February looks a bit suspicious. This is January, so I can't check on our classroom calendar. Jackson, could you bring me the calendar that hangs inside of my coat closet? We can check that for the correct spelling of February. That has all the months of the year. Now how about Altona Elementary? Since this is the name of our school, we can't take any chances. It has to be spelled perfectly.*

Come to Our Author Tea

Febrary 1 in Room 15

Altona Elemntary School

Sample Modeled Writing

TURN &TALK *Put your heads together. Altona Elementary is not on the word wall. It isn't in a dictionary. What resources could we use to check the spelling?*

Analyze

STEP 3: Reread and reflect.

Possible Think-Aloud: *I am going to start a list of resources that help us to check our spelling. I remember that we used the word wall. I will place that on the list. Next, we used a song chart and checked the word "tea." That should be on the list as well. We used the calendar, too. Put your heads together. What other resources should be on our list of tools that can help us check spelling?*

Sum It Up

Writers, we have a lot of resources to use when we edit. We can use familiar books, charts, songs, and the sign on the front of the school! We can also use a classroom word wall, a Portable Word Wall, or an Alphabox. We have a lot of tools to help us be great spellers, so I know I can count on you to use resources strategically as you check your spelling.

VARIATIONS

For Less Experienced Writers: Guide these writers in learning to use the Portable Word Walls that are on the Resources CD-ROM. Provide personal copies so writers have them close at hand when drafting and editing.

For More Experienced Writers: Have experienced writers keep track of the tools they used while editing, and have them write a reflection focused on the tools that they thought were most helpful.

Navigating Homophones

WHEN TO USE IT: When you see evidence of homophones appearing in student writing

FOCUS THE LEARNING

Homophones are words that sound the same, but the spelling and meanings are different. (Example: their, there, they're; chili and chilly; bored and board.) Homophones are particularly challenging for spellers, because they must think about meaning to select the correct spelling.

Model

STEP 1: Provide an opportunity for writers to think about homophones. (Provide copies of the Homophone References from the Resources CD-ROM.)

Possible Think-Aloud: *As writers, we need to be very careful of homophones. These are words that sound the same, but they are spelled differently and they mean different things. One of my favorite homophone pairs is "no" and "know."* (Write them in a visible place for your writers to see.) *I am aware that "no" means that you are rejecting something. I also am aware that to know something is to understand. Those meanings are really different.*

TURN &TALK *Think together. What are the meanings of pear and pair? Let's try ate and eight!* (Write the homophones so writers can see the spellings.)

STEP 2: Continue drawing attention to homophone pairs, and analyze the sample email provided.

Homophone Pairs:

no	know
pear	pair
ate	eight
our	hour
write	right

Hour dog eight a pear of shoes and I don't no what to do.

Sample Modeled Writing

Possible Think-Aloud: *Here is an example of what happens to writers when they forget to think about homophones. The sentence says, "Hour dog eight a pear of shoes, and I don't no what to do." Let's look at this in parts, beginning with "Hour dog." Let's think together. This classroom belongs to us. It is our classroom. Watch as I write the homophone pair* hour, our. *This should have said, "Our dog." With homophones, you have to think about spelling and meaning. The next part of the sentence says "eight a pear of shoes."*

TURN &TALK *Think about "ate" and "eight." Which one means to eat, and which one is the number? What about "pear" and "pair"? Which one means a fruit, and which one means two? What do we need to do to navigate these homophones?*

Analyze

STEP 3: Reread and reflect.

Possible Think-Aloud: *I brought along a reference page for you to add to your writing notebooks. It is a tool that can help you when you need to know which spellings to select for homophones. The first example listed includes* our, hour. *There is a sentence for each. Read the sentences together, and decide which one of these I should use if I want to say, "Our window is open."*

Sum It Up

Homophones are fun to learn. To help us be the best spellers we can, we need to learn the meanings of a variety of homophones and focus on using the correct spelling for each. Over the next few weeks, let's all make a point to notice homophones in both reading and writing and create a helpful poster with lots of homophone pairs that we can reference when we are writing.

VARIATIONS

For Less Experienced Writers: Provide a smaller list with a limited number of high-frequency homophones, and guide these writers in learning to refer to the list as they write.

For More Experienced Writers: Introduce these writers to homonyms in which the spelling is the same but the pronunciation and meaning are different. Examples: minute, bow, and so on.

LINKS TO CD-ROM:
• Spelling Reference: Homophones

CD-ROM INDEX

Section	Lesson #/Focus	Topic/Format
Record Keeping Forms		Record Keeping Grid
		Trait Scoring Guide
		Demonstration Lesson Trackers
Research	1. Identify Facts in a Visual	Visual: Sea Turtle
		Visual: Science and social studies visuals
	2. Locate and Use Important Words and Phrases: Alphabox	Teacher Tool: Alphabox
	3. Locate and Use Facts From Multiple Sources	Thinking Challenge: Research with More than One Book
	4. Create a Visual that Contains Facts	Visual: Labeled diagrams
	5. Place Labels on Illustrations	Visual: Reproducible version of Kyle's Big Tractor
	6. Use *I Remember!* to Summarize Information	Strategy: *I Remember!*
	7. Sketch to Stretch: Visual Summary	Student work: Sketch to Stretch
	8. Use the Very Important Points (VIP) Strategy for Key Information	Shared Reading: Walking on the Moon
	9. Use a Pocket Organizer	Shared Reading: Made for a Frozen World
Planning	1. Draw Pictures Before You Write	Graphic Organizer: Getting Ready for School
		Checklist: Pre-Writing Checklist: Getting Ready to Write
	2. Talk Before You Write	Reflection: Talk Before You Write
	3. Create a Labeled Diagram	Visual: Animal photo
		Visual: Labeled animal photo
	4. Map Out Your Writing with Informational Pictures	Graphic Organizer: How to Make a Paper Snowflake
		Graphic Organizer: Blank storyboard
	5. Planning Page Layout and Paper Selection	Teacher Tool: Sample Page Layouts

Section	Lesson #/Focus	Topic/Format
Planning *(cont.)*	6. Gather Information with the Key Word Strategy	Student Writing: Kindergarten Key Words
		Student Writing: Grade 1 Investigation
		Student Writing: Grade 2 Investigation
Drafting	2. Stretching Words . . . Listening to Sounds	Teacher Tool: Alphabet Strips
	3. Using a Picture Alphabet Card	Teacher Tool: Alphabet Card Teacher Tool: Portable Word Walls
	6. Scratching Out . . . Changing Your Mind	Checklist: Sloppy Copy Checklist
Revising	1. Revising to Add Details	Visual: Detailed photograph
	3. Revising a Lead to Make It Stronger	Chart: Lead Comparison Chart
	4. Sentence Combining	Thinking Challenge: Combing Sentences
	5. Adding Ideas by Cutting and Taping	Visual: Cut and Paste Revision
	6. Revising to Add Variety to Sentence Beginnings	Checklist: Beginning Words Tally Sheet
	9. Recasting a Single Page as a Book…	Student Writing: Wolves Big Book
	12. Using a Revision Checklist	Checklist: Revision Checklist A
		Checklist: Revision Checklist B
		Checklist: Revision Checklist C
Editing	1. Word Boundaries: Keep Letters in a Word Close Together	Teacher Tool: Spacing Buddy
	2. Reread and Touch Each Word	Teacher Tool: Editing Helper
	4. Reread to Add Letters to Words	Thinking Challenge: Caterpillar Story
	5. Using Spelling Consciousness While Editing	Checklist: Spelling Consciousness Checklist A
		Checklist: Spelling Consciousness Checklist B
		Checklist: Spelling Consciousness Checklist C
		Checklist: Spelling Consciousness Checklist D

Section	Lesson #/Focus	Topic/Format
Editing *(cont.)*	6. Using an Editing Checklist	Checklist: Editing Checklist A
		Checklist: Editing Checklist B
		Checklist: Editing Checklist C
		Checklist: Editing Checklist D
	7. How to Peer Edit	Checklist: Peer Editing Checklist I
		Checklist: Peer Editing Checklist II
		Interactive Assessment: A Celebration
		Interactive Assessment Example
	8. Use Familiar Resources to Help You Edit	Teacher Tool: Portable Word Wall Grades K-1
		Teacher Tool: Portable Word Wall Grades 1-2
Presenting	5. In Final Drafts Most Words Are Spelled Correctly	Chart: Classroom Resources I Can Use to Check My Spelling
	6. About the Author	Sample Template: About the Author
Ideas	1. Creating a Topic List	Checklist: Evaluating My Topic List
	2. Write About Pictures	Visuals: Photo from modeled writing
		Visuals: Additional images
	3. Narrow the Topic	Graphic Organizer: Narrowing the Topic
		Thinking Challenge: Which Topic is More Specific (and Interesting)?
	6. Make the Setting Stand Out	Graphic Organizer: Sensory Image
	7. Teach Your Reader Something New	Thinking Challenge: Analyzing Facts About My Topic
	8. Separating Fact and Opinion	Thinking Challenge: Fact and Opinion Chart
	10. Using Comparisons	Teacher Tool: Comparisons in Literature
	11. Focus on "One"	Book List: Mentor Books

Section	Lesson #/Focus	Topic/Format
Organization	1. Main Idea Maintained Throughout	Graphic Organizer: Main Ideas and Details
	3. Plan the Beginning and End... Then the Middle	Graphic Organizer: Beginning...End, Then Middle
	4. Use a Logical Sequence	Graphic Organizer: Planning Sheet for Sequencing Events
		Graphic Organizer: Life Cycle Planning Sheet
	8. Organizing With a Graphic Organizer	Graphic Organizer
		Graphic Organizer: Instructional Writing Organizer
	10. Paragraphs	Reference Chart: T.I.P.S. When to Start a New Paragraph
	12. Sharing Information as a List Poem	Student Writing: List Poems
Text Features	1. Choose a Title That is Interesting	Thinking Challenge: Team Title Challenge
	2. Headings Help Your Reader	Shared Reading: No Wooden Teeth text
	3. Questions Make Great Headings	Shared Reading: The Earthworm
	4. Add Captions to Illustrations	Visuals: Palomino horses
	5. Diagram with Labels	Diagram: Bee diagram
		Diagram: Grasshopper diagram
	6. Bold Words	Shared Text: How Does a Butterfly Begin?
	7. Table of Contents	Student Writing: Emergent Writing Sample
		Student Writing: Developing Writing Sample
	9. Chart/Table/Graph	Student Writing: Animal Movement Chart
Word Choice	1. Use Descriptive Words and Phrases	Visual: Snake's Tongue
	2. Target Powerful Action Verbs	Teacher Tool: Powerful Verbs, Powerful Writing list
	3. Select Word That Show Order or Sequence	Chart: Words that Show Order or Sequence
	5. Beginning Sentences with 'ing' Words	Student Writing: Red-Eyed Tree Frog
	6. Add Action: Group 'ing' Words Together	Student Writing: three examples

Section	Lesson #/Focus	Topic/Format
Word Choice *(cont.)*	7. Use Onomatopoeia	Visual: Frog Call!
	8. Compound Descriptors and Hyphens	Teacher Tool: Compound Descriptors
	10. Transition Words to Add Information or Conclude	Teacher Tool: Transition Words and Phrases list
Sentence Fluency	1. Sentences are of Varying Lengths	Checklist: Varying Sentence Length Checklist Checklist: Sentence Fluency Checklist
	2. Reading Aloud to Check Sentence Fluency	Shared Reading: How to Make a Whisper Phone
	3. Varied Sentence Beginnings	Checklist: Sentence Beginnings Checklist
	4. Varying Sentence Beginnings With Prepositional Phrases	Thinking Challenge: Personal Sentence Planning Chart
	5. Varying Sentence Beginnings with Phrases Focused on Time	Teacher Tool: Phrases that Focus on Time
Voice and Audience	1. Developing an Awareness of Voice	Teacher Tool: How to Tell if Your Writing Has Voice
	3. Consider: Capture the Interest of Your Reader	Graphic Organizer: Note Taker Graphic Organizer
	5. Pick an Enticing Title	Chart: An Enticing Title
	11. Draw Your Reader Into the Setting	Visual: Red-Eyed Tree Frog
	12. Shifting Point of View	Student Writing: I Am a Tornado Student Writing: I Am a Raindrop
Punctuation	1. End Punctuation (statement)	Shared Reading Samples: Writing without Punctuation
	4. Comma in a Series	Student Writing
Grammar	3. Verb Tense	Teacher Tool: Regular and Irregular Verbs chart
	4. Pronoun Order	Student Writing: Fire Blizzard Teaching Tool: Invitations for Analysis
	5. Single vs. Double Subject	Practice Passages (4)
	6. Open with an Adverb	Teacher Tool: Adverbs Primary Students can Use to Open Sentences

Section	Lesson #/Focus	Topic/Format
Sentence Structure	1. Two-Word Sentence	Shared Reading: Weather text
		Shared Reading: Koala
	3. Compound Sentences	Thinking Challenge: Orcas
Capitalization	2. Proper Nouns: Name and Places	Teacher Tool: "Do you Have a Dog?" survey
Spelling Consciousness	1. Spelling Consciousness: Notice When Words Are Not Spelled Correctly	Checklist: Spelling Consciousness Checklist
		Checklist: Spelling Consciousness: Self Reflection
	5. Navigating Homophones	Spelling Reference: Homophones

INDEX